D1351491

The Delirious Museum

The Delirious Museum:

A JOURNEY FROM THE LOUVRE TO LAS VEGAS

Calum Storrie

I.B. TAURIS
LONDON · NEW YORK

Reprinted in 2006 by I.B.Tauris & Co Ltd
6 Salem Road, London W2 4BU
175 Fifth Avenue, New York NY 10010
www.ibtauris.com

In the United States of America and Canada
distributed by Palgrave Macmillan a division of St Martin's Press
175 Fifth Avenue, New York NY 10010

First published in 2006 by I.B.Tauris & Co Ltd
Copyright © Calum Storrie 2006

ISBN 1 86064 569 0
EAN 978 1 86064 569 3

A full CIP record for this book is available from the British Library
A full CIP record is available from the Library of Congress

Library of Congress Catalog Card Number: available

Typeset in Gill Sans by JCS Publishing Services
Printed and bound in India by Replika Press Pvt Ltd

Calum Storrie is supported by

Arts & Humanities
Research Council

Contents

LIST OF ILLUSTRATIONS

ACKNOWLEDGEMENTS

The work that formed the basis of this book was financed by the Martin Jones Award, administered by the Royal Incorporation of Architects in Scotland. My thanks are due to the Martin Jones Awards assessors and the RIAS. Martin Jones himself was also a source of inspiration to me so I am grateful to him on two counts. In the early stages of my research my employers at the former British Museum Design Office under Margaret Hall granted me time off for travel and encouraged the project. The British Museum itself haunts this book. Chapter 6 is an amended version of an article originally published in the journal *Inventory*, vol. 2, no. 2. I would also like to thank the Arts and Humanities Research Council who funded research travel through Kingston University.

Many individuals have helped during my work: Murray Grigor and Richard Murphy both impressed on me the importance of Scarpa's Palazzo Abatellis; Leslie Dick was my host and guide on two visits to Los Angeles; David and Diana Wilson who generously invited me to stay in one of the trailers at the Museum of Jurassic Technology and who spent more hours than was reasonable discussing the museum with me; all the staff at the Museum of Jurassic Technology who were so patient with me during my stay; my old friend Jon Cairns proved to be an expert guide to the Staatsgalerie, Stuttgart on which he worked with James Stirling; Danielle Olsen, formerly of the Wellcome Trust, who suggested I should visit the Grant Museum of Zoology; Marketa Uhlirova who undertook picture research at short notice and hunted down images that seemed to be beyond reach; Jessica Cuthbert-Smith who copy-edited the book so expertly; and my editor, Philippa Brewster at I.B.Tauris, whose patience has been exemplary. I extend my gratitude to all of these people.

Other colleagues and friends have read versions of the manuscript: Mel Gooding has read more than one draft and has been a source of great encouragement to me; John Reeve, Joe Kerr and Peter Wollen also made useful suggestions and moved the project forward. In addition I would like to thank Dinah Casson, Jill Hughes, Andrea Easey, Neil Cummings, James Putnam, Jude Simmons and Bob Wilkinson. Fred Scott probably was not aware that he was helping with this book, but talking to him and teaching with him informed much of my treatment of architecture. I would also like to thank everyone who over more years than I care to think has asked me how the book was progressing; I hope my elaborate excuses for missing my deadlines at least provided some entertainment.

Lastly, I want to thank Caroline Evans and our children Caitlin and Ivo who have brightened every day on which I was engaged on this work, no matter how far away I was. Without Caroline's skills as a reader and critic this book would not have existed. Her belief in both the project and in me has made *The Delirious Museum* possible.

For my father, NORMAN STORRIE
and in memory of my mother, MARY

1. The Delirious Museum

INTRODUCTION

Museums should be invisible. I like art works and institutions that escape any physical presence. Things you can carry in your mind or in your pockets. It's not a matter of laziness or frustration: maybe it's a form of asceticism. With an imaginary museum you can do whatever you want, you can think about it before falling asleep, or you can go out in the morning and build it from scratch. And if it doesn't work, there is nothing to be ashamed of. You can always say that it was simply an exercise in loss. In the end, I just think there is a certain strength in being invisible.

Maurizio Cattelan[1]

The title of this work has two sources. One source is an essay called 'The Delirious Museum', by David Mellor, in a book of photographs by David Ross.[2] Mellor discusses the photographs in the context of two texts. The first of these is by Jacques Derrida and deals with the way in which the 'frame' insinuates itself into the view of the object. The second text discussed by Mellor is Theodor Adorno's *The Valéry-Proust Museum* which examines how the spectator is drawn into an intimate relationship with the displayed object through the paraphernalia of the immediate museum environment.

The second source for the title is *Delirious New York* by Rem Koolhaas. This is described by the author as a '*retroactive manifesto* for Manhattan'.[3] Koolhaas' book could also be seen as a selective, maverick history of New York. This book predates Koolhaas' involvement with museum architecture and is a paean of praise to the urban condition exemplified by the 'Downtown Athletic Club' with its fictional representation of naked 'metropolitan bachelors' wearing boxing gloves and eating oysters.

I first began to unearth the Delirious Museum in a conversation with colleagues some years ago. We were discussing the pros and cons of museum admission charges. This is a discussion that for peculiar political and historical reasons might only occur in Britain. I am in favour of free admission to museums and I was then. At the time there was a split between museums in London over this issue; the British Museum, the National Gallery and the National Portrait Gallery all had free entry; the 'South Kensington' museums: the Victoria & Albert Museum, the Science Museum and the Natural History Museum, all charged for entry. I defended my position by saying that 'museums should be a continuation of the street'. I did not mean that they should have to compete with the street in terms of their speed of communication or that they should appeal to passers-by in the same way as, say, a shop or a games arcade. Instead, I was suggesting that there should be ease of access to both building and collection that in effect integrates them into the life of the city. This premise has led me to look in more detail at the relationship between museum and city. In some ways any city is a Delirious Museum: a place overlaid with levels of history, a multiplicity of situations, events and objects open to countless interpretations. If there was a single starting point for this train of thought it would be Christopher Alexander's essay from the 1960s, 'A City is not a Tree', in which he describes the city as a 'semilattice' of interconnections and overlaps.[4] The Delirious Museum that I will examine has continuity with the street and it aspires to the condition of the city. What I want to do is to reclaim the museum on behalf of the city and vice versa. By shifting the perception of the collection and the container – for want of a better word, the 'architecture' – it is possible to re-evaluate the relationship between museum and city in terms of shared experience.

Most cities have evolved over a long period of time and they have often done so with very little control. The museum, however, is traditionally associated with order and classification. 'Neutral' taxonomic systems have been used as a means of 'clarification' and education. Often this neutrality has meant limiting, either by accident or by design, the possible interpretations of the museum. I argue that it is possible to subvert this position.

All museums carry within them the seed of their own delirium. To a greater or lesser degree they can be re-interpreted in terms of the breakdown of control and classification. This can happen in a number of ways: an obsessive level of control can be self-subverting, while its opposite, a state of chaos, can up-end perceived notions of the museum. Messiness, category confusion, theatricality, elaborate historical layering and museological fictionalizing can, singly or in combination, go towards creating the Delirious Museum. It is as if some of the museums I describe are about to loose their grip on their contents and themselves. When asked by the curators of the Palais de Tokyo the question 'What do you expect from an art institution in the 21st century?' one participant said 'Cheap, fast and out of control'.[5] This description applies equally to the Delirious Museum and to the delirious city.

In *Complexity and Contradiction in Architecture*, Robert Venturi wrote:

> I am for messy vitality over obvious unity. I include the non-sequitur and proclaim the duality. I am for richness of meaning rather than clarity of meaning; for the implicit function as well as the explicit function. I prefer 'both-and' to 'either-or', black and white, and sometimes gray, to black or white.[6]

The Delirious Museum does not replace the museums that we know; it exists in parallel to the museum as it has evolved. It brings a new level of 'messy vitality' and 'richness of meaning' to the museum.

I confess to an anxiety that the Delirious Museum cannot be made; that it can *only* be brought into existence retroactively and it is, in effect, a construction of nostalgia. Perhaps it is the re-realization of the museum that transforms it, that makes it *delirious*. Acknowledging this, I have tried to prove that the Delirious Museum *can* be designed and constructed. So my study moves from 'history' to contemporary architecture and back again. My own background is as an architect who designs exhibitions. I have worked in a number of the museums discussed, most notably the British Museum,[7] so many of the observations made are based on an intimate knowledge of particular places. In creating exhibitions, I have been aware of the way these ephemeral events pass into the history of a place. I see the exhibitions I have designed as experiments where unpredictable ingredients are combined. Sometimes the result is quiet resolution and sometimes the consequences of the combination are explosive. By extension these experiments are part of the life of the city too.

What is the Delirious Museum of the title? It is something both built and unbuilt. It *inheres* in certain buildings and museums, in some artworks, and some unplanned city spaces. The Delirious Museum is nebulous and slippery. It is a parasitical idea found in the fabric of cities, in urban practices and fragments, that is, in *space*. But you also find it in *narratives,* both in and out of time – in fictional fragments, in historical anecdote and near-forgotten detail.

This book weaves together myths, histories and buildings. It tracks the Delirious Museum first as an idea that is embodied in several forms – chapters that are, respectively, a story, a theory, a laboratory, a collection and a walk. The idea of the Delirious Museum is 'grown' in the first six chapters, like a culture in a lab. In the Petri dish in the lab it looks very different from how it will appear later in the book, out there in the world, in the built environment. In the lab the microscope takes the familiar and magnifies it into the strange and mysterious.

Yet once it does move out into the world, it is no less strange and mysterious, merely differently so. Subsequent chapters look at the Delirious Museum as architecture, not as a finished 'thing' but as a new mutation. Escaped from the lab, it settles into its new host, the building. There it mutates into several forms, all of which can go unnoticed – but, equally, can be perceived by the naked eye if you know where, or rather, how, to look. You need a different way of looking to access London of the 1800s, Paris of the 1840s, Las Vegas of the 1990s, and to tie these in with certain European artistic and architectural projects of the 20th and 21st centuries. You need historical knowledge and visual and conceptual acuity to see what is already there but that goes unnoticed, incognito, as if in a parallel universe.

All the forms that constitute the Delirious Museum also determine the form of the book. It is neither pure architectural analysis, nor urbanism, nor history nor literature alone; instead it weaves these forms together. Perhaps the book itself is a Delirious Museum mimicking what it describes, for it is, among other things, a repository of anecdotes and arcane facts. It is my collection.

If the Delirious Museum is first and foremost an idea, the second half of the book pursues the Delirious Museum from urbanism, image and idea into architecture. Key practitioners include Soane, Scarpa and Libeskind. But the idea escapes again, makes its own way, and scuttles into the New World of the late 20th century – the rampant capitalism of Las Vegas via the global art brands of Guggenheim and Getty. This is not so different from the origins of the Delirious Museum in other moments and places of rapidly expanding consumer culture: Soane's London during the Industrial Revolution and mid-19th-century Paris.

The book suggests a historical moment in the development of capitalism and its offshoots after the Enlightenment as a conceptual framework for the context in which the Delirious Museum can lodge itself and grow in its various mutations – image, idea, architectural form, historical fragment, cemetery, department store, fiction, motel, museum, film or artwork. The Delirious Museum makes its way into the cracks and crevices of many aspects of commodity culture; there it lodges and grows in all its forms, in a parallel life but still dependent upon its 'host'.

The chapters are numbered in a conventional way but they can also be read as one might visit the rooms in a museum, visiting different collections of interest, doubling back, taking the shortest route or heading straight for a particular exhibit or the café (though I do not know which chapter that might be). I begin with a convulsive moment for Modernism, one of the events that make up the history of the Delirious Museum. In Chapters 2 and 3 I develop the ideas created in the preceding narrative in terms of a theoretical background. This is, in effect, my own 'manifesto' for the Delirious Museum and it will draw on a series of modernist views of the city: the flâneur, as identified by Baudelaire and theorized by Benjamin, Surrealism and the Situationists. Chapter 4 describes the ephemeral experiments of the early history of the Delirious Museum. Chapter 5 is a description of an imaginary museum devoted to the work of artists who worked or are working with the idea of the museum. Chapter 6 constructs, from existing fragments of a real city – London – an unstable and restless version of the Delirious Museum. Chapter 7 expands on the peculiarly interdependent relationship between the mausoleum and the museum, between the deathly and the displayed. Chapter 8 deals with the particular delirium induced by obsessive architectural (and curatorial) control as exhibited in the work of Carlo Scarpa. The following chapter takes a broader view of the architecture of the museum in the 20th century. Chapter 10 is an examination of the work and ideas of Daniel Libeskind. Chapter 11 represents a geographical and historical shift to a relatively new city on the 'Pacific Rim', Los Angeles, and concentrates on two museums that exemplify separate museological tendencies. The first of these is the acropolis that is Richard Meier's Getty Center. In contrast, the second, the Museum of Jurassic Technology, almost disappears behind a Culver City shopfront. The final chapter tentatively suggests a re-reading of the fantastic urbanism of Las Vegas in terms of the Delirious Museum; a place containing both 'spectacle' and 'situation' and where the museum exists alongside the museum's antithesis.

1

THE LOUVRE: AN ABSENCE

Our civilization will leave to the future ages only its roundhouses and its railroad tracks. Scholars will perish trying to decipher the inscriptions.

Guillaume Apollinaire to Max Jacob[1]

The snare

So much starts at the Louvre. This place is where the private collection, the *wunderkammer*, was transformed into the public museum. Although the idea of making the collection and the building accessible was mooted before 1789, this proposal came to nothing. It took the modern convulsion of revolution to bring the museum into existence. Within a few days of the setting up of the revolutionary government in 1789 a decree was passed to open the palace to the public. This duly happened on the first anniversary of the creation of the Republic. At the core of the collection are the riches of the aristocracy and the loot of France's imperial past. Baudelaire in his poem 'The Swan' speaks of seeing a confusion of bric-à-brac glittering through the windows of the Louvre, while outside in the street he watches the ridiculous wanderings of the creature escaped from a menagerie.[2] In Zola's novel *L'Assomoir* of 1876, the members of a wedding party, after much discussion about how to spend time on a rainy afternoon, take a walk round the museum en route from ceremony to banquet. Only one of the party has visited the Louvre before; the poverty of their lives has restricted them to a small geographical area around Barbès-Rochechouart. Inevitably, as those out of their class and out of their depth in Zola's moral tale, the visitors get lost in the museum:

'Seized with alarm and despondency, they wandered aimlessly through galleries, still in crocodile behind Monsieur Madinier, now mopping his brow and beside himself with rage against the authorities, whom he accused of having changed the position of the doors. Attendants and visitors watched them go past and marvelled.'[3] The museum, brought into being with the best of intentions, has already become both labyrinth and snare.

In 1993 the American architect I. M. Pei completed the glass pyramid that now marks the entrance to the museum and to a subterranean shopping mall. The pyramid is the centre point of a re-development scheme called the Grand Louvre; it serves both as an entrance and as an organizational point for the whole complex, creating routes into the separate wings of the museum. The pyramid forms a hub that is meant to clarify the layout of the museum labyrinth. It is a comprehensible space that uses the architectural language, at its most luxurious, of the adjoining shopping mall. But the pyramid also has an inherent element of parody as befits an object created in the first flush of architectural post-modernism. Is it meant to reinforce the widely held view that all museums are tombs and that they are full of grave goods? Or is the intention to mock the imperial ambition, not just of Napoleon but of the Louvre itself? In its ghostly transparency it could even be read as parodying its own architectural antecedent. The pyramids of Egypt were meant to be impenetrable, not spaces at all but solid geometric artefacts. Even this architectural spectre has international influence: it is seen as a prototype for the re-organization of unruly national collections and their buildings. The British Museum in the creation of its Great Court has a similar ambition. A by-product of the pyramid is the way in which it has become possible to visit the Louvre without visiting the museum of the same name. The institution is thus magnified and made more pervasive in the minds of visitors. Simultaneously, the Louvre is made diffuse and colonises sections of the city intended for other activities. Some years before the construction of the pyramid, the Louvre colonized other bits of city such as the Metro station Louvre Rivoli. The platforms of the station were occupied by vitrines containing plaster copies of the artefacts. The walls, dressed in stone, featured niches within which could be glimpsed life-size photographs of exhibits. Today, in the tra-

dition of out-moded and neglected museum display, the contents of
the vitrines are looking faded and tired.

The space

Zola identified the seed of delirium in the labyrinth of the 19th-
century Louvre but it was not until 1911 that this delirium took root
in the museum. Not only is the Louvre among the first public museums, but it is one of the biggest and it contains artefacts with the
status of cultural icons. The Venus de Milo and 'Mona Lisa' are, perhaps, the two most famous museum exhibits in the world. The fame
of the latter was enhanced by its disappearance for two years. On the
morning of 22 August 1911, the painter Louis Béroud entered the
Salon Carré in order to make some sketches for a satirical painting of
the recently glazed 'Mona Lisa'. He intended to show a fashionable
Parisienne arranging her hair in the reflecting mirror of the glazed
painting. Where the painting should have been there was a gap. The
attendant suggested that the painting had been removed for photography. On investigation it emerged that 'Mona Lisa' was not in the
photography studio and when the curator of the department of Egyptian Antiquities initiated a search it could not be found elsewhere in
the building. By midday the police had sealed off the museum, allowing
visitors out one by one. Eventually the glass and frame of the painting
were discovered in a small access staircase but there was no trace of
the painting itself.

Apollinaire imprisoned

In the end you are tired of that world of antiquity
    O Eiffel Tower shepherdess the bridges this morning are a bleating
                                                                    flock
You have had enough of living in Greek and Roman antiquity . . .[4]

(above) 3. The space vacated by 'Mona Lisa' in the Salon Carré, *L'Illustration*, 26 August 1911.

(facing page) 2. The door onto the Visconti Courtyard forced open by the thief as he made his escape with 'Mona Lisa'. *L'Illustration*, 26 August 1911.

The moment at which the disappearance of 'Mona Lisa' was discovered also marked the beginning of a chain reaction of events that act as a metaphor for modernism's ambivalent relationship with the museum. The two main characters in this story, the artist Picasso and the poet Apollinaire, are bound up in the creation of modern art. There seems to be no agreed version of the events that preceded the arrest and imprisonment of Apollinaire. Opinions vary about the sequence of events surrounding the affair but they were certainly precipitated by the scandal not just of the theft of 'Mona Lisa' but of the ease with which it was taken from the gallery. Apollinaire's friend and sometimes secretary, Géry Pieret, had a history of stealing from the Louvre. He had a number of histories: at the time of the scandal he was not long returned from the Klondike Gold Rush and was still sporting yellow chaps and a stetson around Paris. Apollinaire portrayed him as 'Baron Ignace d'Ormesan' in L'Hérésiarque et Cie. Pieret subsequently adopted this title as his pseudonym. In 1907 he had acquired two Iberian statuettes that he subsequently passed to Picasso. Whether Picasso knew of the origin of the pieces is uncertain, but some versions of the story suggest that Picasso was told by Pieret to keep the sculptures secret. When 'Mona Lisa' went missing, Pieret returned another piece of sculpture that he had also stolen from the Louvre to a newspaper office as a publicity stunt and, ostensibly, to attract attention to lax security at the museum. Apollinaire had already published an article in Paris-Journal on the same subject, saying: 'The Louvre is less well protected than a Spanish Museum'.[5] The sculpture that Pieret returned had sat on the mantelpiece of Apollinaire's apartment during Pieret's stay. Apollinaire, knowing of his friend's actions, thought that Pieret might also have stolen the famous painting and became worried that the statuettes held by Picasso would also come to light. Picasso, the Spaniard, and Apollinaire, born in Rome, were both already exercised by the possibility of being deported as aliens, and then decided to dispose of the incriminating pieces by throwing them into the Seine. On the night they had planned to do this, Apollinaire and Picasso spent the evening playing cards '. . . while they sat waiting for the fatal moment when they would set out for the Seine – "the moment of the crime" – they had pretended to play cards all evening, doubtless in imitation of certain bandits they had read about'.[6] Eventually they set off with the stolen statuettes in a suitcase. After walking the streets of Paris for a large part of the evening they abandoned the plan. Perhaps they felt guilty about disposing of something so valuable or perhaps the opportunity to drop the pieces quietly into the river did not present itself. In most accounts it was Apollinaire who, the next morning, took the statuettes to the same newspaper office previously visited by Pieret.[7] A promise of secrecy was extracted as to who had delivered the statuettes. But the following day the police came to search Apollinaire's apartment, finding incriminating evidence regarding the Louvre statuettes. He was subsequently arrested for handling stolen property and for suspicion of involvement in the theft of 'Mona Lisa'.

A few days after the arrest of Apollinaire, Picasso was brought in by the police and under questioning he mysteriously denied that he even knew Apollinaire. Picasso was allowed to leave and was not charged. Apollinaire was eventually freed on a provisional basis and, after much agitation from influential friends, charges were dropped. But he was affected by his time in prison and although he and Picasso did not fall out, their friendship cooled. In his poem 'Zone' Apollinaire wrote:

> Now you are in Paris at the examining magistrate's
> They have placed you under arrest like a criminal[8]

In *L'Antitradition Futuriste,* a 'Manifeste-synthèse' issued in Milan on 29 June 1913 in support of the Italian Futurists, Apollinaire offered a 'Rose' to his many artist friends and 'MER . . . DE . . .' to: 'Académismes . . . Historiens . . . Museés . . .'. In this, he may have been venting his spleen against the Louvre, but he was also entering into the spirit of the Futurist Marinetti's proclamation:

> Museums: cemeteries! . . . Identical, surely, in the sinister promiscuity of so many bodies unknown to one another. Museums: public dormitories where one lies forever beside hated or unknown beings. . . . Turn aside the canals to flood the museums![9]

Found and lost

Later that year in Florence an art dealer received a letter offering 'Mona Lisa' for sale. He took it as a hoax and replied that he only dealt in originals and that he was unable to visit Paris to view the painting. Soon afterwards he was visited by a man calling himself Leonardo Vincenzo who said that 'Mona Lisa' was in his hotel room and that he required half a million lire and a guarantee that the painting would remain in its homeland, Italy. The dealer alerted the director of the Uffizi and the police, who then infiltrated the hotel. The next day, Leonardo Vincenzo was visited in his hotel room by the dealer, accompanied by the director. Here they saw 'Mona Lisa' being taken from a secret compartment at the bottom of a travelling trunk. This trunk was at once an echo of the suitcase within which Apollinaire and Picasso had concealed the Iberian statuettes and a pre-echo of the *Boîte-en-valise* (the 'Portable Museum') created by Marcel Duchamp years later. The dealer, the director and the thief then took the painting to the Uffizi to verify that this was indeed 'Mona Lisa' and not a copy. Vincenzo was immediately arrested and his name was revealed to be Vincenzo Peruggia, a workman who had been engaged some years previously at the Louvre. His naïve attempt at a kind of cultural restitution (with a price tag) met with limited success: the painting was then displayed in Florence, Rome and Milan before its triumphant return to Paris.[10]

The Italian poet and militarist D'Annunzio tried to reclaim the whole story of the theft for himself. He first hinted that he had commissioned Perrugia to steal the painting then, in 1920, said that 'Mona Lisa' had passed through his hands but that he arranged for its return to the Louvre due to his 'satiety and disgust' with it.[11]

Some years later, the Surrealists (given their name by Apollinaire) were to appropriate the painting for their own ends. 'Mona Lisa' was now fair game. In 1919 Marcel Duchamp added a moustache and goatee to a cheap reproduction and made it the vehicle for one of his risqué puns.[12] Subsequently, Duchamp was to make a postcard-sized reproduction of this work for the *Boîte-en-valise*. Salvador Dali, taking his cue from Duchamp, exaggerated the moustache and egotistically turned 'Mona Lisa' into a self-portrait. In 1930 Fernand Léger incorporated a copy into his painting *Gioconda with Keys,* claiming that it was 'an object like any other object'.[13]

But the story of the return of the painting, and the resolution of the narrative, is a blind. The theft marks the moment when the Delirious Museum infects the Louvre. 'Mona Lisa's' absence changed its meaning forever – Leonardo's famous painting had encountered modernity. In a sense it was 'removed for photography' to be endlessly reproduced mechanically. 'Mona Lisa' was packed up and concealed and, instead of being an object fixed in place both on the wall and in the imagination, it became nomadic. It may never have returned. Now the painting is impossible to see. The space that 'Mona Lisa' occupied on the morning of 22 August 1911 is taken up by a glass box and a crowd of people. Henri Lefebvre wrote:

> The tourist trade – whose aim is to attract crowds to a particular site – historic city, beautiful view, museums etc. – ruins the site insofar as it achieves its aim: the city, the view, the exhibits are invisible behind the tourists, who can only see one another.[14]

How many photographs taken by these museum visitors show nothing but the reflection of the photographer or the camera's white flash? By photographing the painting, the box within which it is contained has become the mirror prophesied by Louis Béroud. The crowds are still looking for the lost painting. But 'Mona Lisa' is forever missing. At the heart of the Ur-museum there is an absence. Melancholy permeates the Salon Carré and seeps out into Paris; a city of lost things.

I have retrospectively appointed Apollinaire as the first curator of the Delirious Museum in compensation for his wrongful imprisonment. The coincidence of his temporary possession of the stolen statuettes from the Louvre and his troubled involvement in the story of 'Mona Lisa' grants him a special relevance to the history of the museum. Inadvertently he was the subversive at the heart of a re-interpretation of the Louvre and, by extension, the institution of the museum itself. At this point the space of the museum changes from presence to absence. The messages of the objects in the collection shift, becoming fluid and uncertain.

2

THE ENDLESS MUSEUM: A 'HOUSE OF DREAMS'

In order to piece together the scattered fragments of the Delirious Museum, a museum in ruins, it is necessary to excavate streets, explore urban spaces and examine ways of looking at cities. The genesis of the Delirious Museum lies not in the history of the museum itself but in ideas about the city, as articulated by Baudelaire, Benjamin, Aragon and Breton. Their ideas constitute both a history and the Delirious Museum itself. Though the 'map is not the territory'[1] the diagram of the labyrinth is also a labyrinth. The anecdotes and stolen manifestos here are at once both theory and collection.

At Charlie Brown's

There is a photograph taken by Bill Brandt in the 1930s. It shows a young couple kissing in a London pub. Next to them sits another man, apparently oblivious to his neighbours. On the wall behind the three people is an assortment of pictures; a sailing ship, a caricature, a soft-edged photograph of the king. Brandt's photograph is called: *At Charlie Brown's*. This pub, also known as the Railway Tavern, was located on West India Dock Road, at the north end of the Isle of Dogs. It sat at the crossroads of a number of routes to the docks and, as such, it became a haunt of sailors setting out on, and returning from, sea voyages. From around the turn of the century many of the sailors deposited artefacts collected on their trips in lieu of payment. Instead of selling these things, the proprietor began to cover the walls of the pub with them. Guidebooks, when they referred to the East End at all, would refer to Charlie Brown's as a pub/museum. The *Guide to London*

4. Bill Brandt, *At Charlie Brown's* (1938).

Pubs (1968) says: 'Part of this collection, which includes weapons of all kinds and ages, matchboxes, antlers, opium pipes and Japanese temple shoes, can still be seen in the Saloon-Lounge, with its curved ceiling, which is actually under the railway bridge. The rest of the collection is, apparently, now divided between a Woodford pub and a private house.'[2] The small photographs in the book show an arched room festooned with objects, including a number of stuffed alligators. Charlie Brown himself died in 1932 and today the pub is gone, swept away for the approach roads to the Canary Wharf office development.

There is a tradition of public house decor in Britain that could be called 'accretion';[3] this is characterized by a slow build-up of objects that have come to belong to the interior. Some pubs buy this look: books are purchased by the metre and left to gather dust, framed pictures come off-the-shelf to give the interior the look of age. In London there are a number of pubs that have 'frozen interiors' with the contents left untouched from a particular moment in time. Charlie Brown's seems to have transcended both of these styles. To be described as a 'pub/museum' suggests that some value could be attached to the collection. This belongs within a separate tradition that began with the collections put together by the proprietors of certain London coffee-houses and taverns in the 18th century. These places had an ambiguous rôle that straddled entertainment and education. The most famous of these was Don Saltero's Coffee House in Cheyne Walk, Chelsea. James Salter, its proprietor, is reputed to have been a servant in the household of the scholarly collector and founder of the British Museum, Sir Hans Sloane. Indeed, Salter said his collection was based around duplicates and copies from Sloane's collection. Thus the history of the popular museum shadows that of the institutional collection though both arise from the private collection, the *wunderkammer*. The artefacts exhibited at Don Saltero's were a mixture of natural history specimens and man-made curiosities. The catalogue for 1732 listed a petrified cat found between the walls of Westminster Abbey, a rose from Jericho, 'the Pope's infallible candle' and 290 other objects.[4] The Royal Swan Tavern in Shoreditch, London, listed 567 items in its catalogue of 1756 including Chinese chopsticks and Charles of Swedeland's boots. In 1752 this pub/museum put on show the rope used to hang a murderer at Execution Dock. The rope was said to cure ailments.[5]

The Bill Brandt photograph, though clearly not a documentary picture of the interior, provides a clue to a particular quality of the Delirious Museum. Brandt's image shows people kissing and drinking in the pub. Incidentally, it shows the same activities taking place in a 'museum'. These are activities that are not meant to happen in a museum, except maybe in the museum café. Yet here the life of the street is brought into the museum in an extreme way. Of course, all museums have this imposed on them to some degree. Despite the fact that parallels are often drawn with the cathedral, most museum buildings are social, rather than religious, spaces, with all the complications that 'social spaces' implies. The former Bankside power station, Tate Modern, has been especially prone to the cathedral comparison. The architects, Herzog & de Meuron, and numerous critics referred to this before and immediately after the opening.[6] The vast entrance space has obvious parallels to the nave of a cathedral, though it is more obviously a turbine hall.

Another, richer, comparison made with museums is to the department store. Both institutions were born out of the same modern impetus and they have many features in common: display, repetition and classification, not to mention commerce.[7] By 1855, Paris boasted two Louvres: the former palace turned museum and its double, the Louvre department store. Walter Benjamin recognized this relationship:

> There are relations between department store and museum, and here the bazaar provides a link. The amassing of artworks in the museum brings them into communication with commodities, which – where they offer themselves en masse to the passer-by – awake in him the notion that some part of this should fall to him as well.[8]

The Delirious Museum acknowledges and even celebrates this ambiguous relationship and welcomes the intrusions and complications that come from the museum being seen as a social space.

Far from consenting to be 'educated' by museological displays and their didactic labels, visitors frequently use museums to other ends: as shelters from the rain, as places of assignation or ancestor worship or as through-routes. At both the British Museum and the National Gallery in London it is possible to traverse city blocks along north/ south axes. The route through the National Portrait Gallery in

London slices a slender triangle off the same block that houses the National Gallery. In Amsterdam's Historical Museum, a painting gallery dramatically colonises a public passageway. This is one component in a series of complex urban spaces that move unnervingly between public and private, open and concealed.

These other 'uses' bring an element of the arcade, the café, the church and the city's streets and parks into the museum. Similarly, the street is a type of museum with its accretions of history, its relics, its wall texts and its patina of age. The visitor to the museum may not even care about the particular history of the museum's objects; her or his interest may be that of a cat-lover, an embalmer, an occultist or a student of industrial design. In *The Museum of Unconditional Surrender* the Croatian Dubravka Ugrešić uses the metaphor of the museum to attempt to regain some form of collective memory for people whose lives have been irrevocably changed by political implosion and war. In the short prologue to the book she lists the contents of a vitrine that are all the items found in the stomach of a deceased walrus.

> The visitor . . . cannot resist the poetic thought that the objects have acquired some . . . secret connections. Caught up in this thought, the visitor then tries to establish semantic coordinates, to reconstruct the historical context (it occurs to him, for instance, that Roland [the walrus] died one week after the Berlin Wall was erected) . . .[9]

The Delirious Museum sits firmly within the city, that most complex of social spaces and the language used here derives from certain urban theories and stratagems relating particularly to walking.[10] Movement through the Delirious Museum is also characterized by wandering or drifting and getting lost. The associations generated by the objects in my imagined museum are open-ended; meanings are un-fixed and transient. The city in flux is the model for the Delirious Museum. To read my museum it is necessary to look at ways in which the modern city has been anatomized as found, as opposed to planned, space. And, as the city and hence the 'museum' under consideration here are constructions of modernity, the theoretical context also belongs within that 'tradition' of modernity. Much of the theoretical language to be used has its origins in studies of modern Paris and in the city itself. In his autobiographical essay 'Hermit in Paris' Italo Calvino wrote:

Paris has the kind of shops where one feels that this is the city which gave shape to that particular way of regarding culture which is the museum, and the museum in turn has given its form to the most varied activities in daily life, so that the galleries in the Louvre and the shop-windows form a continuum. Let's say that everything in the street is ready to go into the museum, or that the museum is ready to absorb the street.[11]

The *flâneur*

Charles Baudelaire in his essay of 1859, *The Painter of Modern Life*, refers to the work of an artist engaged in the description of the spectacle of 'modern life', not just the city street but also, for example, modern warfare and make-up. The artist whom Baudelaire used as his example was the relatively obscure Constantin Guys, but he could have been referring to Edouard Manet, Edgar Degas or Gustave Caillebotte. These painters all addressed the urban scene, which was in the process of being transformed by the boulevards planned by Baron Haussmann from the 1850s onwards. These cut through the proletarian rookeries, the *faubourgs* of Paris with their constant potential for revolution, not just providing slum clearance and easy movement for troops, but also creating a theatre of the street. Wide pavements and roadways set the individual and the crowd on a stage upon which to be viewed. Baudelaire paraphrases Edgar Allan Poe's story 'The Man of the Crowd':

> In the window of a coffee house there sits a convalescent, pleasurably engaged in gazing at the crowd, and mingling, through the medium of thought, in the turmoil of thought that surrounds him. But lately returned from the valley of the shadow of death, he is rapturously breathing in all the odours and essences of life; as he has been on the brink of total oblivion, he remembers, and fervently desires to remember, everything. Finally he hurls himself into the midst of the throng, in pursuit of an unknown, half-glimpsed countenance that has, on an instant, bewitched him. Curiosity had become a fatal, irresistible passion.[12]

In his essay Baudelaire first establishes the status of the *flâneur*:

For the perfect *flâneur*, for the passionate spectator, it is an immense joy to set-up house in the heart of the multitude, amid the ebb and flow of movement, in the midst of the fugitive and the infinite. To be away from home and yet to feel oneself everywhere at home; to see the world, and yet to remain hidden from the world – such are a few of the slightest pleasures of those independent, passionate, impartial natures which the tongue can but clumsily define. The spectator is a *prince* who everywhere rejoices in his incognito.[13]

Baudelaire then goes on to promote what he calls the 'man of the crowd':

Be very sure that this man, such as I have depicted him – this solitary, gifted with an active imagination, ceaselessly journeying across the great human desert – has an aim loftier than that of the mere *flâneur*, an aim more general, something other than the fugitive pleasure of circumstance. He is looking for that quality that you must allow me to call 'modernity' . . .[14]

Walter Benjamin situated the *flâneur* of Paris somewhere between the street-corner idler of Berlin and the man of the crowd of London. Benjamin notes:

There was the pedestrian who would let himself be jostled by the crowd, but there was also the *flâneur* who demanded elbow room and was unwilling to forego the life of a gentleman of leisure.[15]

Benjamin, like Poe, saw the man of the crowd as someone whose 'composure has given way to manic behaviour'.[16] The *flâneur*, the gentleman of leisure, on the other hand, was of the crowd but set apart from it. Like him, the inquisitive modern urban observer, the visitor to the Delirious Museum, moves freely between these rôles. He or she can be both 'of the crowd' and, like the *flâneur*, detached from it.

The desire of the Delirious Museum is that every visitor should succumb to curiosity, that 'irresistible passion' described by Baudelaire. In 1879 Edgar Degas began a series of drawings and etchings of his fellow artist, the American Mary Cassatt, with her sister, in the Louvre.[17] Twenty years prior to this he had been a registered copyist in the museum and this might have kindled his interest in the idea of 'looking' as a subject for his art. The drawings of Mary Cassatt show her from the back so that the viewer is, as it were, looking over her shoulder. Degas drew her leaning on her umbrella, clothed in black and he repeats this silhouette in each of the compositions, moving her like a mannequin from room to room. In *At the Louvre: Mary Cassatt in the Etruscan Gallery* her sister Lydia's attention is drawn away from the guidebook in her hand to gaze at Mary or beyond her. From a vitrine, the two faces of reclining, dead Etruscans gaze out beyond the edge of the picture. Lydia may be a little distracted but Mary seems engrossed in the act of looking. Thus, the viewer of the picture is engaged in a myriad act of looking that involves Degas, Mary Cassatt, Lydia Cassatt and the Etruscan figures. It is tempting to describe this as 'just looking' yet the looking provides the way into the experience of the museum and its objects. There is a particular kind of looking going on here; it is both looking at and looking through. It is also about reflection; the reflection of the glass and the reflection generated by the relationships between objects and their context. In order to get more out of this experience it is necessary to make some kind of imaginative leap, as it is when gazing out, like Baudelaire's man of the crowd, through the shop window.

Despite being historically and socially specific, the *flâneur* – the 19th-century white, upper-middle class male – is still an emblematic figure for modernity.[18] At the same time the presence and pursuit of leisure has become a commonplace for working people. Museums often aspire to the educational and these aspirations are reinforced by the need for public bodies to identify targets that will justify funding. But the basis of the museum's 'use' remains within the broad sphere of leisure. The counterpoint to the rigour of the organized visit is the random process of visual consumption in which the individual and the small group engage. This creates, in Peter Campbell's phrase, an 'unresolved narrative'.[19] When the museum is (mis)read by the cat-lover or the occultist, the narrative may go beyond the unresolved to become deviant: a reading against the grain of the museum. Inevitably, the viewer makes her or his own connections; constructs a series of relationships and a line of questioning that is particular to that individual.

Walter Benjamin and the arcades

The idea of the museum-goer as *flâneur* has been explored by Pierre Missac in his detailed discussion of Walter Benjamin's Arcades Project.[20] He extends the idea of the arcade to include glass architecture and the atrium. Naming the *flâneur* on this occasion the 'art lover', Missac describes how he

> contents himself with a fairly brief tour of some rooms, a rapid flânerie to see new acquisitions or a restoration. He quickly finds himself in an atrium that is not only characterized by greater and greater square footage but also occupied by fixtures that have nothing to do with the works on display.[21]

Missac suggests that this extends Benjamin's notion of the arcade as the 'collective's house of dreams' to include the museum. Not only the museum, but also the objects, their relationships to each other and their relationships to their surroundings, are inextricably connected to this proposition.

The work of Walter Benjamin forms a series of links between the spaces of 19th-century Paris, the writings of Baudelaire, the idea of collecting and the convulsive city that the Surrealists were to inhabit in the 1920s. Benjamin himself was a collector of books and he wrote about this in his celebrated essay 'Unpacking My Library'.[22] Elsewhere he wrote about other collectors[23] and, in one of his radio broadcasts for children, about stamp collecting. But his most ambitious engagement with the collection was the Arcades Project. There seems to be no consensus of what Benjamin meant the final form of the Arcades Project to be. Was it a book or the research for a book? Was it, indeed, a kind of *objet deluxe* created under the influence of Surrealism? Today, it exists in book form (in German since 1982 and in English since 1999) as an assemblage of other people's texts put together and classified by Benjamin the collector. At the same time, though, it is also many of the things described within it: a city, a ruin, a panorama and a museum.

> Method of this project: literary montage. I needn't *say* anything. Merely show. I shall purloin no valuables, appropriate no ingenious formulations. But the rags, the refuse — these I will not inventory but allow, in

the only way possible, to come into their own: by making use of them.[24]

If the collection that is the Arcades Project is a kind of museum, it is as if Benjamin is here proposing a museum without labels and without explanation; a museum in which the role of the curator is returned to being the custodian rather than the interpreter.

Throughout his writings Benjamin returned to the theme of the city. Berlin was the site for reminiscences of his childhood, Marseilles was experienced under the influence of hashish, Moscow was the scene for his pursuit of Asja Lacis and, writing with Lacis, Naples became a place of delirium:

> As porous as this stone is the architecture. Building and action interpenetrate in the courtyards, arcades, and stairways. In everything they preserve the scope to become a theatre of new, unforeseen constellations.[25]

It is as if Benjamin sees Naples as the unconscious of Paris:

> . . . one can scarcely discern where building is still in progress and where dilapidation has already set in . . . Porosity results not only from the indolence of the Southern artisan, but also, from the passion for improvisation, which demands that space and opportunity be at any price preserved. Buildings are used as a popular stage.[26]

This is Benjamin's retro-active, collective dream for Paris:

> To construct the city topographically – tenfold and a hundredfold – from out of its arcades and its gateways, its cemeteries and bordellos, its railroad stations . . . just as formerly it was defined by its churches and its markets. And the more secret, the more deeply embedded figures of the city: murders and rebellions, the bloody knots in the network of the streets, lairs of love, and conflagrations.[27]

Here, in these 'lairs of love' and in these 'conflagrations' lies the link to the Surrealists. Theirs was an imagined city lying just beneath the surface and behind the history of the visible. For Benjamin, Surrealist writing opened up a way to see Paris in these terms, as a place with associations beyond the closed descriptions of Baedeker and the Haussmannization of the street pattern. Surrealist readings of Paris created a porous, dream city.

> At the centre of this world of things stands the most dreamed-of of their objects, the city of Paris itself. But only revolt completely exposes its surrealist face . . .[28]

If there was a single image that made this possibility manifest, it was the arcades. These were fissures in the urban fabric, spaces that opened up the possibility of the subversive theatre of city life. If the boulevards were about control and spectacle, then the arcades allowed for the possibility of a rending of the fabric, places in which to wander, cutting through city blocks, both man-made caves and urban labyrinths. 'The father of Surrealism was Dada; its mother was an arcade'.[29] The particular arcade upon which the Surrealists alighted – the movement's 'mother' – was the Passage de l'Opéra.

Aragon and Breton; the passage as museum

The Passage de l'Opéra was demolished in 1929 to make way for the latest phase of urban improvements to Paris, the extension to the Boulevard Haussmann. In this arcade had been the Certa Café, the favourite meeting place of the Dadaists and those who would eventually break from them under André Breton's influence. Among these was the other prime mover of early Surrealism, Louis Aragon, who in his 1926 book *Paris Peasant,* inventorized the interior of the arcade in detail. Described by the author as a 'Modern Mythology', the book was split into two parts discussing first, the Passage de l'Opéra and then the 19th-century park, the Buttes Chaumont. These sites held a particular resonance for Aragon and the Surrealists. The part dealing with the park is a description of the topography of the place and the associations that various features have with human activities (for example love-making and suicide). The larger first part, where Aragon describes the passage, is more complex. Here the description of 'topography' is taken to an extreme. Aragon notes the details of shop signs and the exact placement of rooms and doorways. He not only describes the drinks available at the Certa Café but also reproduces the tariff list. The fascination with the minutiae of this place points

(facing page) 5. Passage de l'Opéra.

towards a curatorial concern. There is an emphasis on the windows of the arcade and the, sometimes surreptitious, act of looking:

> . . . the Librairie Rey, with its window displays of magazines, popular novels and scientific publications. It is one of the four or five places in Paris where one can glance through magazines at leisure without buying them. So it usually has its quota of young people reading busily, making a little tent of the uncut pages to squint inside, and others for whom this illusory occupation provides a screen from behind which they can keep an eye on the comings and goings in the passage . . . A single cashier surveys the bookshelves, from his perch in a little glass-panelled booth equipped with a frontal grille through which business is transacted.[30]

Aragon then goes on to describe a concièrge, elsewhere in the passage, inhabiting his glass cubicle at the foot of the stairs leading to a set of furnished apartments: 'watching skirts and trousers pass by as they climb up towards their assignations'.[31] He scrutinizes the windows of the champagne seller and the truss shop and he remarks on a melancholy vitrine:

> Directly opposite the tailor and the hairdresser's, a showcase belonging to the Restaurant Arrigoni, in which a coloured picture of a memorable banquet holds the place of honour amid a display of long-necked, straw-corseted Italian wine bottles . . .[32]

This interest in detailed description is not dissimilar to the photographic work undertaken between 1909 and 1915 by Eugène Atget in his *Seven Albums*, which meticulously, even obsessively recorded hitherto uncelebrated fragments of the fabric of Paris. One of the albums, *Métiers, boutiques et étalages de Paris*, was a record of the ephemeral fragments of street displays: kiosks, market barrows, the stalls put on pavements outside shops. Another album, *Enseignes et vielles boutiques de Paris*, documented shop façades. These pictures fix moments and places that are largely gone; when Atget photographed them he knew they were either temporary by nature or were endangered by development. At the same time, these photographs, along with those in the other albums, are a means of classifying the city, a kind of archive of the streets; a Delirious Museum of photographs. Atget became at once photographer and curator, in fact he preferred the term 'archivist' to 'artist'. Atget's images undoubtedly influenced the Surrealists though he preceded them and was wary of being linked to them.[33]

The information in *Paris Peasant* is drawn together in an analytical manner that is almost like re-assembling the clues on an archaeological site. What Freud suggested as a metaphor for uncovering the unconscious, the Surrealists extended into the realm of the city. Aragon, by reconstructing the Passage de l'Opéra in a text also transforms it. The passage or arcade is anyway an ambivalent kind of urban space. It is enclosed yet open, inside yet top lit, both public and private. While it is a space that clearly belongs to the street it is something separate from it. 'What I forgot to say is that the Passage de l'Opera is a big glass coffin . . .'.[34] Aragon goes on to describe 'the changing light of the arcades, a light ranging from the brightness of the tomb to the shadow of sensual pleasure . . .'.[35] This is an echo of Zola's description of the fictional Passage du Pont Neuf in *Thérèse Raquin*:

> . . . the arcade takes on the sinister look of a real cut-throat alley; great shadows creep along the paving-stones and damp draughts blow in from the street until it seems like an underground gallery dimly lit by three funereal lamps.[36]

Knowing of the imminent demolition of the Passage, Aragon writes it back into existence as a 'mythological' subject. In his unfinished Arcades Project Walter Benjamin took the idea of the arcade to represent the birth of the modern city. Aragon, in choosing to document this particular arcade, acknowledged the importance of this kind of space to the city, while recognizing the possibilities of a longing for that which is about to be lost. Benjamin acknowledged the particular delirium of both place (the Passage) and the written word (*Paris Peasant*): '. . . evenings in bed I could not read more than a few words of it before my heartbeat got so strong I had to put the book down . . .'.[37]

There is, of course, no trace of the Passage de l'Opéra. Under its site is the small ticket hall of the Metro station Richelieu-Drouot. This is dominated by a large, black, marble war memorial. The memorial, to employees of the Metro who died in the First World War, covers an entire wall with names inscribed into its surface from Abraham, through Breton to Zoeller. It appears to be sinking; the base is several centimetres below the level of the floor. The central figure is of a woman with arms stretched upwards to the vault of the ceiling. It is as if the roof of the station needs to be supported by the statue but it is still too heavy and the memorial is slowly descending into the earth. Above ground, the site is occupied by the confluence of two boulevards and that most impervious of all architectural forms: a bank. For my purposes there was nothing there, but on my visit I took consolation in small discoveries: I noticed numerals, like catalogue numbers, impressed into the tar – after rain these took longer to dry than the surrounding pavement. I also found a small white sticker on the bus shelter on the site. This showed the head of a dog in three-quarters view stamped onto a blank manufacturer's checking label. The image had run in the rain or faded through time so the dog's head was a ghostly remnant. But the ghost was not that of the Passage.

Benjamin also noted the physical similarities and the common use of iron as a building material in both arcades and exhibition halls. By extension it is useful to apply this comparison to museum galleries: long, high spaces with central access lit by daylight from above ('the brightness of the tomb' or what John Soane called a *lumière mys-térieuse*). Both spaces are semi-public and used for display. And, returning to the shop window through which Baudelaire's 'man of the crowd' views the city, the shop windows of the passage have similar-ities to museum showcases. These vitrines, of course, work in both directions: they are seen into *and* out of, and this ambiguity marks them out as fragments of the Delirious Museum.

Nadja, written by André Breton and published in 1928, also describes fragments of Paris. In this work Breton describes his encounters with the elusive Nadja in various streets and cafés haunted by the Surrealists. The narrative is mainly made up with a series of wanderings starting and ending almost arbitrarily. One such walk, before Nadja herself is introduced in the book, describes Bre-ton and Marcel Noll's visit to the flea market at Saint Ouen. He talks about previous visits:

> I go there often, searching for objects that can be found nowhere else: old-fashioned, broken, useless, almost incomprehensible ... like, for example, that kind of irregular white shellacked half cylinder covered with reliefs and depressions that are meaningless to me, streaked with

horizontal and vertical reds and greens, preciously nestled in a case under a legend in Italian, which I brought home and after careful examination I have finally identified as some kind of statistical device, operating three-dimensionally and recording the population of a city in such and such a year, though all this makes it no more comprehensible to me.[38]

This near hysterical passage sparks off a long sequence of descriptions of similarly 'incomprehensible' objects: a glove, a sign with a double meaning and a picture incorporating three separate images, a *tableau vivant* of a tiger, a vase and an angel. In *Mad Love*, published in 1937, Breton returns to the flea market, this time with the sculptor Giacometti and once again he encounters 'the *catalyzing* role of the found object'.[39] They each discover an object on the stalls that Breton claims has striking associations for them: Giacometti a mask with odd louvred eye-slits and Breton a large wooden spoon with a tiny shoe carved into its end. But it is striking that Breton does not see the same possibilities in the museum nor, indeed, in the museum object. Breton seems intent on possessing the object of his desire rather than just recording it visually. In his essay 'Surrealism and Painting' of 1927 Breton wrote:

Now I confess that I have passed like a madman through the slippery halls of museums. But I am not the only one. In spite of some marvelous glances thrown to me by women similar in every way to those of today, I have not for an instant been fooled by what those subterranean and immovable walls had to offer me of the unknown . . . Outside, the street prepared a thousand more real enchantments for me.[40]

Then in *Nadja*, these 'glances' come back to haunt him:

How much I admire those men who decide to be shut up at night in a museum in order to examine at their own discretion, at an illicit time, some portrait of a woman they illuminate by a dark lantern.[41]

Side-by-side on the Boulevard Montmartre are the entrances to the Musée Grévin waxworks and that of the Passage Jouffroy. The museum was opened in 1882 and houses the usual displays of the famous and infamous. On the ground floor are the Salles des Colonnes and La Coupole which are devoted largely to contemporary displays. On the first floor there is a hall of mirrors called the Palais des Mirages. In *Nadja*, Breton admits that his own desires have been thwarted:

the impossibility of obtaining permission to photograph an adorable wax-work figure in the Musée Grévin, on the left, between the hall of modern political celebrities and the hall at the rear of which, behind a curtain, is shown 'an evening at the theatre': it is a woman fastening her garter in the shadows, and is the only statue I know of with eyes, the eyes of provocation, etc.[42]

There is no evidence to suggest that Breton snatched his own 'illicit time' in the Musée Grévin. Maybe, instead, he did this at the claustrophobic Musée Gustave Moreau, a short walk from both the waxworks and Breton's own home. In 1961 Breton wrote:

Discovering the Gustave Moreau Museum when I was sixteen permanently formed my manner of loving. It was there that beauty and love were revealed to me in the many faces and postures of women. That 'type' of woman obstructed my sight of all others – I was absolutely enchanted.[43]

André Breton's house and studio was in the rue Fontaine. Its façade gives little away. The doorway is part of the wall of a theatre designed in a vaguely modernist style. To see anything of Breton's studio and proto-museum it is necessary to make a detour to the Centre Georges Pompidou where the part of the collection taken in lieu of death duties is kept. Embedded in their gallery of 20th-century art is one whole room of Breton's collection. Displayed within a large vitrine is the faithfully recreated display of the Surrealist and African art objects that Breton juxtaposed in his studio at rue Fontaine. Some of these, along with pieces from the collections of, amongst others Paul Eluard, Louis Aragon and Tristan Tzara, formed part of the exhibits in the Counter Colonial Exhibition of 1931. This was set up in opposition to the official Colonial Exposition and was an attempt to undermine the imperialist message with one sympathetic to the Communist Party. The Surrealists' exhibition was held with the support of the Soviet Union and was housed in Melnikov's Soviet Pavilion, itself a vestige of the 1925 exposition.[44] In retrospect it is more difficult to distinguish between the intention of the Colonial Exposition and that of Breton's obsessive collecting. And, of course, the stolen Louvre statuettes would have looked perfectly at home here.

In 2003 the remainder of Breton's collection was put up for sale by his daughter. At the auction disgruntled 'surrealists' circulated fake

Euro notes showing the head of Breton and bearing the legend: 'Your money for the stinking corpse of a poet . . .'.[45]

Afraid of the institutional power of the state museum, the Surrealists seem to have shied away from direct links to it. At one point in the narrative, Nadja seems to be leading Breton to the Louvre but they stop in the Tuilleries, it is late and they go to a café. One of the early Paris Dada events attended by Aragon and Breton was held in the churchyard of Saint Julien le Pauvre in 1921. The announcement for the meeting proposed other sites for the next events 'which really have no reason for existing . . . To participate in this first visit is to become aware of human progress in possible works of destruction . . .'.[46] Among the list of proposed sites for other meetings was the Louvre. As if in acknowledgement of their fear of the museum, the Dadaists' planned visit to the museum with 'no reason for existing' never took place. Other connections between the Surrealists and the museum may be tangential but they are numerous. A 'catalogue' of painted Surrealist museums would include René Magritte's label/object paintings ('In my pictures I showed objects situated where we never find them'[47]), Paul Delvaux's *The Spitzner Museum* of 1943 and de Chirico's still-life assemblages. Joseph Cornell, working in the United States at some distance from 'official' Surrealism, made boxes that were clearly influenced, as much by museums and archives, as by his personal obsessions. The influence of Marcel Duchamp on Surrealist exhibition installations and, by extension, the museum gallery, is discussed in Chapter 4.

Lautréamont's words, borrowed by Man Ray for the first issue of *La Revolution Surréaliste*, are often seen as a dictum for the early phase of Surrealism: 'as beautiful as the chance meeting on a dissecting table of a sewing machine and an umbrella'. That the Surrealists never made a direct connection between this dictum and the museum display is remarkable. The museum cabinet (and not just the cabinet of curiosities) brings together a huge range of artefacts in an attempt at forming some cohesive history or narrative through 'things'. There is certainly a degree of pleasure to be had by visitors (and here we could include the 'group' visitor too) in the looking, not just at the individual object but at the display itself.

3

Beneath the Museum, the Street

So now we are entering into the limitless Paris adored by collectors,
this city which invites you to make collections of everything, because it
accumulates and classifies and redistributes, where you can search as in
an archaeological excavation.

Italo Calvino[1]

*Leonardo Vincenzo created a nomadic museum when he took 'Mona Lisa'
back to Italy in a suitcase. He left behind him a space in the Louvre that
the Delirious Museum filled. The Louvre was no longer a closed system. It
was now open-ended and its meanings were fluid and un-fixed. Baudelaire,
Benjamin, Aragon and Breton looked at the city in a new way — reading
between the lines and against the grain. In post-war Paris ideas about
display and the city resurfaced in the work of both artistic and political
groups. Each strand identified the spectacle as important despite having
very different agenda.*

Klein/Arman

In the aftermath of the Second World War, Paris lost its reputation
for being the world capital of art. When artists left Europe before and
during the war, many moved to New York and it was here that the
last influential developments of Surrealism were played out, most
publicly in the exhibition First Papers of Surrealism.[2] While in New
York abstract expressionism took hold in the galleries, in Paris there
was a less seemly scramble for recognition. Developments in the
New York art world fitted seamlessly into a trajectory leading from
studio, via gallery, to museum. In Paris this was not the case. Instead,

across various movements, there was an antipathy towards the idea of the museum and its stultifying effect. One of these was a group centred on Yves Klein and Arman, who came to be known as the Nouveaux Realistes. Their work returns this narrative briefly to the rarified world of the art gallery but it mirrors the agitational activities of other, more revolutionary, groups. Klein had already established a reputation with his monochrome paintings (in International Klein Blue) in exhibitions in Milan and Paris in 1957, but it was his show at the Iris Clert Gallery, Paris, in the following year that became the *coup de théâtre* that he sought.

The exhibition, 'Le Vide' (The Void), involved Klein and Clert in elaborate preparations. An application was made to the City of Paris to illuminate the Place de la Concorde obelisk in blue light. Two Republican Guards were secured for the *vernissage* and the gallery's exterior was transformed by draping a huge blue curtain over the adjacent archway and painting out the gallery window (also, needless to say, in blue). Klein spent the days before the opening in the gallery covering the traces of any previous exhibition and covering every surface in white paint that he called 'immaterialized blue'. The night of the opening justified all the preparations, and though the lighting of the obelisk was cancelled at the last moment, other events compensated. Huge crowds gathered (Klein had sent out 3,500 invitations) and queued to enter an interior that was emptied of content. Specially prepared blue cocktails were served which turned the urine of those who drank them blue. The police and the fire brigade turned up after a hoax phone call only to find it impossible to enter the street due to the number of people. In the ensuing days Clert and Klein were interrogated over the apparent misuse of the Republican Guards but were let off the hook because government ministers had been on the guest list.

Klein was jubilant over the success of the event. Here was a void creating a complex series of reactions. By clearing the gallery of content, it was as if Klein had been able to start from scratch. Klein wrote:

> Some people were unable to enter, as if an invisible wall prevented them. One day, one of the visitors shouts to me: 'I will come back

when the void is full . . . .' I respond to him: 'When it is full you will no longer be able to enter.'[3]

'Le Vide' was not 'about' museums. Klein wanted art to transcend daily life and this exhibition of de-materialized blue and spectacle was his attempt at this. But the opening of 'Le Vide' and the installation, particularly the photograph of the empty vitrine, haunt museology. This was the museum laid bare as if all its contents had been returned to their rightful owners or re-buried in the sites from which they had been excavated. Klein inadvertently exposed both the desire and the fear inherent to the Delirious Museum.

Though Arman suggested 'filling up' the void created by Klein as the follow-on exhibition, it took him two years to convince Iris Clert that it was acceptable to fill the same rooms with rubbish. The original idea for 'Le Plein' (Full-up) had been to empty the contents of refuse trucks into the gallery, but this was seen as too disgusting and the compromise was to collect discarded items from Paris streets instead. Even this proved difficult and eventually the hoard was supplemented with other material to add bulk. This included old art catalogues and, to Clert's consternation, the unsold works from an exhibition of 'miniatures' (which apparently included a very small Picasso). A tiny space was left for visitors to enter, but otherwise the space was crammed from floor to ceiling with detritus. The opening was once again an event of some note, though not on the scale of Klein's exhibition. The space inside the gallery was so restricted that it was necessary for the guests to assemble in the street. Of the exhibition Klein wrote:

> After my Void, Arman's Full-Up. The universal memory of art lacked this definitive mummification of quantitavism. Reassured at last, all of nature will from this moment begin, as of old, to address us directly and with clarity.[4]

After a few weeks the small amount of rotting organic matter left among the rubbish began to have its effect and it was necessary to close the exhibition before its scheduled run.

Situationists

> What were we to do after we had painted a moustache on the *Mona Lisa*? Did we really wish Genghis Khan to stable his horses in the Louvre?
>
> Alexander Trocchi[5]

The Situationist International was a movement that developed out of various Surrealist splinter groups in the 1950s. If the relationship between Surrealism and the museum is tangential, then that between the Situationists and the museum is antagonistic. However, the Situationists negotiated and understood the city in a way that has parallels to the reading of the Delirious Museum. The primary site for situationist action was the street. The Delirious Museum is an extension of the street. Some of the strategies devised by the Situationists in order to dismantle the meaning of the city can also be used to take apart and re-invent the language of collection and display.

The Situationist International was formed at a conference in Cosio d'Arroscia in Italy in 1957. The founding members had previously belonged to other groups. From Paris there were those who had belonged first to the Lettrists then to the Lettrist International (Guy Debord, Isidore Isou, Michele Bernstein). Another group was artists associated with CoBrA (Copenhagen, Brussels, Amsterdam) and the Movement for an Imaginist Bauhaus (Asger Jorn, Constant, Giuseppe Pinot-Gallizio). There was one member who was the sole represent-ative of the Psychogeographic Committee of London (Ralph Rumney). Between 1958 and 1969 the Situationists published various magazines that expanded on their ideas, initially about art and urban-ism and increasingly, as the movement evolved, about politics. The stated aim of the Situationists was to disrupt and eventually dismantle the 'spectacle' of capitalist society by creating subversive 'constructed situations'. These were defined as: 'A moment of life concretely and deliberately constructed by the collective organization of a unitary ambiance and a game of events.'[6] It was recognized within the move-ment that capitalism has a tremendous power to recuperate subversion, to turn it to its own ends. This recognition bore the seeds

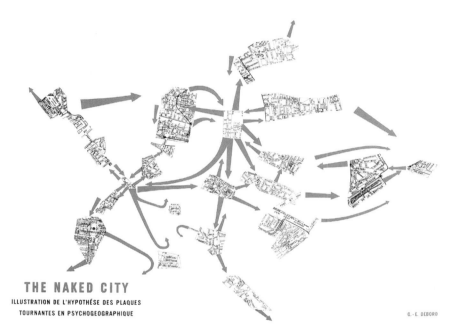

THE NAKED CITY
ILLUSTRATION DE L'HYPOTHÉSE DES PLAQUES
TOURNANTES EN PSYCHOGEOGRAPHIQUE

G.-E. DEBORD

6. Guy Debord with Asger Jorn, *Naked City* (1957).

of the Situationists' own destruction. By the early 1960s the Situationists realized that artistic practice, far more than theoretical texts and
revolutionary acts, was vulnerable to this recuperation. Almost from
the moment of the inception of the Situationist International, members, especially the artists, either left or were expelled from the
movement. In 1962 a breakaway group made up almost entirely of
artists from Scandinavian countries formed the Second Situationist
International. Other artists, such as Rumney, though no longer formal
members, kept up contacts with the group long after expulsion. In
1967 Guy Debord, who had established himself as the single most
powerful force within the movement, published his book *La Société du
Spectacle*.[7] This set out the ideology of Situationism in its post-art
phase and is seen as one of the major influences on the radical student
movements of Strasbourg and Nanterre and on the events of May
1968 in the streets of Paris. These events were as close as the Situationists came to realizing their desire for revolution. The streets were
transformed into places of spontaneous action as the barricades went
up and the walls were covered with graffiti and posters. The ideal,
that the workers and the students should join in self-governing workers' councils, was never quite achieved, even within the limited,
temporary autonomous state of the Sorbonne during its occupation.
When a degree of peace was restored and de Gaulle and his right-
wing party emerged unscathed, it was recognized that the uprising
had been a failure. With that failure came the slow deterioration of
the Situationist International. In 1972, Debord and his remaining
cohorts voted the movement out of existence.

Though formally wound up, the Situationists continued to exert an
influence. The most visible manifestation of this was in the taking up
of situationist slogans, if not always ideology, by Malcolm McLaren,
manager of the Sex Pistols in 1976 and in the accompanying graphic
designs of Jamie Reid. Here subversion was put to use to undermine
the record industry and the production of popular music. Of course,
this too was open to recuperation. There is also a strong vein of situationist thought running through the actions of adherents to the
anti-capitalist movement of the 1990s and into the beginning of the
21st century. But another strand of situationist theory also retains a
resonance and refuses to disappear: that of the project of re-

imagining urban life. This strand can be put to use in assembling the non-museum that is the Delirious Museum.

In the 1950s the Situationists, while building their armoury against the spectacle, defined a number of techniques for use in their version of urban life. Their notion of *dérive*, literally 'drift', is part of a modernist tradition of an almost casual engagement with the city. Not only does it link to Breton's wandering through Paris in his hopeless pursuit of Nadja, but it also has echoes of Baudelaire's 'man of the crowd'. *Dérive* depends on chance and a degree of chaos. The first issue of *Internationale Situationniste* defined *dérive* as 'a mode of experimental behaviour linked to the conditions of urban society; a technique of transient passage through varied ambiences'.[8] What the *dérive* allows the city dweller (or the museum visitor) to do is to create a new kind of map of the city (the museum). The Situationists called this mapping 'psychogeography'. In the psychogeographic map the seen, the known and the experienced are amalgamated. The Situationists did produce some of these maps, thereby, of course, courting recuperation. The English artist Ralph Rumney made a record of a *dérive* around Venice in 1957. This is a composition made up of a deliberately obscure map, small photographs of bars and street scenes linked in a narrative by oblique captions.[9] 'It is our thesis that cities should embody a built-in play factor. We are studying here a play-environment relationship'.[10] For Rumney, 'Venice, like Amsterdam and the Paris of yesteryear, offer[ed] many possibilities for disorientation'.[11] Rumney avoided making proposals for Venice. Instead he treated it as a found place, a museum of spaces and accidental encounters. By selecting sites and routes with particular resonances, Rumney became a nomadic curator of the city. Other experiments in *dérive* took place over the following years, but Rumney's idea of combining text and photographs was not repeated.

In the same way that Rumney used the archetypal melancholic city, Venice, as the site for his explorations, other *dérives* were based around areas of Paris that were doomed or in states of transition. The montage, *The Naked City*, made by Guy Debord and Asger Jorn in 1957 shows fragments of a map of Paris connected by graphic red arrows. The areas featured were not only sites of the correct Situationist ambience, they were also places that were threatened by development. This echoes the Surrealists' fascination with the Passage de l'Opéra and the possibilities of creating 'modern mythology' from that which has been destroyed. Thus, the *dérive* could occupy an ambiguous position between the melancholy of nostalgia and the desire for total transformation. And, of course, the Delirious Museum occupies a similar position: it is both an existing and a potential space. It is a space that exists hidden within the visible, where there is always the possibility of disorientation and the probability of getting lost.

In his psychogeographical description of Les Halles, the Situationist Abdelhafid Khatib wrote:

> The first step, architecturally, would obviously be to replace the current pavilions with an autonomous series of small situationist architectural complexes. Among these new architectures and on their peripheries, corresponding to the four zones we have envisaged here, ought to be perpetually changing labyrinths, and this with the aid of more adequate objects than the fruit and vegetable panniers which make up the sole barricades today.[12]

Here the *dérive* leads to a psychogeographic analysis and hence to 'détournement'. Guy Debord defined *détournement* as 'the re-use of pre-existing artistic elements in a new ensemble'. He went on to say:

> The two fundamental laws of détournement are the loss of importance of each détourned autonomous element – which may go so far as to lose its original sense completely – and at the same time the organization of another meaningful ensemble that confers on each element its new scope and effect.[13]

In the context of urbanism, *détournement* could subvert the way in which the capitalist 'spectacular' city could be read and used. In Les Halles the existing four zones of ambience would be 'détourned' by the demolition of the pavilions and the superimposition of 'Situationist architectural complexes'. Other, more detailed, suggestions for the improvement of Paris were suggested in the journal *Potlatch*:

> The rooftops of Paris should be opened to pedestrian traffic by means of modifications to fire escape ladders and construction of catwalks where necessary ... All street-lamps should be equipped with switches; lighting should be for public use ... Cemeteries should be

eliminated. All corpses and memories of that sort should be totally destroyed; no ashes and no remains . . . Museums should be abolished and their masterpieces distributed to bars (Phillipe de Champaigne's works in the Arab cafés of rue Xavier-Privas; David's 'Sacre' in the Tonneau in Montagne-Geneviève).[14]

Here is the real space of Charlie Brown's pub with its collection of exotica moving back into the theoretical world of conscious category confusion.

The most thorough Situationist architectural project was New Babylon, undertaken by the Dutch artist Constant Nieuwenhuys between 1956 and 1974. This project began as a series of proposals for insertions into existing cities but developed into a scheme that would replace and extend whole urban areas. Its starting point was a future nomadic culture brought about by technological liberation. Here was a society that no longer needed to work but instead could indulge in play and continuous *dérive*. Constant proposed a labyrinthine net structure that could accommodate this ludic desire. There are elements in this project that were picked up in, for instance, the Walking City of Archigram and Cedric Price's Fun Palace in the 1960s. Ironically, these were to influence, in turn, Piano and Rogers' designs for the Centre Pompidou – a building that Debord refused to enter.[15] The building was not only named after one of Debord's natural enemies, but it was also an embodiment of the way in which society recuperates the potential of the 'situation' and transforms it into spectacle.

It is in the openness of New Babylon that there is a link back to the Delirious Museum and its experiments, losses, wanderings and accidents. The Delirious Museum is also a labyrinthine network; objects linked in an attenuated space and in disrupted time. Each has a nomadic existence. The glass vitrine of the museum acts both as barrier and as an environment of unresolved connections and relationships: between people and things, between the living and their predecessors and between things and other things.

Situationist theorists, especially Debord and Raoul Vaneigem, developed the theme of subversion throughout the 1960s. However, they became increasingly distanced from visual culture and began to move closer to direct political action. The barricades that disrupted the street pattern around the Sorbonne in May 1968 created a particular form of *détournement*, but they were limited in terms of what the Situationists called 'unitary urbanism'. They were never to return to the ideas expressed in the pre-Situationist document: 'Formulary for a New Urbanism' written by Ivan Chtcheglov in 1953. This text, reprinted in the first issue of *Internationale Situationniste*, describes a possible future for the city (Paris is, not surprisingly, the only real city mentioned), which is responsive to human needs. Partly this is done through the creation of zones such as the Sinister Quarter, the Bizarre Quarter and the Historical Quarter. The text posits a place that is resistant to the 'museumization' of city life and especially the city fabric. The city of 'unitary urbanism' achieves this through flux and redefinition: 'The architectural complex will be modifiable. Its aspect will change totally or partially in accordance with the will of its inhabitants . . .'.[16] Chtcheglov's city is neither utopia nor dystopia, rather it is an intensification of existing cities.

In a similar way the Delirious Museum is not an alternative to existing museums; it is the existing museum re-interpreted, '*détourned*' and intensified through its interaction with the city. If the Situationist city was a labyrinth in which to get lost and a site for play, if it was a place where misreading and subversion of the predictable were there to be discovered, so too is the Delirious Museum.

4

THE TOTALMUSEUM:
EXHIBITIONS/EXPERIMENTS

The artists' exhibitions and installations described here have disappeared, have been damaged or have been put beyond use. The chapter excavates these exhibitions and experiments in order to establish a relationship to the idea of the Delirious Museum. Some of these were meant as temporary constructions, others have been shattered in transit or have been destroyed by bombs. One was destroyed, re-assembled and reproduced in multiple versions. Another, created in a series of 300, was intended as 'portable' but each edition has, inevitably, become the object of private or museological veneration and has reached a point of stasis. Yet others exist as documents or memories. So the descriptions and cross-references here are archaeological in nature. They are important to the development of the Delirious Museum because they are attempts to reconfigure the language of display. Unlike the urban strategies discussed in previous chapters these experiments were contained within the laboratory that is the museum. And they existed within a different chronological frame so it will be necessary to move back in time as well as travel to different locations.

Lissitzky/Schwitters (Hanover)

In 1922 the Soviet artist El Lissitzky, alongside others, exhibited his work at the First Russian Art Exhibition in Berlin. The following year, after a successful show at the small gallery of the Kestner-Gesellschaft in Hanover, he produced a series of prints called the Kestner Portfolio. These prints were part of an ongoing project that Lissitzky called Proun – an acronym for 'project for affirmation of the new'. Lissitzky wrote: 'Proun begins as a level surface, turns into a model of three-dimensional space, and goes on to construct all the objects of everyday life'.[1] The prints, and other Proun works, were created using dynamic abstract shapes and a limited colour range – usually black, white and red. They are recognizably Constructivist or Suprematist in style. One of the prints is an isometric projection of adjoining walls, actually an exploded view of a simple box, laid out by Lissitzky in the print to show all the surfaces. There is a single doorway and a series of rectangles and rods applied to the walls and floor. The various groups of geometrical elements wrap around corners, connecting one plane to the other in a continuous composition. The print is Lissitzky's design for the Proun Room in the Berlin exhibition. This was his starting point:

> Given were the six surfaces (floor, four walls, ceiling); they are to be designed, but, mind you, not as a living room, for there is an exhibition going on. In an exhibition people keep walking all around. Thus, space has to be organized in such a way as to impel everyone automatically to perambulate in it.[2]

The idea of articulating a rectilinear space by utilizing the corners was not new. In the pivotal 0.10 Exhibition in Petrograd of 1915 both Malevich, El Lissitzky's teacher, and Tatlin used the corners in their installations. Malevich, referring to the traditional placing of icons, hung one of his black square paintings high in a corner of the gallery. Tatlin's installation was more radical in that he created sculptural pieces that were created expressly for corners, parts of the room that were usually reserved for furniture. Lissitzky, in his Proun Room, extended the idea of connecting one plane to another to include the whole room and began to work towards a symbiotic environment for artworks.

Lissitzky continued his Hanover connections the following year when he worked on issue 8/9 of Kurt Schwitters' magazine *Merz*. The work of these two artists could hardly be more different. Schwitters, though working with a certain modernist economy of means, was unafraid of the detritus of the past, incorporating it, often chaotically, into his collages and sculptures. Lissitzsky was fascinated by the new:

new typography, new materials, new technology. The way their interests overlapped is reflected in the layout of the magazine. Alongside pictures of the work of Modernist architects framed with bold graphic devices, there are found photographs.

In 1926 Lissitzky was asked back to Germany, this time to Dresden, after his wife-to-be, Sophie Küppers, agitated on his behalf with the architectural director of the Dresden International Art Exhibition, Heinrich Tessenow. Four years after the experiment of the Proun Room Lissitzky wanted to extend the possibilities it had presented:

> While passing along the picture-studded walls of the conventional art exhibition setup, the viewer is lulled into a numb state of *passivity*. It is our intention to make man *active* by means of design. This is the purpose of space.[3]

Writing to Sophie Küppers, he said: 'The room must be a kind of showcase, or stage on which the pictures appear as the actors in a drama (or comedy).'[4] In Dresden Lissitzky was presented with a fairly small cubic room with a central doorway. In his design there was no emphasis on the axis, instead, he composed the walls of the room to act in balance as a whole. The most striking display features are all commentaries on movement and change. The ceiling of unbleached, stretched calico allowed for diffuse colour to be projected down into the space, so that, on either side of the doorway, one wall was yellow and the other was blue. Some of the walls had superimposed vertical slats, painted white and black on alternate faces, the background of the wall being grey. As visitors moved round the room, therefore, the walls changed from black to grey to white and vice versa. Lastly, Lissitzky made a series of vertical sliding screens allowing for the doubling-up of pictures on display. Visitors were expected to slide these planes up and down, making a choice about which pictures they wanted to look at. The pictures actually dropped behind a perforated steel screen so that they remained partially visible at all times. The work displayed was not only that of Lissitzky; Léger, Picabia, Moholy-Nagy, Mondrian and Gabo were also shown. So this was not just a showroom for Lissitzky but an attempt to re-frame the work of art and re-imagine the art gallery.

The director of Hanover's Landesmuseum, Alexander Dorner, was, at this time, in the process of re-organizing the museum's displays.[5] After seeing the Dresden installation he approached Lissitzky to design a permanent room for the collection of modern works. This space came to be known as the Abstract Cabinet. Lissitzky illustrated it in another isometric drawing that, in its dynamism, could itself be mistaken for an abstraction. Some of the devices developed for Dresden were used again in this design; the ideas of the sliding screens and the slatted walls were retained. Lighting was from a window occupying one side of the room. Lissitzky wanted to manipulate this light by artificial means, introducing colour and dimming but there was no electric power available for the room so these ideas were not realized. The window wall incorporated two vitrines with rotating planes on which works on paper could be shown, and a sculpture plinth with a mirror at its back. The adjacent wall had a horizontally sliding screen containing four works, two of which were visible at any time. In 1930, Dorner commissioned László Moholy-Nagy to design the next room in the chronolgical sequence in the museum. This was called the Room of Our Time and was devoted to film, architecture and design. If anything, this display was more radical than Lissitzky's in that it contained no artefacts, only models and reproductions. But, like so many galleries using new technologies, it was plagued by malfunctioning machinery and had to open without many of the devices specified by its designer.

Matthew Drutt has pointed out that some of the effects created by Lissitzky for the Abstract Cabinet had echoes in his photographic practice (such as the use of contrasting positives and negatives and semi-transparent screens placed over images)[6] and thus it was a precursor to the graphic work that Lissitzky developed in ensuing years. In 1927 he returned to Moscow and began to design a series of large-scale propaganda exhibitions for the Soviet state, such as pavilions for Pressa in Cologne, 1928, and for the International Hygiene Exhibition, Dresden, 1930. These were spectacular montages of photography and graphics, set in complex spatial compositions and in their juxtapositions of materials and techniques they have continued to exert an influence on exhibition design. The propaganda installations continued some of the themes of the Dresden and Hanover installations.

Lissitzky's description of the Dresden room: 'Thus an optical dynamic is created as a result of human motion. The game actively involves the viewer',[7] could equally apply to one of the displays at Pressa. But the display of art as artefact, however active and dynamic that display was, did not form a part of these exhibitions. The ideas embodied in the Abstract Cabinet were, instead, picked up by a strand of modernism running through Dada to Surrealism. When they re-emerged, these ideas manifested themselves in a very different image.

Kurt Schwitters, the one-time Dadaist and Lissitsky's erstwhile collaborator, forms the link here. While El Lissitzky appropriated territory in exhibitions and existing museums to create his publicly accessible 'Totalmuseum', Schwitters embarked on a programme of re-imagining the interior of his own house in Waldhausenstrasse, Hanover. Where Lissitzky had Proun, Schwitters had 'Merz'. Schwitters' re-invention of the world as 'Merz' began with him lifting a syllable from one of his own collages. In Merz he was making a new practice that, while building on the ruins of the past, could transform both the present and the future.

> I called it 'Merz', it was a prayer about the victorious end of the war, victorious as once again peace had won in the end; everything had broken down in any case and new things had to be made out of fragments and this is Merz.[8]

This re-use of the fragment has within it a pre-echo of the situationist method of *détournement*.

The Merzbau's starting point seems to have been the placing of a cumulative, sculpture – the *Merz-Column* – in Schwitters' studio in 1919. Over the years this work was moved from room to room as tenants moved into the Schwitters' home. As the column moved and grew, encompassing small found objects and niches into which the artist placed significant objects, he began to consider its relationship to the surrounding walls, also covered in detritus, and the source material for his collage work. In 1923 this relationship between sculpture and wall crystallized into an intention to make a complete environment when the Merzbau's construction was begun. The structure of the piece is still difficult to grasp. This is not helped by its destruction, though there have been numerous attempts to reconstruct it in whole or in part. One major element of the Merzbau was still based around the idea of the column and was called the *Kathedral des erotischen Elends* (Cathedral of Erotic Misery). Schwitters often referred to this element as the *KdeE*. Sometimes the whole installation is referred to by this name; elsewhere there are references to there being several columns. The Merzbau grew from one room in 1923 to three by 1926. In the late 1920s Schwitters took over an attic room from which a staircase was built through the skylight onto a roof platform. Some years later he cut through the floor of the house into a courtyard in which a well was found and a Merz construction was inserted in it. Thus the Merzbau actually reached from the subterranean onto the rooftop but the bulk of the installation remained in the three rooms on the ground floor of the house.[9]

There are two reasons that the Merzbau is relevant to the Delirious Museum. First, it is a total environment that was meant to be viewed and experienced rather than lived in, a space recognizably different, like the Proun rooms, from the domestic. Secondly, it incorporated numerous displays of 'found' objects dedicated to particular narratives or people.[10]

Schwitters had been active in the Berlin Dada movement and the first column, incorporating a doll's head, displays some of the distorted anthropomorphism associated with that movement. The First International Dada Fair in Berlin in 1920, in its chaotic way, was also a total environment, so Schwitters' Merzbau had a background in Dada exhibitions. Schwitters must also have found inspiration in the work of the Russian Constructivists, particularly El Lissitzky with whom Schwitters worked closely, and in the artists of the Dutch De Stijl movement with whom Schwitters also had connections. John Elderfield, in his monograph on Schwitters has pointed out the relationship between the Merzbau and a curious text of 1923 regarding some fictional experiments:

> All that I can say now is that experiments are being undertaken with white mice, which live in *Merzbilder* especially constructed for this purpose. Also under construction I have *Merzbilder* that will restore by mechanical means the balance disturbed by the movements of the mice. As they bump into wires, the lighting changes automatically.[11]

This fanciful description is not so far away from the 'mechanical' rooms (or exhibitions) that Lissitzky had begun to develop for human beings.

The inclusion of discreet displays for particular people seems to belong more to the world of the social history museum rather than the art of the 1920s. Schwitters developed the niches in the original *Merz-Column* into much more elaborate displays that he called 'grottoes'. These ranged from the specific to the general. There were grottoes devoted to Mies van der Rohe (containing the stub of a pencil filched from his office), to Goethe (also containing pencils and a relic purporting to be Goethe's leg) and there were much larger arrangements called the Gold Grotto and the Love Grotto. These larger arrangements seem to have been based around conventional museum displays using glass vitrines for displaying and protecting the objects. Many of the more personal collections were stored in archive-like conditions such as drawers and hidden niches. Visitors to the Merzbau were shown different parts of the installation; Schwitters seemed to control access to the material like a protective curator. As the Merzbau grew, the various displays were buried in newer constructions so that parts were forever covered yet also preserved.

Schwitters fled Germany to Norway in 1936, leaving the Merzbau intact but unfinished. Like any museum, it had within it the possibility of infinite growth and its destruction in an air raid in 1943 ensured that it would remain eternally unfinished. He subsequently built two other Merzbau; the first in Lysaker, Norway, which was destroyed by fire in 1951and was never photographed and the second near Ambleside in the Lake District, parts of which are preserved in the collection of the University of Newcastle. The last of these was much more organic in form than the Constructivist inspired Hanover Merzbau and it was a construction that had its roots in the rural rather than in the city. Schwitters, in his Hanover years, was like Baudelaire's *flâneur*, a detached wanderer in the city, observing and collecting, creating what Dorothea Dietrich has called 'an inventory of fragments'.[12] He prefigured the ways in which the Surrealists and their successors were to re-read the possibilities thrown up by urban life.

Duchamp/Keisler (Paris/New York)

> Everything important that I have done can be put into a little suitcase.
>
> Marcel Duchamp, 1952[13]

Like Schwitters, Marcel Duchamp was a refugee from Dada. By the middle of the 1920s Duchamp had ostensibly given up on the art world in order to concentrate on chess. But before he did this he had decided to leave the *Large Glass,* also known as *The Bride Stripped Bare by her Bachelors, Even*, 'definitively unfinished'. In 1927 it was smashed whilst in transit between the Brooklyn Museum and the home of its owner, Katherine Dreier. Some years later Duchamp supervised its re-building, when it was put back together and sandwiched between two more sheets of glass. Its destruction and re-making became, in effect, a part of the work, extending its narrative into time and making this highly wrought artwork into a kind of ready-made.[14]

In a note of 1913 Duchamp wrote:

> The question of shop windows :.
> To undergo the interrogation by shop windows :.
> The necessity of the shop window :.
> The shop window proof of existence of the world outside :. _____
> When undergoing the interrogation by shop windows, you also pronounce your own Condemnation. In fact, the choice is a round trip. From the demands of shop windows, from the inevitable response to shop windows, the conclusion is the making of a choice. No obstinacy, ad absurdum,: in hiding this coition through a sheet of glass with one or more of the objects in the shop window. The penalty consists in cutting the glass and in kicking yourself as soon as possession is consummated. q.e.d. _____[15]

Then in 1916 he added:

> I. Showcase – with sliding glass panes. place some fragile objects inside. – Inconvenience narrowness – reduction, of a space . . .[16]

Duchamp, in making the *Large Glass,* constructed his own 'shop window', one that avoided any 'penalty' because possession could not be consummated. So instead of placing the objects for display inside the

window/vitrine, Duchamp applied their enigmatic images to its surface – a reduced space. The viewer of the *Large Glass* is at once
looking into it, at it and beyond it. The mirroring effect of the glass
means that the viewer is even 'in' the work, so, like the Merzbau, the
Large Glass is an environment. It is, simultaneously, both window and
vitrine. In a lecture made in 1957 Duchamp said:

> . . . the creative act is not performed by the artist alone; the spectator
> brings the work in contact with the external world by deciphering and
> interpreting its inner qualifications and thus adds his contribution to
> the creative act.[17]

This expands the possibilities of viewing into an infinite number of separate experiences. Instead of a closed reading of the object, Duchamp
suggests a series of delirious and open-ended interpretations.

Even after he 'gave up' art, Duchamp was revered by the Surrealists
and particularly by Surrealism's 'Pope', André Breton, and he continued to collaborate with him on projects. In 1937, the Surrealist Paul
Eluard was approached by the commercial Galerie Beaux-Arts in
Paris to organize a retrospective of Surrealist art. Duchamp was then
engaged to create the *mise-en-scène* for the exhibition called Exposition Internationale du Surréalisme. The artworks represented a large
selection of those involved in the movement, covering past work and
artists, such as De Chirico, who had parted company from the group.
The opening night of the exhibition in January 1938 has been well documented with many contemporary accounts of the anarchy that
ensued. There were so many people in attendance that it was necessary to call for the police in order to control the crowd.[18] In the
courtyard was Salvador Dali's *Rainy Taxi*, a Paris cab in which two
mannequins sat covered in ivy and live snails, water pouring from the
ceiling of the cab and out onto the pavement. The exhibition space
consisted of four rooms, two of which were conceived by Duchamp,
the other two smaller spaces being set out by Georges Hugnet. One
of these latter rooms had a chandelier made from underwear as might
have been worn by a giant can-can dancer, the other had a *trompe-l'œil*
skylight painted onto the ceiling. More spectacular were the entrance
corridor, or the rue Surréaliste, and the main exhibition space. The
first of these comprised 16 mannequins (17 if counting the single male

mannequin prone on the floor at the feet of Max Ernst's *Widow*) dressed by members of the Surrealist movement (both artists and writers), including Duchamp himself.[19] This corridor acted as an extension of the street, first by the parade of mannequins (open to interpretation as street walkers or as the occupants of non-existent shop-windows), then by the inclusion of enamel street-name signs on the wall behind the mannequins. These acted as an homage to the city that had nurtured and inspired the Surrealists. Some were actual places in Paris: rue Vivienne, rue de la Glacière, rue de la Vieille Lanterne, with particular associations for the Surrealists. Another corridor, the Passage des Panoramas, made a link back to Walter Benjamin's Arcades Project and Aragon's *Paris Peasant*. (Aragon had broken with the Surrealists in 1932 when he had joined the Communist Party – a move that led eventually to this organization becoming the owners of Duchamp's *LHOOQ*.) Other signs were for streets that the Surrealists were willing into existence: 'rue de la Transfusion de Sange', 'rue des Tous les Diables'. The second room, which contained the bulk of the exhibited work, had at each corner a made-up bed, suggesting that the space could double as the 'brothel' implied by the petrified prostitutes lining the corridor. In addition, Duchamp festooned the ceiling with 1,200 used coal bags. Though empty, these continued to disgorge coal dust over visitors for the duration of the exhibition. In the centre of the space was a brazier, glowing, not with coal due to the risk of fire, but with electric light bulbs. Brian O'Doherty has pointed out Duchamp's subversive intent in this:[20] the ensemble amounts to a reversal of floor and ceiling, the coal sacks being the floor and the brazier acting as a chandelier. Duchamp had wanted to use individual lights triggered by 'magic eyes' to illuminate the paintings on the wall, but this proved impractical. Instead the 'Master of Lighting', Man Ray, provided guests with torches for viewing the work. These all disappeared at the opening, so permanent lighting was subsequently installed. Graphic works were displayed on revolving doors and behind the scenes coffee was brewed in order to create a suitable olfactory environment for the exhibition. On the evening of the opening, Duchamp inspected the installation then, before visitors arrived, caught the boat-train bound for London.

Duchamp's next encounter with the Delirious Museum had less of the laboratory about it. The *Boîte-en-valise* (also called the *Portable Museum, From or by Marcel Duchamp or Rrose Sélavy* and *Box in a Suitcase*) was less an experiment, more a re-imagined, yet fully formed version of the museum. In an interview in 1955 Duchamp said:

> Instead of painting something the idea was to reproduce the paintings that I loved so much in miniature. I didn't know how to do it. I thought of a book, but didn't like that idea. Then I thought of the idea of the box in which all my works would be mounted like in a small museum, a portable museum, so to speak, and here it is in this valise.[21]

From the mid-1930s Duchamp set about making scaled-down, two- and three-dimensional reproductions of his work up to that date. In 1941, in German-occupied Paris, he produced the first *Boîte-en-valise*, a deluxe version, for Peggy Guggenheim. The remaining reproductions were shipped out of Paris via Grenoble to New York with Guggenheim's personal effects. When Duchamp arrived in New York in 1942 he set about assembling the other deluxe editions of the box. The first 20 boxes were in small leather-covered suitcases with handles and each had a unique artwork included with the 69 other exhibits filed into folders. Subsequent editions were installed in simpler boxes without the 'carrying' handle. In 1966 another 12 reproductions were included in the box to bring it up to date. The last box of the total edition of 300 was completed in 1971.

By making the *Boîte-en-valise* his own 'museum', Duchamp was erecting a barrier to the conventional museum from behind which he could continue to work. Furthermore, by containing the miniatures within a mundane valise, Duchamp placed his own mediator between the work and the 'real' museums and galleries into which the *Boîte-en-valise* would inevitably be placed. Susan Stewart, in her book *On Longing*, says:

> The reduction in scale which the miniature represents skews the time and space relations of the everyday lifeworld, and as an object consumed, the miniature finds its 'use value' transformed into the infinite time of reverie.[22]

7. Marcel Duchamp, *Boîte-en-valise*, 0/XX (1943), closed.

8. Marcel Duchamp, *Boîte-en-valise*, 0/XX (1943), open.

Even in the rarified 'lifeworld' created by Duchamp's works of art, the box and its miniature reproductions skew the time and space of the museum.

Duchamp was also commenting on the condition of the museum itself. By producing the box as a multiple Duchamp 'devalued' the work in question but, at the same time, each item in the box is properly labelled with dimensions, dates and collection details. These details refer back to the original objects, so this 'museumized' version of the work is not 'authentic'. Duchamp actually creates a museum of devalued objects in a devalued container that can be, theoretically at least, picked up by its handle and carried away. The *Boîte-en-valise*, however, escapes the linearity of the *catalogue raisonée* as a book by making its contents three-dimensional and movable. The construction of individual pieces in frames and mounts made it easy to display them. The complexity of the *Boîte-en-valise* suggests an awareness, not just of the ambiguity of the work reproduced, but of the ambiguity inherent in the 'container', the museum.

In the actual *catalogue raisonée*[23] of Duchamp's work, his installation of the exhibition First Papers of Surrealism in New York, 1942 is no. 488, *Sixteen Miles of String*. (His *mise-en-scène* for the 1938 Paris exhibition is no. 461, *Twelve Hundred Coal Bags Suspended from the Ceiling over a Stove*.) In fact, in the installation only one mile of string was used. According to Arturo Schwarz, 'During installation the string caught fire through spontaneous combustion and had to be replaced with another mile of string'. Duchamp gave the other 14 miles of string away to an unnamed person. The exhibition was a fund-raising event for French prisoners of war organized by the designer Elsa Schiaparelli; the venue was a former mansion in Madison Avenue. Breton was involved in the selection of work for the exhibition and, once again, he called on Duchamp to provide the *mise-en-scène*. The existing rooms were elaborate domestic interiors with heavy mouldings and painted ceilings. In order to display the works, most of which were paintings, conventional freestanding screens were installed. On top of these and the pictures, Duchamp then stretched the string in an elaborate web. This turned the whole space into an impenetrable labyrinth. Visitors had to step over and through the network of string, which also partially obscured the works on show.[24] On the night of the opening Duchamp had arranged for children to play ball games in the midst of the gallery. The children were told by him not to speak and to play on when asked to stop by the guests, saying only that they were acting under the instructions of Mr Duchamp. As the evening progressed, a number of adults joined in the games but, as usual, Duchamp did not attend. In the March 1943 issue of the Surrealist magazine VVV Duchamp reproduced a photograph of the First Papers of Surrealism installation upside down, completing the inversion begun with the coal sacks on the ceiling. From now on the art gallery could be rotated at will.

One week after the First Papers of Surrealism event, Peggy Guggenheim opened her museum, Art of this Century, in two converted tailors' workshops on the top floor of a building in West 57th Street, New York. This was a display of the collection with which Duchamp's miniature reproductions had been shipped out of Marseilles. Guggenheim had originally installed a version of her museum in London but eventually settled on New York, far away from the war that had been brewing in Europe at the time. Subsequently the works in her collection were given a permanent home in Venice and were to be subsumed into the global 'Guggenheim' brand. To design the New York installation, Guggenheim engaged the Romanian émigré Frederick Kiesler. His designs for the gallery may not have suggested any 'share in the ownership' of the artworks but they certainly addressed 'mood' as one of its central themes.

Kiesler had arrived in the Unites States in 1926 from Vienna via Paris. He had strong links with the European avant-garde and, particularly, with the Surrealists. In the early 1920s Kiesler had designed a spiral 'Space Stage' in Vienna that developed into the 'Endless Theatre' projects of 1925 and 1926 where the barriers between audience and performers were broken down through dynamic and flexible forms. Also in 1925 he made a maquette for an abstract City in Space for the Paris International Exhibition of Decorative Arts. This was influenced by both the Constructivists and by the De Stijl movement and was itself a development of Kiesler's own, earlier exhibition installations in Vienna. In 1927, the year after his arrival in the United States, Kiesler completed his first building project: the Film Guild Cinema in New York. Like the exhibition and theatre projects that preceded it, this was meant to de-materialize the formal space of presentation and display. The screen of the cinema could be set to different sizes and formats by means of an eye-shaped moving shutter. The auditorium's walls and ceiling could be used for projection anticipating the complex audio-visual displays of later years. Kiesler wrote: 'The spectator must be able to lose himself in an imaginary, endless space even though the screen implies the opposite'.[25] In 1929, Le Corbusier dreamed of the Museé Mondial, a Tower of Babel for the League of Nations,[26] and the following year Kiesler imagined a prototype of the virtual museum:

> The Telemuseum. Just as operas are now transmitted over the air, so picture galleries will be. From the Louvre to you, from the Prado to you, from everywhere to you. You will enjoy the prerogative of selecting pictures that are compatible with your mood or that meet the demands of any special occasion. Through the dials of your Teleset you will share in the ownership of the world's greatest art treasures.[27]

This was published in Kiesler's book, *Contemporary Art Applied to the Store and its Display*. Kiesler explained the need for his book: '. . . the store window is a silent loudspeaker and not dead storage'.[28] There are echoes in Kiesler's text of Duchamp's own inquisition of the shop window and of his development of the *Large Glass* as, simultaneously, barrier, mirror and vitrine. Kiesler wrote: 'We have discussed new uses of the sides of the show window resulting in a contracted or diminished spacing. Now we must consider the results of the opposite process: expansion.'[29] Under the heading 'A DREAM OF A KINETIC WINDOW' he wrote: '. . . push button/open and close windows at will – bring merchandise close for inspection and reveal price – revolve, focus light and buy'.

Between 1938 and 1942 Kiesler developed an idea for the 'Vision Machine' that was to extend the possibilities of getting lost in imaginary space. The *Vision Machine* drawings could be fragments of works by the Surrealist Yves Tanguy or collages by Max Ernst; free-flowing organic forms of tubes and eyes. But in their ambition Kiesler sets out his interest in perception and the relationship between eye, object and brain.

Through the demonstration we learn that neither light, nor eye, nor brain, alone or in association, can see. But rather, we see only through the total co-ordination of human experiences; and even then, it is our own conceived image, and not really the actual object that we perceive. We learn, therefore, that we see by creative ability and not by mechanical reproduction.[30]

The theme of endlessness was one that Kiesler was to return to throughout his career, but in his designs for Guggenheim's gallery it was ideas of de-materialization and the extension of human perception that predominated.

Art of this Century was divided into four galleries, each designed to reflect its content while fulfilling Kiesler's view of the role of the art gallery. Echoing Aragon's intention in *Paris Peasant*, Kiesler said: 'These galleries are a demonstration of a changing world, in which the artist's work stands forth as a vital entity in a spatial whole, and art stands forth in a vital link in the structure of a new myth.'[31] The Abstract Gallery showed abstract and Cubist paintings and sculptures hung on wires stretched diagonally between ceiling and floor. Existing walls were concealed behind a curving screen of ultramarine fabric. The floor was painted turquoise. The 'daylight' gallery was for temporary exhibitions and was situated along the 57th Street façade, its windows were covered in white 'ninon' (a material usually used for lingerie, apparently) to diffuse the light. Paintings and prints could be viewed on specially designed units that doubled as seating and storage. The Surrealist Gallery had curved walls of South American gum wood from which paintings were cantilevered on brackets reputedly made from baseball bats – though photographs show arms of square section. The paintings were displayed without frames, at Guggenheim's insistence and with Kiesler's approval, and were lit by individual spotlights. The two sides of the gallery were originally lit alternately so that at any one time only half the paintings were visible. After many complaints this feature, like Man Ray's torches in Paris in 1937, was abandoned and replaced by permanent lighting. Both the Abstract and Surrealist Galleries were furnished with 'organically' shaped rocking-chairs that could become benches when joined together, fixed seats or, when turned on their sides, sculpture plinths. The fourth gallery housed various kinetic displays and, according to

Guggenheim, was dubbed by the press 'Coney Island'.[32] Visitors turned a wheel and looked through a window at a revolving display of 14 of Duchamp's miniatures from the *Boîte-en-valise*. A series of paintings by Paul Klee were displayed on a 'pater-noster' activated by the visitor breaking a light beam. André Breton's 'object poem' *Portrait of the Actor A.B.* was visible through a peep-hole also operated by a handle. Kiesler intended that the street should be brought into a direct relationship with the museum through the installation of an elaborate telescope. This delirious viewing device seems never to have been constructed. In her autobiography Guggenheim wrote:

> Keisler really created a wonderful gallery – very theatrical and extremely original. If the pictures suffered from the fact that their setting was too spectacular and took away people's attention from them, it was at least a marvellous décor and created a terrific stir.[33]

But Kiesler clearly did not consider his installation to be a distraction:

> Today, the framed painting on the wall has become a decorative cipher without life and meaning . . . the frame today reduced to an arbitrary rigidity, must regain its architectural, spatial significance. The two opposing worlds must be seen again as jointly indispensable forces in the same world. The ancient magic must be recreated whereby the god and the mask of the god, the deer and the image of the deer, existed with equal potency, with the same immediate reality in one living universe.[34]

At the time of the opening of Art of this Century, Marcel Duchamp was staying with Kiesler and his wife in their New York apartment, so it would seem fairly certain that a dialogue was taking place around both this installation and that of the First Papers exhibition. This dialogue continued in the following years, first in publications, then in the creation of another exhibition.

The special Duchamp edition of the magazine *View* had a fold-out triptych created by Kiesler showing Duchamp in his studio. A portion of the right-hand panel of the triptych is a photograph printed in negative of shelving stuffed with objects. Duchamp sits in the centre surrounded by pieces of machinery and collaged elements of the *Large Glass*. The left hand panel is inscribed: 'POEME ESPACE . . . dedié à H(ieronymous) Duchamp'. Parts of the image fold out to reveal further fragments of the *Large Glass* and sections of text. The reverse is a photograph of the First Papers installation. Kiesler here acknowledges the influence of the *Large Glass* on his own work and draws attention to the point at which the interests of the two artists most obviously overlapped. Kiesler, as hinted at in his book on the shop window, was fascinated by the prospects opened up by the *Large Glass*. He connected it back to architecture in an essay of 1937,[35] saying 'Glass is the only material in the building industry which expresses surface-and-space at the same time'[36] and described it ecstatically: 'a vibrant mass of luminous densities, transparent, lucidly shivering with its tender layers of colour-coverings'.[37] He extended further its possible readings into the ambiguous homage printed in *View*.

The final collaboration between Kiesler and Duchamp took place in 1947 between Paris and New York, summing up the shift that had occurred in the art world after the Second World War. By this point Surrealism had arguably lost its power to shock, so the Exposition Internationale du Surréalisme could be read as a footnote to an avant-garde. The show took place in the Galerie Maeght in Paris. Breton was once again involved as overall organizer, while Duchamp's rôle seems to have been as a kind of remote director – accounts vary as to who was responsible for what. Duchamp suggested the Salle de Superstition and other spaces that were subsequently designed and carried out by Kiesler who, unlike Duchamp, was present on site. Some of the same motifs present in Art of this Century re-appear (such as the curving fabric wall), but here the programme, written by Breton, was linked to the creation of a *mise-en-scène* more akin to the 1938 exhibition. The entrance was via a staircase in the form of a stack of suitably evocative books, each relating to a card of the tarot. Rooms were linked by a continuous thread evoking, not only the labyrinth of the Minotaur, but also Duchamp's *Sixteen Miles of String*. The rain of Dali's taxi re-appeared here as a multicoloured shower in a room with a billiard table. Kiesler, who designed the overall *mise-en scène*, exhibited a sculpture and created Duchamp's installation *Green Ray* according to his instructions. A second Duchamp piece was assembled by Breton and the painter Matta – further emphasizing Duchamp's absence. The exhibition caused none of the furore of its predecessors; Surrealism's influence was slowly and inevitably being overtaken by diverse younger movements in France but particularly in America.

In 1948 Duchamp fell out with Kiesler over the expulsion from the Surrealist movement by Breton of Matta following the suicide of Arshille Gorky. Duchamp went on secretly working on his last major work, the peepshow *Etant donnés*. This work stands in contrast to the openness of the *Large Glass* – an enclosed world visible to only one person at a time, through a small hole in a door. Kiesler, meanwhile, switched his attention from display to the utopian domestic project, the Endless House, and the writing of his own 'Manifesto of Correalism'. The fusion of art and architecture of his exhibition designs shifted into a search for spiritual space.

Each of the works described here can now be seen as part of the development of strands of modernist art practice. The Merzbau was a forerunner of installation art. The Proun Rooms anticipated the power of graphics and communication. Art of this Century was a progenitor of organic architecture. The various perverse projects of Duchamp were inspiration for the conceptual art of the late 20th century. But the Delirious Museum retrieves the events, narratives and ideas surrounding these projects and, *post-facto*, claims them for its own history. The Delirious Museum occupies an ambiguous position: it does not belong within the mainstream of modernism and yet it could not exist without modernity. It contains not only the clutter and dust of history but also, the ghosts that the modern would deny: the ghosts of modernity itself.

5

THIS IS NOT A MUSEUM

Visiting a museum is a matter of going from void to void. Hallways lead the viewer to things once called 'pictures' and 'statues'. Anachronisms hang and protrude from every angle. Themes without meaning press on the eye. Multifarious nothings permute into false windows (frames) that open up onto a verity of blanks. Stale images cancel one's perception and deviate one's motivation . . . . The museum spreads its surfaces everywhere, and becomes an untitled collection of generalizations that immobilize the eye.[1]

Robert Smithson

Schwitters, Lissitzky, Duchamp and Kiesler conducted experiments with the idea and form of the museum. The subjects of this chapter are more like parasites, feeding off the institutional body of the museum while trying to take it over. This is a process of re-investment rather than reinvention. In order to draw the various strands of this geographically and chronologically diverse practice together I have invented a fictional museum or a Theatre of Memory in which the manifestations of this project can be displayed. The following is a description of the Department of Art, the Delirious Museum.

The **Architecture** of this museum is neither here nor there. Suffice to say that it has steps on axis, the vestiges of a portico, a more-or-less symmetrical arrangement of galleries ranged around a central rotunda. The museum spans a city block with entrances on the north and south sides. Its entrance is almost lost among other buildings that have been inserted into the space that once stood in front of its façade. It is a large thing inside a small thing.

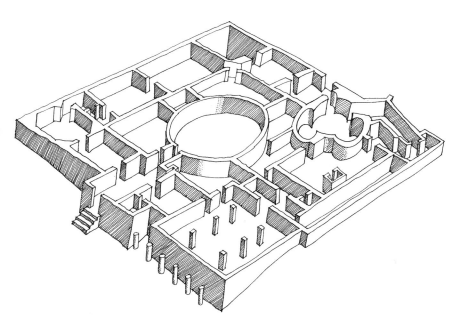

9. Department of Art, the Delirious Museum (2005).

The **Entrance** is through the porch also referred to, misleadingly, as the portico. It is an ordinary porch of an ordinary house in Utopia Parkway in Flushing, Borough of Queens, New York. This is the actual structure of the house where Joseph Cornell lived and worked throughout his life until 1972. It is hard to believe that this building of a domestic scale could conceal such a large collection, but in that respect it is like one of Cornell's own boxes. He was a self-taught artist who associated himself with the Surrealists, although he was never formally recognized as a member of the group. In 1931 he produced his first collage influenced by the work of Max Ernst. He then experimented with tiny amended pillboxes and constructions in glass belljars. In 1936 he made his first 'shadow box'. These were glass-fronted wooden boxes containing two- and three-dimensional 'found' objects. Each box marks the edges of a complete world – contained in its spatial configuration but infinite in its possible readings. Cornell meticulously collected the contents of the boxes from book and junk stores in Manhattan and, occasionally, from the pavements of the city. Walking the streets of New York in the act of collecting became a part of the process of making his collages. The boxes were, therefore, the product not just of selection and composition but also of the same random drifts undertaken by Breton and later, with different intent, by the Situationists.[2] Many boxes were dedicated to individuals, living and dead, like shrines to home-made saints . . . movie stars and singers. The Cornell archives – his own store of materials and his papers – have been reproduced and are stored in the basement galleries of the museum.[3] This facility is open by appointment.

The **Main Hall** is a larger space than the entrance would suggest. The turnstile[4] is part of *Samson* by the artist Chris Burden. This work was made in 1985 and first installed in the Henry Museum of Art, Seattle. This piece is comprised of the turnstile, a winch, worm gear, a 100-ton jack, timbers and steel plates. *Samson* is designed to be placed in the entrance to a museum where visitors will pass through the turnstile. With each rotation of the mechanism the large horizontal timbers push against the walls of the museum. Cracks are now visible in the two lateral walls of the Main Hall. As this institution does not exist there is no danger to visitors. Chris Burden has confirmed the

10. Chris Burden, *Samson* (1985).

conceptual nature of *Samson*: 'If enough people come to the show, the museum is destroyed. But in fact that doesn't happen, because not enough people ever come.'[5] Also, the movement of the arms is infinitesimal: 'It's like looking at a glacier'.[6] The possibility, even probability, of failure often lies at the centre of Burden's work.

Samson was shown at Newport Harbor Art Museum in 1988 but it had to be removed after complaints from the fire department. When installed at the MAK in Vienna in 1996, *Samson* was accompanied by a text documenting the number of people who would have to pass through the turnstile in order to bring the building down. In 2001 the piece was put up for auction at an estimated value of between $250,000 and $300,000. It remained unsold. *Samson* is now on long-term loan to the museum.

The décor for the surrounding space refers to the work of Marcel Broodthaers. This museum was constructed on the ruins of his Musée d'Art Moderne, fragments of which are visible at various points throughout the galleries. Potted palm trees are placed axially on either side of the doors and around the room alongside other vestiges of Broodthaers' works: a cannon, a picnic table and chairs and so on. A number of short introductory films (such as Broodthaers' film on London shop windows and Jeremy Bentham, *Figures of Wax*) are shown in the **Annexe** (Cinema Broodthaers) at intervals throughout the day. The uniformed guards in this space will direct you to seating and ensure that the museum regulations are observed at all times. (enfants non admis, Nicht Rauchen, NO PHOTOGRAPHS ALLOWED, etc.) On the wall above the door is the following inscription:

> Fiction enables us to grasp reality and at the same time that which is veiled by reality.[7]

Guidebooks and plans are available at the enquiry desk in this space but these are unreliable. Members of staff are available to give further information on the museum and collections.

The room beyond, the **Rotunda**, is also dedicated to Broodthaers and sits on the site of the original Musée d'Art Moderne, Département des Aigles.[8] The displays deal with each of the sections of Brood-thaers' museum:

> Section XIXème Siècle, Section Littéraire, (Each of these was housed in Broodthaers' apartment in Brussels between 1968 and 1969. The former began when a truck delivered a series of packing crates to the front door and ended when these were removed a year later), Section XVIIème, Section XIXème Siècle (Bis), Section Documentaire, (this consisted of the floor-plan of a notional museum drawn on the beach at Le Coq, Belgium, in 1970. Signs in French and Flemish were placed at the corners reading: 'Touching the objects is absolutely forbidden'. The incoming tide destroyed the Section Documentaire forever. All that is left are texts, photographs and the hats inscribed 'MUSEUM' worn during the drawing/building of this fragment of the museum.) Section Cinéma, Section Financière, (During this piece the museum was put up for sale 'due to bankruptcy'), Section des Figures (Der Adler vom Oligozän bis Heute), Section Publicité, Section d'Art Moderne (These last two were presented at Documenta 5 in Kassel, 1972, and marked the permanent closure of the museum).

In addition there is a display covering the Musée d'Art Moderne, Galerie du XXème Siècle. The largest exhibit, located in the centre of the Rotunda, is normally devoted to the Section des Figures (The Eagle from the Oligocene to the Present) but, as this is currently closed for conservation, it is worthwhile to describe it here. In fact Broodthaers said: 'I am against the museum as a center of research for avant-garde art. The museum should emphasize its role as being strictly a place of conservation.'[9] Broodthaers organized this section of the museum for the Düsseldorf Kunsthalle in 1972. Artefacts deal-ing with eagles of many kinds were borrowed from various collecting institutions. These ranged from a large stone carving to three eagle eggs from a science museum. Each exhibit was displayed in the proper museological manner, mostly in desk-type vitrines, but without set-ting up particular relationships between individual artefacts. All eagles/exhibits here were treated non-hierarchically. Labels were in engraved black plastic with the relevant catalogue number and the words 'This is not a work of art' in English, German or French. At the end of the exhibition the works were returned to their collecting bodies leaving the Section des Figures permanently empty.

To talk about my museum means discussing the ways and means of analyzing fraud. The ordinary museum and its representatives simply present one form of truth. To talk about this museum means speaking about the condition of truth. It is also important to find out whether or not the fictional museum casts a new light on the mechanisms of art, the artistic life, and society. I pose the question with my museum. Therefore I do not find it necessary to produce the answer.[10]

Adjacent to the exit an improbable glass lift takes visitors to the museum's Contents Room.

Coming back into the Main Hall, visitors can turn to the west into the **Critical Wing**. Even as fiction most of this wing has not been constructed, but visitors are advised to persevere in order to get the fullest understanding of the whole museum. Each of the artists in the Critical Wing is, in their different way, actively involved in a critique of the museum (any museum) and its collections (whatever they may be). This can be seen as a political engagement with the institution and in each case it manifests itself through unconventional approaches to display. Though inherently critical, the displays described here revel in the visual possibilities of objects and embrace a sense of re-discovery through visual pleasure. However, visitors with children may wish to turn east into the **Pop(ular) Wing** at this point.

The first gallery adjacent to the entrance (**Room V**)[11] is devoted to the work of Mark Dion, whose practice falls broadly into two categories: Natural History and Archaeology. Both strands of his work depend on the relationship between work in the field (collecting and taxonomy) and in the museum (taxonomy and display). His natural history pieces explore themes of bio-diversity and the history of science through a re-examination of the work of key scientific thinkers such as Darwin. The displays mix Dion's own collected specimens with those of the museum and with contemporary artefacts. Typically, his natural history exhibits create a narrative using these varied elements. His piece *Extinction, Dinosaurs and Disney: The Desks of Mickey Cuvier* is due to be installed in this gallery. This series of works has Baron Georges Cuvier, the 19th-century scientist, represented by an animated Mickey Mouse figure, expounding his theories of taxonomy, extinction, deep time and the fixity of species. Each of these lectures turns to criticism of the Disney Corporation. The work was originally installed in Paris in 1990 to coincide with the opening of EuroDisney.

The display in Room V will be installed as soon as the museum completes construction work. In the meantime, visitors are invited to inspect work to the foundations of the building. It is possible to see the remains of various other structures of unknown use that have previously occupied the site. The museum's curators are divided on this point; both a 'Fun House' and a department store have been suggested. Earlier claims that the walls were those of a temple have been dismissed. From time to time visitors will be inveigled into assisting with the dig that is planned for the exposed area of the foundations.

Until internal discussions with the curators of the parent organization – The Delirious Museum – are resolved the installations planned for Rooms IV, III, II and I will remain at a conceptual level. In each of these spaces a small area has been set aside for presentations of the invited artists' relevant work.

Room IV: Barbara Bloom, *The Reign of Narcissism*.[12] Presented originally in the exhibition A Forest of Signs at MOCA, Los Angeles, in 1989, this work subsequently toured to Stuttgart, Zürich and London. In each location an identical set was created – an octagonal room with soft grey painted walls and white plaster neo-classical details. The exhibits, consisting of chairs, vitrines and busts on pedestals, ranged around the edge of the room. Each exhibit contained either a portrait of the artist or some explicit reference to her biography, from wall-mounted plaster reliefs to chocolates showing her silhouette and a row of identical books claiming to be 'The Complete Works of Barbara Bloom'. The seat-covers were printed with a pattern made from X-rays of the artist's teeth. The conventional style of the display was undermined by its obvious transience, there was no ceiling to complete the illusion suggested by the walls, and on closer examination the walls were actually far too thin to be convincing. The accompanying book expands on the iconography of the room, reinforcing the solemnity of the biographical exhibit while simultaneously revelling in the kitsch often attached to hero worship. Bloom plunders the work of a wide range of writers, including Virginia Woolf, Walter Benjamin and Oscar Wilde, in a self-conscious effort to lend the enterprise gravitas. In other works Bloom bridges the role of artist and designer in a direct engagement with display. In her installation of Art Nouveau chairs at the MAK in Vienna, 1993, the objects are at first seen in silhouette behind long, transluscent screens; the austerity of the display technique is countered by the exuberant lines of the chairs themselves.

Room III: Fred Wilson, *Mining the Museum*.[13] This exhibition was created for the Maryland Historical Society under the auspices of the Contemporary, Baltimore in 1992. Wilson used the collection of this gallery of historical artefacts to re-appraise the existing top-down narrative. In this process the means of display (plinths, mounts, vitrines) all came into play. In the painting displays, Wilson drew attention to and questioned the positions of various black attendants on the edges of the works. In the section labelled 'Cabinetmaking 1820–1960' he positioned a set of elaborate 19th-century chairs around a whipping post. In the metalwork case he showed not only silver *repoussé* vessels but also a set of slave shackles. In another room cigar store Indians are turned away from the viewer, facing a wall of photographic portraits of Native Americans.[14] The adjacent label says: 'Portraits of Cigar Store Owners' suggesting that these clichés tell us more about their owners than about those depicted.

At the British Museum in 1997 Wilson took over a small gallery in the Egyptian Department for his work *In Course of Arrangement*.[15] Using a selection of redundant 19th- and 20th-century object mounts from the museum's stores, this focused on the language of display and the authority that a museological language brings to bear on the reading of the collection. At the same time it pointed out that the museum itself has a history, one that is often confined to the storeroom. Wilson's work, while continuing its political engagement, is strongly rooted in the act of looking and the enquiry that this act sets up. The installations are beautiful compositions that, by sleight-of-hand, trick the viewer into an involvement with the dialogue imagined by the artist.

Room II: Joseph Kosuth, *The Play of the Unmentionable*.[16] This exhibition, made for the Brooklyn Museum in 1990, was a direct response by Kosuth to the exhibition's funding source (The National Endowment for the Arts). By juxtaposing works from a number of time periods that had all, in their different ways, courted or attracted controversy, with a variety of textual quotations the artist made an unapologetic attack on right-wing censorship. The way the work was displayed placed it firmly within a didactic context, to the anxiety of many of the curators involved.[17] Paintings, instead of being hung according to a centre line were arranged in compositions with the silk-screened texts. In this layout the paintings and sculptures were no longer seen as autonomous artworks but were placed within the overall frame of the artist's argument.

Like Wilson, Kosuth is aware of the need for a visual hook for his argument. In some ways, Kosuth is heir to the collaged exhibitions created by El Lissitzky in the 1930s, both in terms of the idea of the visual as a bearer of meaning, and in the way that text and image can be mixed. *The Play of the Unmentionable* was a complex installation that, in order to convey its message, depended on exemplary graphic clarity. Against the grain of much current museum practice, Kosuth's exhibition was what is often referred to derisively as a 'book on the wall'.

There is still discussion within the museum as to whether Kosuth's work belongs in the Critical Wing. A suggestion that there should be an Adjunct Curator of Justifiable Propaganda is currently under consideration.

Room Ia occupies the north-west corner of the museum and is easily missed as the main visitor route cuts across the corner joining Rooms II and I.[18] (This short corridor also gives access to the museum Library.) The work installed in this space is by Christian Boltanski. This room was, until recently, given over to the museum offices. There is a proposal currently under discussion that the artist should be given access to all the museum records (payroll, acquisition, donations, personnel, restitution files and so on[19]) to make an installation. At the time of going to press the details of this work are unavailable.[20] Note: there is restricted lighting in this room.

Room I: Hans Haacke, *Ansichts Sachen: Oben* (*Viewing Matters: Upstairs*).[21] In 1996 Haacke was asked by the director of the Museum

Boijmans Van Beuningen, Rotterdam, Chris Dercon, to be the fourth in a series of guest curators to make a special exhibition. Previous participants in this programme had been the curator Harald Szeeman, the film-maker Peter Greenaway and the artist/director Robert Wilson. Subsequently Hubert Damisch has organized an exhibition. Haacke began to think about how he would approach the exhibition while in the galleries of the Metropolitan Museum, New York, and was especially struck by the juxtaposition of artifice and 'reality' in Degas' sculpture of the *Little Dancer Aged 14*. Visiting the museum in Rotterdam he was taken to the stores where he saw the painting, drawing and photography collections hung, puzzle-like on racks.

> I thought it worth using the central space of the exhibition to baffle and disturb visitors, and to provoke them to think, thus matching the experience I had in the depot. This process offered an opportunity to render visible how the institutions of the museum and of art history (also I as a guest curator) influence social consciousness. In other words: to exhibit the exhibition.[22]

In the exhibition, Haacke used a number of striking visual display devices. While the works from the stores were exhibited packed onto the wire racks in the centre of the room, there was a considered and ostensibly conventional display of paintings and photographs around the walls. These were pieces selected by Haacke so that they would become part of a purposeful 'conversation' between one another. This conversation is drawn out in the book produced to document the exhibition. Texts point out political and social undercurrents that were at play in the making of the artworks and document acquisition histories and commercial transactions relating to them. The conservative nature of the display was undermined by the row of empty picture frames running cheek-by-jowl around the whole room at the top of the wall.

In one of the two small side-rooms of the exhibition space Haacke placed the Rotterdam museum's own version of Degas' *Little Dancer* facing Rodin's huge bronze *Man Walking*, which is normally displayed out-of-doors. Haacke described this work as 'a majestic ruin: headless, armless and without a dick'.[23] Behind these two figures was hung Andy Warhol's large silk-screened *The Kiss (Bela Lugosi)*, showing the film

Dracula at the moment of a fatal bite into the neck of his woman victim. These three works thus entered into a strange and disquieting dialogue.

In the second of the two small rooms Haacke picked up on the clues provided by Man Ray's *The Enigma of Isidore Ducasse*. Man Ray's work is a mysterious object wrapped roughly in felt and tied in rope. In Haacke's installation this was placed on top of a 17th-century Dutch dresser. On one side was a genre scene by Gabriel Metsu of a similar age to that of the dresser and on the other a seemingly blank white canvas, *Achrome* by Piero Manzoni. On the top of this wall, Haacke displayed a row of television sets collected by the Product Design Department of the museum. The blank screens echo the empty frames in the adjacent room and refer to the sightlessness of Man Ray's sculpture below.

Viewing Matters was a delirious, inquisitive and ambiguous, celebration of the museum's collection in particular, and the idea of the collection generally that stands in contrast in its playfulness to many earlier works by Haacke. In 1975 he made a work detailing the history of a single painting: *Seurat's Les Poseuses (Small Version) 1888–1975*. This documented the painting's progress from being a gift given by Seurat to an anarchist friend to its being acquired by an American corporation then being sold on, with profit, to a Paris art dealer. His text/photo work of 1981, *The Chocolate Master*, was a didactic enquiry into links between the exploitation of workers, business and the art world centred around the Museum Ludwig in Cologne.[24] In 1983 he began his work *Taking Stock (Unfinished)* that explored the relationship between Margaret Thatcher, the advertising firm of Saatchi and Saatchi and the art collecting activities of Charles Saatchi. This relationship reached its logical conclusion in the installation, in 2003, of the Saatchi Collection at the former home of the Greater London Council, a tier of government dismantled by Thatcher and the Conservative Party during their administration in the 1980s.

In both the Rotterdam exhibition, where he spoke of the museum stores as the '*wunderkammer* par excellence'[25] and his exhibition, *Mixed Messages*, based around the collection of the Victoria & Albert Museum, London, Haacke has referred back to this historical precedent. As part of the temporary display the museum curators have installed two *wunderkammern*. The first of these is the room of an unknown scholar in Ulm from the 17th century[26] – from the historic collection, containing amongst many other things, a number of globes, nautilus shells, books, a skull, small cannons and at least one eagle. The second is shown in Hogarth's picture *Hudibras Beats Sidrophel and his Man Whachum*. The scene here has overtones of the alchemist's laboratory; here too there are globes and books but there is also a stuffed crocodile hanging from the ceiling, a skeleton in the cupboard and a homunculus in a jar.

The **Library** is entered through a doorway between Rooms II and I. All the publications mentioned in this guide are available here for consultation by visitors. The following four books, which together form the beginnings of an encyclopaedia, are 'chained' and left on lecterns for ease of access:

- *Museums by Artists*, edited by A. A. Bronson and Peggy Gale.
- *The Museum as Muse*, by Kynaston McShine.
- *Art and Artifact; The Museum as Medium*, by James Putnam.
- *Deep Storage; Collecting, Storing and Archiving in Art*, edited by Ingrid Schaffner and Matthias Winzen.

In addition there is documentation of work by a number of artists that are in the collection of the museum, but are not included in the galleries due to restrictions of economy and scale.[27]

The centrepiece of the **North Gallery**, which is also the back entrance, is the ziggurat-like *Palace of Projects*[28] by Ilya and Emilia Kabakov. The form of this structure has been described by the artists as a 'snail', but it also invites comparisons with the Tower of Babel and with Tatlin's *Monument to the Third International*, if on a humbler scale. The spiral structure is of timber covered in white semi-transluscent panels so that the external lighting makes it glow on the inside. There are 65 'projects' on show arranged in three sections: 'How to make yourself better?', 'How to make this world better?' and 'How to stimulate the appearance of projects?'. The projects cover a wide range of ideas from 'Punishment of household objects' through 'Resurrection of all the dead' to 'Project "horse on the stairs"' each explained in text, drawings and models. The installation is designed to be rebuilt in a variety of indoor locations, a building within a building, but it has become a cumbersome semi-permanent construction here, making it necessary for anyone using the back door to pass through it. Visitors going between the Critical and Pop wings also have to negotiate the structure, though this degree of complexity of movement is not, actually, physically possible. It is also theoretically possible to enter the Rotunda from the North Gallery or to leave the museum entirely from this room.

Kabakov's previous installation in this space, called *Incident at the Museum, or Water Music*, originally made for Ronald Feldman Fine Arts, New York, in 1992, consisted of a leaking roof and the dark red walls of the museum hung with paintings.[29] Buckets were placed to collect the dripping water. The sound of the drips was 'scored' by the composer Vladimir Tarasov. This work has had to be removed from the museum for technical reasons.

To the east of the **North Gallery** is the **Pop(ular) Wing** of the museum. The first room (Gallery 8) here is the **Mouse Museum** by Claes Oldenburg. This version was created for Documenta 5 in Kassel, 1972 (at which Broodthaers closed his museum). Like the original, the form – the head of a 'Geometrical Mouse' that Oldenburg had developed as a rubber stamp some years earlier – is embedded within the form of the room. In creating this and the adjacent space the formal plan of the museum has been disrupted and the enfilade of symmetrical doors has been lost. The entrance to what Oldenburg called his 'museum of popular culture' is through the 'nose' of the mouse. The exhibits are unlabelled but are documented and keyed in the inventory. They are of various types: found objects, found objects with a known maker, amended objects, casts and development models of the artist's work. To give a flavour of this collection – there are 385 exhibits – here is a short passage from the catalogue:

> The largest object, about 87 cm, is the **Inflatable leg** (MM inv. no. 31) and the tallest, about 50 cm, is the **Study for a sculpture in the form of a ketchup bottle**, 1966 (MM inv. no. 102). The smallest objects are the **tiny eraser on chain**, 1971 (MM inv. no. 76) and the **Buttons in the shape of cigarette packs** (MM inv. no. 108), each 2 cm long.[30]

The next gallery (Gallery 7) expresses the shape implicit in its title visibly on its exterior. The entrance to the **Ray Gun Wing** is through the handle of the gun-shaped room. Its exit is through the barrel. Here the objects have been collected for their, often very vague, resemblance to ray guns. Thus there are more found objects (often detritus), 'ray guns' constructed by others (such as examples by Jim Dine and 'fag ends' twisted into shape by guards at the Venice Biennale), ray gun toys and models made by Oldenburg. There are also photographs of immovable 'ray guns' (such as fractures in the pavement and marks on walls) that are termed 'Certified Ray Guns'. This uncritical curatorship of the Mouse Museum and the Ray Gun Wing is at odds with the, sometimes enigmatic, relationships explored by Broodthaers, but the museum has no difficulty in containing both. This is at once its strength and its weakness.

The barrel of the gun points south into the **East Wing** (Gallery 6) which is awaiting installation of works created by Andy Warhol. The museum's curators are developing ideas to represent the exhibition made by Warhol in the Museum of Art, Rhode Island School of Design, Providence, in 1970, Raid the Icebox. Warhol was invited to use the archives and stores of the museum to create a special exhibition that would tour to Houston, New Orleans and return to Providence. It was expected that Warhol would choose the 'best' objects from the holding. Instead, he alighted on particular types of objects and asked that they should all be displayed. This process began when, on his first visit to the stores, he was shown a row of cupboards full of shoes. These all went into the exhibition exactly as Warhol had first seen them, including the cupboards. Instead of picking outstanding furniture or a representative selection, he chose to exhibit a row of Windsor chairs stacked on a shelf. The same manner of selection was applied to baskets, umbrellas and hatboxes. Warhol was shown potential paintings for the show on racks in no particular order:

> At first Warhol considered borrowing five racks of paintings and installing them close together and perpendicular to the wall, just as he found them. 'You couldn't walk in but you would know they're there. And you could put the best ones in front. Or should I just pick famous or valuable paintings?'[31]

In the end, Warhol selected paintings that were then shown on wire racks but that were made visible by providing ample space between them. The catalogue lists the exhibits by type either alphabetically by maker or in the order of the museum acquisition numbers. 'Warhol made a specification . . . he requested that the catalogue entry for each be as complete as possible . . .'. In effect Warhol handed the exhibition back to the 'real' curators of the museum in a damaged form. He had established an implied set of relationships between exhibits to which they would have to apply the usual standards of their profession. In distancing himself from connoisseurship, Warhol, in his genial way, subverted both the collection and the institution.

The galleries in which this work will be installed are currently closed for the first stage of their renovation. Lining the corridors there is a special display of Warhol's *Time Capsules* on loan from the Warhol Museum in Pittsburgh. Writing in his diary on 24 May 1984, Warhol said: 'I opened a Time Capsule and every time I do it's a mistake, because I drag it back and start looking through it'.[32] He had started making the *Time Capsules* when moving house in 1974. They became depositories for almost anything that came his way over the following years. There was always one opened at the end of his desk that was sealed and stored when full – eventually he made over 600 Time Capsules. Here is a selection of items from no. 113:

- bumper sticker, 'Who is John Gault?'
- unopened air mail envelope from International Biographical Centre, London
- orange t-shirt, 'PARIS' in black velveteen, 100% cotton
- postcard from Frank
- film screening program, *Rancho Deluxe*
- wanted criminal poster, May 7 1975
- model's headsheet, Jay Johnson for Zolli Models[33]

There are about 195 objects in this *Time Capsule*. Alongside the *Time Capsules*, Warhol assembled scrapbooks and 'idea boxes' containing source material for his work at the Factory. He also collected a huge amount of material at his home (this was auctioned after his death). In order to visit the next gallery it is necessary to take a detour through the **Shop**. The Shop can also be reached through the Oldenburg rooms. The doorway linking the Warhol and Fluxus galleries is fundamentally unstable and will be closed until further notice.

The Shop has a number of functions and sometimes blends in with the adjacent galleries. As well as selling a large selection of mass-produced souvenirs, readymades and *objets trouvées* ('as found' as well as amended) it also stocks a selection of facsimile 'charged' objects created during the 'performances' of Claes Oldenburg's *The Store* in New York in 1961. As the artist is not available to undertake these performances actors have been employed to re-enact the piece at regular intervals.[34] Oldenburg said: 'These things [the charged objects] are displayed in galleries, but that is not the place for them. A store would be better . . .'.[35] The inventory for December 1961 ranged from item 1: '9.99 . . . free . . . hanging . . . $399.95' through to item 107: 'Oval photograph . . . free . . . $21.79'.[36]

From time-to-time the shop also stocks objects rubber-stamped 'ATTENTION OEUVRE D'ART DANIEL SPOERRI'. The stamp was first used by the artist at the Galerie Addi Koepke, Copenhagen, in 1961:

> The entrance to the gallery, arrayed with shelves like a grocery store, presented a display of colonial goods (preserves, canned foods, etc.). The application of the rubber stamp elevated all of these wares to the status of works of art, which then were sold at their usual retail prices.[37]

The next two rooms of the Museum, the **Fluxgallery** (Gallery 5) and the **Spoerri Room** (Gallery 4) are empty. The first of these was to house a series of works created under the name Fluxus in the 1960s and 1970s. Fluxus was dedicated to the democratization of art practice and to the use of the 'everyday' as the material of art. The display was to include a number of Fluxkits and Fluxus Year Books assembled by the group's founder and leader, George Maciunas.[38] The centre-piece of the display was to be his last work, and the last collective Fluxus work, the *Flux Cabinet* of 1977. This set of drawers contains the work of a number of artists associated with the group, including Ben Vautier, George Brecht, Robert Watts and John Lennon. It is, in effect, a museum of Fluxus or, at least, a major retrospective in miniature of the group. Maciunas' own contribution includes his unfinished *Excreta Fluxorum* or 'Shit Anthology', consisting of the dried droppings of 36 different animals. The drawers are arranged as an interconnecting labyrinth with holes through which pinballs can run.

One of Brecht's drawers has a rubber band attached so it resists being opened, another is designed to shoot out when opened slightly. In a Fluxus newsletter in 1963, Maciunas proposed the following action:

> Propaganda through sabotage & disruptions of . . . museums, theaters, galleries:
>
> 2. Ordering by phone in the name of the museum . . . at the exact (or just prior to) opening various cumbersome objects: rented chairs, tables, palm trees, caskets, lumber, large sheets of plywood, bricks, gravel, sand or coal for delivery at sidewalks.[39]

This animosity to the museum has led to a dispute with the artist (who died in 1978) and the display has had to be delayed indefinitely. The small **Annexe** opening off this gallery contains a hat worn by Robert Filliou in various cities around 1961. Filliou was a Fluxus collaborator who, taking his cue from Duchamp's valise, installed a gallery – called the *Galerie Légitime*, in a number of caps and hats:

> . . . I would walk through the streets and I would come up to somebody walking in the street, and a typical dialogue might be, 'Are you interested in art, monsieur, or madame, or mademoiselle?' and they said, 'Yes, yes,' I would say 'Well do you know that I have a gallery?' If they express some interest, I would say 'Here it is.' There inside my hat were the works.[40]

In 1962 the Misfits Fair[41] was held in a small gallery in London. Filliou's contribution, which, according to Daniel Spoerri, was exhibited at the top of a ladder,[42] was a version of the *Galerie Légitime* in a frozen bowler hat containing small works by all the artists involved in the fair. Subsequent versions of this *Frozen Exhibition* used a flat cardboard bowler hat with exhibits slipped inside.

The adjoining gallery (Gallery 3) will be dedicated to the *Musée Sentimental* of Daniel Spoerri. This has been installed in different manifestations in Paris, Berlin, Cologne and Basel since 1977. Spoerri has compared them to the idea of the *wunderkammer* but, instead of the objects being used by the private scholar, these are meant as public museums relating directly to the cities in which they are installed. In Cologne in 1979, Spoerri worked with local art students with whom he identified 120 key words relating to the city. Exhibits were then collected to illustrate these key words. The exhibition, though conventional in its display, set up a matrix of meanings and associations that mirrored the complexity of the city itself.

As this museum does not belong to any city in particular it is still under discussion how the *Musée Sentimental* can be installed in the gallery set aside for it. Other works by Spoerri can be seen in the museum **Café**.[43]

There may be some confusion as to the status of the **Sound Archive Gallery**. This is located in a space parallel to the main suite of galleries and is accessible through the false door in the east wall. The 'display' is built around a near-forgotten piece of pop music from the 1980s: 'Just Give 'em Whiskey' by the group Colourbox, who recorded on the 4AD label.[44] The culture of sampling and mixing has become pervasive in pop music but this is a relatively early example (1985) of a particular kind of sampling that revelled in the use of film voice-tracks as found sounds.[45] This track forms the centrepiece of the gallery because of its resonance for the curator but also because it samples two sources with unusual relevance to the museum. The first is the film *Westworld*, which features a futuristic theme-park where the robotic characters malfunction and rise up against the visitors. The second is the 1960s British television series *The Prisoner* set in the real pastiche village of Portmeirion in which the story's hero is held captive for no apparent reason. In addition the song samples: *The Andromeda Strain*, *Queen from Outer Space*, *2001, A Space Odyssey*, *2000 Maniacs* and (possibly) *The Stud*.[46] The members of Colourbox went on to collaborate with A. R. Kane in the group M/A/R/R/S who made the ground-breaking 'Pump up the Volume' in 1987 with its eclectic collection of samples.[47] The archive is vast, documenting the works of a huge number of DJs and sound artists, however, the room is seldom open due to a dispute as to its appropriateness to the museum.

The **Temporary Exhibitions Gallery** (Gallery 2) is housed in a wholly unsuitable conversion created in the 1960s. It plays host to various itinerant museums. Some of the past exhibitions have been:

The Maybe by Cornelia Parker and Tilda Swinton. It is, of course, impossible to reproduce this exhibition and it is a matter of wishful thinking that it should have taken place in this museum. (In fact *The*

Maybe was staged at the Serpentine Gallery, London in 1995.) The work consisted of two elements: Tilda Swinton 'asleep' in a glass case and 35 objects with particular significance assembled by Cornelia Parker, also exhibited in cases. The objects were things such as the quill pen with which Charles Dickens wrote *The Mystery of Edwin Drood* and the preserved brain of Charles Babbage. Some were ordinary but for their associations, their 'importance' only being revealed by the labels written by Parker. The power of the exhibition hinged on the relationship between these dead things and the live, dreaming Swinton.

Joni Mabe's *Travelling Elvis Museum* – an obsessive collection of all things Elvis Presley including a preserved wart and a toe nail found in Gracelands, Elvis' mansion in Memphis.[48] This is part archive and part entertainment. The encyclopedic museum has gone to seed here, spawning a wayward kitsch fiction. In this it pays homage to the absurdity of hero worship usually found in the preservation of the homes (Sir John Soane, D'Annunzio, Sigmund Freud, Victor Hugo) or the actual bodies (Jeremy Bentham, Lenin) of the famous.

Eduardo Paolozzi's *Krazy Kat Archive*, on loan from the Victoria and Albert Museum, London – an eclectic collection of ephemera, memorabilia and source material for Paolozzi's work that he has been collecting since the 1960s. Like Oldenburg's 'charged' objects these things are transformed by the process of collection and by the juxtapositions created between sketch models and tin toys, between pulp magazines and quasi-ethnographic objects. Discussing his 'Idea for a new museum', Paolozzi wrote:

> The arrangement and juxtaposition of the objects & sculptures not only superb originals but, fakes combined with distinguished 'reproductions' copies of masterpieces both in painting & engineering. The radial engine & a Leger painting & a Bugatti, wheels, cinema prints, crocodile skulls. All parts movable: an endless set of combinations . . .[49]

The Birthday Ceremony by Sophie Calle. This comprises 15 vitrines that were arranged around the walls of the gallery. Each vitrine contains birthday presents given to the artist at her own dinner parties between 1980 and 1993.[50] Each party was to be attended by a number of invited guests plus one stranger, the total corresponding to the artist's age. In effect there were a number of deviations from the pre-scribed ritual so that some vitrines have fewer exhibits/gifts. The contents of each vitrine are described in a text applied to the glass.[51] In much of her work Calle acts as a curator of her own life, setting up conjectural programmes that leave themselves open to chance and sometimes risk. In 1981 in Paris she first followed a man and then, co-incidentally, was introduced to him at a gallery opening. He revealed that he was planning a trip to Venice and Calle decided to follow him incognito on this trip. This exercise was documented in her work, *Suite Vénetienne*.[52] In 1994 Calle installed a number of her personal possessions in the galleries of the Museum Boymans-van Beuningen, Rotterdam, in an exhibition called La Visite Guidée.[53] The objects (including a bucket, shoes, letters and a razor blade) corresponded typologically with the existing exhibits but were accompanied by text commentaries revealing personal (and often sexual) details of Calle's life. The installation was accompanied by a cassette-tape guided tour read by the artist, further personalizing the objects and hence de-stabilizing the authority of the museum collection.

The final gallery (Gallery 1) on this itinerary is devoted to the work of Mark **Dion** (as is Room V. See above). His archaeological pieces are based on detritus gathered in particular sites. The detritus, trans-formed into museum artefacts, is cleaned, sorted and exhibited. Past excavations have taken place in medieval rubbish heaps in Fribourg in 1995 (though Dion does not distinguish between 'historic' rubbish and contemporary rubbish) and by dredging a canal in Venice in 1997. His *Tate Thames Dig* of 1999 was undertaken on the beaches adjacent to the two London Tate sites and was subsequently displayed in the Millbank building. The finds were sorted according to material and then displayed in a large wooden cabinet with glass-fronted cases and a series of drawers that visitors were invited to open. Dion subverted usual museological practice by simply omitting labels from the display. The only text available to the visitor was one explaining the process by which the objects had been gathered.[54] Dion's attitude to the museum displays some of the ambiguity that lies at the heart of the *Delirious Museum* itself. In his 'Lexicon of Relevant Terms' he writes:

> **Museum** 1. The resting place for souvenirs, trophies, loot, and other objects stripped of function. 2. The location where the history of the

ruling class is passed off as public. 3. Site of the production of the 'official story', be it about art, history, nature or biography. The place of progress.[55]

Elsewhere he says: 'If someone wants to update the museum, they should build a new one. An entire city of museums would be nice, each stuck in its own time.'[56]

Note: At any time there are likely to be interventions in the museum taking place without the knowledge of the curators. The precedents for this are numerous. In 1977 Robert Filliou visited the Louvre and the Musée d'Art Moderne de la Ville de Paris, donned overalls and cleaned the fronts of various paintings and sculptures. Filliou had himself photographed cleaning the paintings and placed the photographs, the cloths used in the cleaning and the dust gathered in the process in archival boxes. It is not recorded if the museum authorities were aware of Filliou's helpful action. In the same year the artist Jeffrey Vallance replaced electrical socket covers at the Los Angeles County Museum of Art with ones he had painted. Like Filliou, this also involved dressing in overalls. The sockets were subsequently painted over during redecoration but the artist believes that his work is still intact beneath the other layers.[57] It is to be hoped that any re-building of the Los Angeles County Museum of Art will take this intervention into account in its conservation plans.[58] In October 2003 the graffiti artist Banksy glued an altered painting from a street market onto the wall of Tate Britain. The picture was of a rural scene with superimposed 'Police Line. Do not cross.' tape. The painting only came to the attention of guards when it fell off the wall.

Visitors are requested not to inform security guards or the information desk if they observe any action or intervention that might ultimately lend the institution more mystique or add to the so-called 'complex layers of meaning' attached to the museum.

The **Index Room** is located in the basement. Here it is possible to track down individual objects in the museum. Various systems of classification have been used: alphabetical, thematic, chronological, geographical and typological. In addition it is possible to locate objects by their medium or substance, if at all.

6

FROM SOANE TO SOANE

Chapters 2 and 3 were a drift around ideas largely generated in and by Paris in the 19th and 20th centuries. Chapters 4 and 5 identified lost and imaginary fragments of the Delirious Museum created as experiments. The following is a search for a version of the Delirious Museum in London (the city in which I live). By undertaking and describing this dérive, I have, of course, destroyed it. It survives as a potential itinerary. This version of the museum uses 20th-century ideas applied retro-actively to the spaces of the 19th century.

> The ordinary practitioners of the city live 'down below', below the thresholds at which visibility begins. They walk – an elementary form of experience of the city; they are walkers, *Wandersmanner*, whose bodies follow the thicks and thins of an urban 'text' they write without being able to read it. These practitioners make use of spaces that cannot be seen; their knowledge of them is as blind as that of lovers in each other's arms. The paths that correspond in this intertwining, unrecognized poems in which each body is an element signed by many others, elude legibility. It is as though the practices organizing a bustling city were characterized by their blindness.[1]

It is possible to trace a crooked line over a map of central London linking a tomb to the occupant's house and museum. This line can be walked over the course of a day, going from death into life, from the end to the beginning. Along the route, tombs and death re-occur, either as architecture or as fragments of narrative. Also along the route, providing a more cohesive thread are a number of real museums, quasi-museums and pseudo-museums.

I undertook the walk I describe here twice in its entirety. The first walk was in 1996 and it still had some of the qualities of a *dérive*. I knew where it was to begin and end but the points along the way were not so predictable. The second version of the walk was in 2003 and by then it was a search for places that I already knew. I had to ascertain if the places were lost or transformed. In this text the two versions of the walk elide. Other fragments come from occasional intersections with the route over the intervening period, so the description is geographically but not chronologically ordered. By 2004 the early part of the route had been radically altered by demolition around St Pancras Station.

I started from King's Cross, my own point of entry to London when I arrived to live here from Scotland in 1980. To get to the beginning of the route I headed north from the station, skirting the edge of the King's Cross goodsyard site, under three railway bridges and through a small gate. On the steps beyond the gate I found a page from a guide-book. Every walk needs a guidebook. On one side was a description of walks in Teesdale and on its reverse a list of museums in Northumbria, including one dedicated to mining and two to railways. Along the route of this walk it will be necessary to read the signs. The city leaves these textual traces to remind us of where, in time, we are placed.

> To him [the *flâneur*] the shiny enamelled signs of businesses are at least as good a wall ornament as an oil painting is to a bourgeois in his salon. The walls are the desk against which he presses his notebook . . .[2]

In this vault are deposited the remains of Sir John Soane R.A., F.R.S., architect of the Bank of England etc. etc. etc. who departed this life on the 20th of January 1837, aged 84 years.
Inscription on the Soane Family Tomb.

Sir John Soane is buried alongside his family in St Pancras Old Churchyard. When he was interred here this was an open space on the edge of the city. During his life Soane romanticized the location by depicting the tomb set in countryside with the tomb of Rousseau in the distance. Today it is wedged between a hospital, a busy road and the railway lines that connect to the station of the same name. The cemetery forms part of a hinterland of railway arches, gasometers, canal

11. John Soane, Design for the Monument to Mrs Soane (1816). Drawn by J. M. Gandy.

buildings and the council housing estates of Somers Town. At its eastern edge is located a coroner's court and mortuary. As a collection of objects, the St Pancras burial ground is historically enigmatic. There is a half-timbered chapel, an elaborate monument – the Burdett-Coutts sundial – guarded by two stone dogs, and two stone lions, the slab which marks the original burial place of Mary Wollstonecraft and a tree called, according to its plaque, the Hardy Tree. This is named after the author and architect Thomas Hardy, who was in charge of the exhumation and removal of bodies from the part of the burial ground that was disturbed when the railway line was built in 1865. Around the base of the tree a confusion of redundant headstones radiate out, the trunk gradually swallowing them up. The Soane Family Tomb is nearby, surrounded by a wide encircling *cordon sanitaire* of railings. It has been proposed at least twice that the tomb be removed from this spot to escape vandalism. The first time that this was suggested was in 1869 when it was thought it should go to Lincoln's Inn Fields.[3] The second time was in 1997 when the suggestion was that it would be safer were it to be re-located to the grounds of Dulwich Picture Gallery. Instead, the railings have been built and a security camera is permanently trained on the structure – the dead are watched over eternally. The tomb is ostensibly a neo-classical construction using an architectural language borrowed from ancient Rome. In detail, however, this straightforward allusion does not hold. By the time that Soane designed this tomb (originally for his wife) he had already completed some of the most important commissions of his career. Significantly, he had built Dulwich Picture Gallery where the founder's mausoleum formed a centrepiece to a building otherwise dedicated to the display of paintings.[4] He had also amended and extended the house at Lincoln's Inn Fields that was ultimately to become his own house/museum. The tomb uses a number of the same devices that Soane had developed in these buildings as well as other commissions: the shallow saucer dome, the aedicular 'pavilions' and fragments of Roman funerary architecture. In the watercolour by Soane's illustrator, J. M. Gandy, the tomb is shown as a huge monument with two figures next to the (unbuilt) gateway. The architectural elements of the tomb are taken apart, as if they are meant to be read separately. The stairs and the balustrade are notional or ceremonial, too small to be functional. In the centre of the sunken well stands the tomb itself, topped by the pavilion with its urns, columns and dome. While this part was meant to be seen rising above ground level, the other elements could be read as an excavation. The ritual staircase has been, as it were, uncovered by the archaeologist/aesthete in his search for antiquity. The new railings make the staircase virtually invisible from ground level; maybe from the vantage-point of the security camera this descent can still be fully appreciated.

Soane was not only re-inventing the antique within which he could literally place himself, but he was also building archaeology. Soane was preoccupied with the architecture of death and the idea of the museum. It is no coincidence that much of his surviving work is imbued with morbid concerns – either through the direct association with the classical architecture of the tomb or through the accumulation of so many objects. The parallels that exist between the grave (the body interred with the goods necessary to ease the passage into the afterlife) and the collection (an attempt to achieve immortality through things) is obvious. Soane's work is a paradigm of this relationship.[5]

The Fleet River flows past the church and immediately south along its course on to St. Pancras Wells . . .

Signboard, St Pancras Old Churchyard

. . . in 1846, the river [the Fleet] – quite literally – blew up, its rancid and foetid gasses bursting out onto the streets above. At King's Cross the road was impassable . . .[6]

Along Midland Road the vaults supporting the railway line have had their façades removed and temporarily look like the ruins of Roman baths. At one point (and at one moment in time) it is possible to see all the way through the vaults to the eastern edge, daylight appearing at the end of the long tunnel for the first time since construction. The screens and spire of St Pancras Chambers colludes in the illusion of ruin. Once, the route of the walk veered off Midland Road up the taxi ramp of St Pancras Station. This is now filled with rubble. The station is a gateway into the 19th-century city. The train shed acts as a reminder of modernity's impact. So the two structures together make a bridge in time. In myth, the station also buries the past; there is a story that the ancient British Queen Boudicca is buried under Platform 7. Where the railway line terminates the scale of the architecture and the intensity of the traffic changes.

MILK
Graffito sprayed in blue paint on the wall of the Great Midland Hotel at the corner of Euston Road and Midland Road

The tiered public open space in front of the British Library to the west forms a continuation of the huge room that is St Pancras Station train shed. But this is only a temporary respite and it is necessary to rejoin the Euston Road and travel upstream, as it were, against the flow of the traffic. On the south side of the road is a reminder of the literal form of architectural style borrowing in the replication of the Erechtheion tacked onto the side of New St Pancras Church and the addition of the Temple of the Winds in the middle of the church tower. Further along the Euston Road are the headquarters of the Wellcome Trust, named for the pharmacist and great accumulator of medical and social artefacts whose collection on his death rivalled the holdings of the British Museum.[7]

The Wilkins Building of University College is approached on axis, but like so many other points along this route there is no door on this axis. The entrances to the quadrangles are insignificant doors to the north and south.

This case contains the skeleton of Jeremy Bentham, one of the founders of University College, dressed in his usual clothes. The wax face was modelled by Jacques Talrich and the head is in the College safe.

Explanatory label on Bentham's cabinet

The 'auto-icon' of Jeremy Bentham is situated in the south quadrangle of University College. Bentham was a contemporary of Soane; he died five years before Soane, in 1832. Bentham's intention in leaving his dressed skeleton to the college was very different from Soane's version of immortality as exemplified by his museum. Bentham asked that his auto-icon be removed periodically from its case to attend meetings, thereby ensuring that he would remain, quite literally, present. By turning 'himself' into a displayed object Bentham denied the possibility of a funeral monument. Marcel Broodthaers made a film about Bentham's auto-icon:

> . . . the figure is seated on a chair at the back of an illuminated cupboard, and observes with his blue eyes the comings and goings of the new generation. Indeed, here is a good scientific subject for a university film. In short, I will make a film if I succeed in waking up . . .[8]

Despite the substantial nature of the auto-icon Bentham has become, in effect, a one-man museum. This condition is usually involuntary. The British Museum is full of bodies who believed they were making their way to another life. They could not have guessed at the possibility that this other life would be as a display. Bentham seems to look more like stuffed clothing as the years pass. His limbs are too thin, his posture is unconvincing. A photograph displayed in a vitrine adjacent to the cabinet shows his spine emerging during conservation treatment. Another shows him looking fuller than he is today and with his mummified head at his feet. Meanwhile he stares blindly out of his case at an empty phone box. The axis here suggests a relationship between the two boxes: the positive and the negative, the occupied and the empty. This axis arcs across London to the Tate on Millbank, site of the penitentiary constructed on the lines of Bentham's all-seeing Panopticon. And from here the connections extend to the tomb of the collectors the Tradescants[9] across the river and beyond to the asylum of Bedlam at the Imperial War Museum in Lambeth.

SEAN MASKEY IS ASLEEP PLEASE PASS QUIETLY

Graffito, Gower Street

Every walk needs a map. The map of the second walk was of the London Underground found on Gower Street; the spaces beneath my feet.

The Grant Museum of Zoology & Comparative Anatomy on Gower Street has almost no external presence, forming, as it does, part of the Department of Biology in the Darwin Building. This sits on the site of one of Charles Darwin's houses. If Jeremy Bentham's presence in the South Cloister is of a solitary nature, here the preserved and stuffed animals crowd together in a wild society. There is no dissimulation here; the animals are displayed as skeletons, as whole and dismembered specimens in glass jars and as examples of the taxidermist's craft. They are suspended in a half-state neither dead nor alive.

NO BLOOD FOR OIL

Sticker on pavement, Gower Street

The Petrie Museum of Egyptian Archaeology is also embedded within the fabric of the university complex.[10] The route to the museum through a library building is contorted; like the Grant Museum, the Petrie has erratic opening hours. Beyond two large rooms of displays a door leads to a staircase lined with vitrines. This staircase descends to a locked (fire) door – an inadvertent reference to the false doors of Egyptian tomb architecture. This door is also like Soane's descent into the ground, however, it is situated on the ground floor, a fact easily forgotten on the tortuous route from the entrance. The rather anonymous door is visible from the outside; an understated face for the museum and an unused exit. At the top of the stairs there is a discreet display installed by the Museum of Jurassic Technology, Los Angeles, made up of stereoscopic viewers presenting the life story of the museum's founder, Flinders Petrie.

AROSFA
HOTEL
MUSEUM 2115

Sign, Gower Street

In the basement of the Habitat shop, under the Heal's building on Tottenham Court Road in amongst the open displays of glass and crockery was a long, narrow floor-to-ceiling showcase. For a time this was a site for a series of visiting objects from Glasgow museums; then it became a showcase used for installations by invited artists. Culture temporarily blended invisibly with commerce.

NO FUN HOUSE

Graffito, Tottenham Court Road

Pollock's Toy Museum in Scala Street had its origins in the shop created for the sale of Pollock's theatres in Hoxton. These are still sold,
cut-out paper proscenium arches and sets, plain or coloured with
characters in costume on long sticks. Whether these are still sold as
toys is doubtful. And, like all museums of childhood or playthings, the
displays upstairs probably mean more to adults than children. For
children's toys are to be played with, not to be looked at.[11]

The museum itself is located within a labyrinth of domestic rooms
and narrow staircases. Small windows open out onto views of the
surrounding streets and light-wells. Fireplaces and mantelpieces
occupy ambiguous positions between the domestic state and display.
The organization of the collection is not clear. Objects are arranged
chronologically, by origin and by type. This serves to make readings
of the displays both difficult and entertaining. If the museum aspires
to a condition where the world is made visible either through categorization or through miniaturization, then what is happening here?
Certainly miniaturization comes into play. Every doll (especially the
doll that cannot be played with) presents itself as 'us' made small. Each
railway station, car, gun and doll's house shows us our world in miniature. Of course, by bringing together different scales of object, this
world is also made absurd. So what, at first, appears as a way of relating simply to the world (the world of made things) is actually a mad
tableau that defies coherence. This brings us to the Surrealists' love
of juxtaposition. The showcases of Pollock's Toy Museum could be
the products of Max Ernst or Joseph Cornell, missing only the enigmatic texts that the Surrealists favoured. And, like the surreal images
created by de Chirico, this interior ultimately defies categorization in
a confusion of half-meanings and misunderstandings. In a room largely
devoted to dolls, out of the way on top of a large glass showcase lies
a tiny doll Ophelia in her own glass box. She seems to be based on
the Millais painting yet evokes comparison with Sleeping Beauty and,
in more recent art practice, with Cornelia Parker's staging of the
recumbent Tilda Swinton in The Maybe. Not dead, only sleeping. An
adjoining sealed room is occupied only by dolls. The crib has 15 dolls

all sitting up around its edge – the dolls have taken over here; it has become their space.

ST GB 1823 REFIXED 1896 ST GF 1823 REFIXED 1896
Parish boundary marker, Keppel Street

On 24 September 1966 the artist John Latham built three towers of books – the *Skoob Towers* – on Montague Place. The first, made of copies of *The National Encyclopaedia*, was at the corner with Malet Street. The second, made of bound copies of *Punch*, was 20 yards down the pavement. The third was built of the journal *Metropolitan Museum Seminars in Art* and was situated outside the north entrance to the British Museum. At around 6:30 in the evening the first tower began to smoke, after being set alight by the artist and was still smouldering an hour later. At 7:30 the second tower also began to smoke but quickly caught fire, soon after which firemen arrived on the scene. As they were training their hoses on the fragile construction, the third tower was lit. As the firemen dealt with the smoking first tower the third sprang up into a 20-foot flame and this too was extinguished. Latham was questioned by the police but not charged.[12] The artist chose the site, no doubt, for its proximity to both the University of London and the British Library at the heart of the British Museum. In 1998 the new British Library building opened next to St Pancras Station. The removal of the books from the Round Reading Room of the British Museum left an absence comparable to that at the centre of the Louvre.

By entering the British Museum through the north door past two massive stone lions it is possible to retrace the fragments of another route from death into life. The villain of Hitchcock's 1929 film *Blackmail*, in his attempt to escape from the police, runs up the steps to the main entrance, then goes through the Egyptian galleries and the triangular Iron Library at the edge of the Round Reading Room. Eventually he emerges onto the dome of the Reading Room from which he falls to his death. Since the construction of the Great Court it is now possible to see the dome and the drum of the library building from within the museum, though, of course, the dome is not accessible. The Iron Library has gone but some of the rest of the route taken by

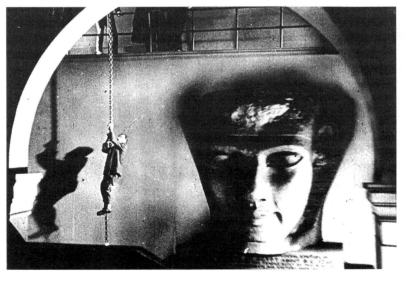

Hitchcock's character can be pieced together. The upper Egyptian galleries were, until recently, still in the same form as they were in *Blackmail*. These rooms contain the museum's collection of sarcophagi, mummies and *shabti* figures. The Egyptian sculpture gallery on the ground floor was remodelled in the 1970s but is still recognizable as the space used in the Hitchcock film. The impact of the Great Court can also be felt here. Previously wide ramps led to side 'chapels' along one side of the sculpture gallery. Now the chapels have been demolished to make way for Norman Foster's Great Court, but the ramps remain as another reminder of the pervasive accidental evocation of the blind in Egyptian architecture: false doors, stairs that lead to dead ends, ceremonial ramps with nowhere to go. Running parallel to this long gallery on its north–south axis are two other suites of rooms. The first is devoted to the collections of the Western Asiatic Antiquities Department. The second has displays of Greek sculpture. Within this collection are the more complete fragments of the Tomb of King Mausolus at Halicarnassus. This structure gave the name to all subsequent mausoleums. The form of the tomb has been the subject of much academic and architectural conjecture and argument. In the British Museum the different types of fragments (architecture and sculpture) are deposited in various rooms, making the job of any mental re-assembly even more complex.

Of course, it is possible to take a number of different routes through the British Museum. The artist Tim Brennan organized a guided tour of the area that starts at the North Entrance of the Museum. His first reference was to the University of London Senate House that is visible to the north. This was Orwell's inspiration for the government buildings featured in *Nineteen Eighty-Four*. The part of Brennan's walk that went through the museum itself was undertaken in silence so as not to add to the babble of voices already permeating the environment. Brennan's book *Museum of Angels*[13] is an unconventional museum guidebook picking out various 'winged creatures' in

(facing page) 12. Stills from Alfred Hitchcock's *Blackmail* (1929).
From top: The dome of the Round Reading Room; the Egyptian Gallery; the Sculpture Gallery.

the collection. The route taken by Brennan in his walk overlaps with one going through the Coptic Corridor to the Hittite Landing and on through the galleries of Celtic Europe and Roman Britain. There is now no trace of the huge wall carving, *Capital*, made by the artist Terry Smith in the plaster of this gallery in 1995. Future archaeology will uncover it as a faint palimpsest written into the brickwork.[14]

Another obvious route would be through the Great Court itself. This route almost manages to avoid the museum completely. The hybrid, open space around the Reading Room is given over to cafés, shops, information desks and a few large museum objects. It is covered by a spectacular glass roof that lends it the air of being a semi-outdoor space, as if it has taken the principle of the arcade and twisted it, by technological virtuosity, into the form of a square enclosing a drum. Its effect, unlike the Louvre pyramid to which it is often compared, is to objectify the rest of the museum. Where once this could only be seen to be happening from the street, the museum is now visible as a freestanding object within itself. The effect on the Reading Room is similar. This was a space designed to have no outside. It was reached by, in effect, a tunnel that opened into the expanse of the library. Now the Reading Room is encased in Portland stone to match the surrounding walls of the museum and it is made to seem smaller by being a detached building within a public open space. On some nights the Great Court is left open later than the museum galleries, further extending the ambiguity of the space.

> **Proposal:** That the Great Court only be opened when the rest of the Museum is closed and vice versa. This would dispel the illusion that the Great Court is part of the Museum and would establish it as an integral part of the street.

Leaving the museum by the main entrance it is possible to see the lion-headed drinking fountains, an echo of the lions at the north door, where Frank Weber, the blackmailer in Hitchcock's film, stopped on his way into the museum. In fact, he never really entered the building. There was not enough light to film within the galleries so Hitchcock employed the Schufftan cinematographic process involving mirrors, photographic transparencies and models filmed alongside the live action.[15]

Many older visitors still associate visits to the museum with the magic-shop that stood for many years opposite the entrance in Great Russell Street. This has now disappeared.

LONDON BOROUGH OF HOLBORN MUSEUM ST. W.

Street sign

St George's, Bloomsbury, was completed in 1731 and was designed by Nicholas Hawksmoor. The orientation of the church is now solely towards Bloomsbury Way, however, Hawksmoor designed it on two crossing axes. The east–west axis with its door under the steeple, which formerly had flights of steps up from the street, is now blocked off, even the yard formed by the adjacent buildings is now locked. Above the present doorway the empty, keystone-shaped lamp is joined by a CCTV camera. The steeple itself brings us back to the Tomb of King Mausolus. The stepped pyramid top of this is one, probably highly inaccurate, interpretation of the tomb. When St George's was built, the building that stood on the site of the British Museum was Old Montagu House, which was not used as a museum until 1754. The sculptures from Halicarnassus were not acquired until 1835. Hawksmoor's imaginative reconstruction therefore pre-dated the arrival of the mausoleum's fragments by more than 100 years. The lamps on the street positioned on either side of the entrance stairs are topped off with miniature models of Hawksmoor's conjectural design. Iain Sinclair in his prose poem 'Nicholas Hawksmoor, His Churches' makes much of the proximity of this church to the British Museum: 'The British Museum . . . The locked cellar of words, the labyrinth of all recorded knowledge, the repository of stolen fires and symbols, excavated god-forms . . .'.[16] Sinclair connects Hawksmoor's London churches by superimposing a pentacle onto the map of London.[17] This pentacle connects another site discussed in this book: Bunhill Fields.[18]

London Borough of Camden WEST CENTRAL STREET WC1 FORMERLY HYDE STREET

Street sign

An address that is now the Cuban Embassy:

... Ferguson's Grand Promenade at 167 High Holborn ... advertised a collection consisting of a Devonshire giant and two dwarfs, all alive, mechanical wax figures of Lady Flora Hastings (the unfairly accused central figure in a scandal at the youthful Queen Victoria's court), John Marchant ('the murderer of his fellow servant in Cadogan Place, Chelsea'), and "the Female School of Nicholas Nickleby"; a mechanical panorama ... of the Grace Darling sea rescue; live serpents; a mummy; numerous mechanical waxworks; and ... the fittings and drapery allegedly used at the enthronement of the queen.[19]

In 1847 Ferguson's Grand Promenade and its remarkable three-dimensional façade was described by *Punch* with an ironic suggestion that the collection should be moved to the British Museum.

WE STARVE LOOK AT ONE ANOTHER SHORT OF BREATH WALKING PROUDLY IN OUR WINTER COATS WEARING SMELLS FROM LAB'RATORIES FACING A DYING NATION OF MOVING PAPER FANTASY LISTENING FOR THE NEW TOLD LIE WITH SUPREME VISIONS OF LONELY TUNES SOMEWHERE INSIDE SOMETHING THERE IS A RUSH OF GREATNESS WHO KNOWS WHAT STANDS IN FRONT OF OUR LIVES I FASHION MY FUTURE ON FILMS. IN SPACE SILENCE TELLS ME SECRETLY EVERYTHING EVERYTHING SINGING MY SPACE-SONGS ON A SPIDER-WEB SITAR

Graffiti in alley between Drury Lane and Shelton Street

The current Freemasons' Hall is a huge wedge of stone occupying the triangular site between Great Queen Street and Wild Street. Like the Wellcome Building on Euston Road, it looks not so much built as carved out of solid rock. The Grand Temple itself sits insulated in the centre of the site, surrounded by ancillary accommodation and meeting rooms. Hidden away amongst these is the museum, a perplexing collection of artefacts so overloaded with symbolism that, to the layman at least, they are impossible to understand. Images of chequerboards, masons' tools, pyramids and the columns of Boaz and Jachim abound. On my first visit the door marking the entrance from the museum to the Temple was flanked by elaborate freestanding columns. The right-hand column had a shaft with terrestrial maps surmounted by a celestial globe. The left-hand column had a shaft with celestial maps; its top was empty. On my second visit these columns had been moved to the opposite end of the museum where they stood on either side of a curious desk, in the top of which was hidden a detailed wooden model of the 'Tabernacle in the Desert'. By this time the single globe had disappeared and both columns had empty tops.

On this site previously stood a Freemasons' Hall built by Thomas Sandby in 1775–76. John Soane added a Council Chamber in 1828 that was demolished in 1864.

CHINA HONG CHINESE KONG INDIA INDIA WE ARE JORDY WE ARE JEWISH WE ARE JEWISH WE ARE JEWISH SYNAGOGUE SYNAGOGUE WE ARE JEWISH ARMY ARMY GREAT BRITAIN CHURCH JORDY BRITAIN CHURCH JORDY BRITISH CHURCH JORDY

Graffiti on fountain, Lincoln's Inn Fields

Lincoln's Inn Fields:

It used to be said that he [Inigo Jones] designed the sq. to be of the same size as the Great Pyramid. This is now discredited. It is not even certain that Inigo Jones made a design for the whole sq. The base of the Great Pyramid is 755 ft. square, and L.I.F. are about 100 sq. ft. more in area.[20]

Lincoln's Inn Fields is oblong.

Circling this oblong leads to the Hunterian Museum – in 2003 'closed till late 2004 for renovation' – on the south side of Lincoln's Inn Fields. This is in the building of the Royal College of Surgeons and is adjacent to the Odontological Museum. It is named after the pioneering 18th-century surgeon, John Hunter, whose collection forms the core of the display. The museum was hit by a bomb in 1941 and nearly three-quarters of the collection was destroyed. The remaining exhibits include the skeleton of an Irish giant, Charles O'Brien and that of a famous Sicilian dwarf, Anna Crachami. The collection also includes the four anatomical tables of John Evelyn. These are the dried arteries, veins and nerves of various bodies pinned onto wooden panels by the Paduan physician Fabricius Bartoletus in 1645. The donors of these distorted and vestigial bodies are not named.

Eternal war against Capitalism. All your financial and media centres will fall to war. And Babylon will fall.

From a poster, Lincoln's Inn Fields

South of Lincoln's Inn Fields, through the lost Clement's Inn is the site of Butcher Row, from which Giordano Bruno set out on an imagined journey to Whitehall to debate his ideas regarding heliocentricity at 'the Ash Wednesday Supper'. His account of this was published as *La Cena de la ceneri* in London in 1584. He describes setting off with his two companions along the streets of the city, then changing plans and going to the Thames in order to take a boat to their destination. After a long wait boatmen arrived, they boarded, then moved sluggishly along the river singing as they went, only to be dropped off well before the desired landing spot. When they set off once again on foot, they found themselves knee-deep in mud and then discovered that they had returned to near their starting point. The narrator of the story exclaims: '. . . O obscure enigmas, O tangled labyrinths, O enchanted sphinxes – Disentangle yourselves or let yourselves be disentangled. At this crossroad, at this doubtful step.'[21] When they set out once more they were assaulted by the London mob: '. . . the Nolan [Bruno] received about twenty . . . violent shoves, particularly at the pyramid near the palace at the junction of three streets . . .'.[22] Soon after, they reached their destination:

> . . . having travelled impassable paths, passed through doubtful detours, crossed swift rivers, left behind sandy shores, forced a passage through thick slimes, overcome turgid bogs, gaped at rocky lavas, followed filthy roads, hit against perilous cliffs, we arrived alive, by the grace of Heaven, at the port, *id est,* at the portal, which was opened as soon as we touched it.[23]

As Frances Yates has pointed out, this journey never took place: 'The journey is something in the nature of an occult memory system through which Bruno remembers the themes of the debate of the "Supper"'.[24]

This imaginary journey leaves us still in Lincoln's Inn Fields.

In the hallway there is a mirror which faithfully duplicates all appearances. Men usually infer from this mirror that the library is not infinite (if it really were, why this illusory duplication?); I prefer to dream that its polished surfaces represent and promise the infinite . . .[25]

Sir John Soane's house, on the north side of the Fields is a museum of blanks, traces and reflections.

Soane intended the projecting bay of his house to be duplicated to the west along the façade looking onto Lincoln's Inn Fields. This was a grand design that would have taken over three adjoining houses. As it is, the three-storey projecting bay has become the external image of the house/museum. For a number of years this architectural feature was an open loggia (Soane extended the space by glazing the arcade in 1829), but even today the transitional quality of this space is clear. The house/museum states its presence in the square (and hence, by extension, in the city) with this device. Standing in the narrow space on the first floor which extends beyond the South Drawing Room, it is possible to turn one's back on the museum and its collection and be, as it were, outside it. This is not possible anywhere else in the building. All the rooms (and that is discounting the first-floor loggia space as a 'room') look inward. The personal collection, as much as that of the public museum, aspires towards the condition of the encyclopedia. Within this assumption is the idea that the museum can be an attempt to re-make the world. Soane's museum does this by intensifying the environment of the collection. At times it is difficult to distinguish the building from its contents. Much of the collection is made up of fragments and miniaturizations of architecture. These are often assembled in such a way as to produce a kind of confusion; models of real projects by Soane are used as lantern lights within ceilings, chunks of masonry are re-assembled into a cod tombstone, or more accurately, a dog tombstone, and neolithic tombs are recreated in cork.

The actual architecture colludes in this confusion: pre-figuring Lissitzky's Proun rooms, walls fold out to reveal other walls which fold out to reveal a narrow atrium, ceilings float off the walls, the corners of rooms are occupied by mirrors. The labyrinthine quality of the museum is essential to the way it works and is not just an accident of

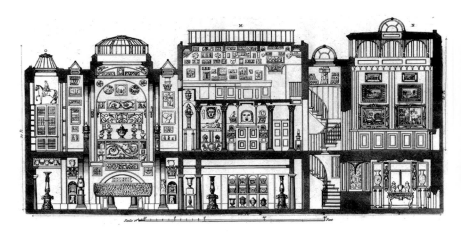

13. Section through the Soane Museum from west to east (1827), from Britton's *Union*. Drawn by C. J. Richardson, engraved by Gladwin.

its evolution. Soane may have considered the asymmetry a flaw born of the order in which the properties were purchased, but without this disrupted development there would have been no opportunity to explore the interstitial; the spaces between the spaces. There are constant reminders in the museum of the orientation of rooms in the form of labels on the walls giving the compass points. The effect of this is to give temporary reassurance to the viewer, however, these notices also blend into the collection. They soon stop being useful and become another blind against clarity.

In the Sepulchral Chamber, at the base of the part of the museum called the 'Museum', under the Dome, sits the empty Sarcophagus of Seti I, also called the Belzoni Sarcophagus. This was bought from the former circus giant and renegade archaeologist Giovanni Belzoni through his agent in 1824. The artefact had first been offered to, and displayed in, the British Museum, but the trustees were unwilling to part with the £2,000 asking-price for its acquisition. In a parallel commercial exhibition at the Egyptian Halls in Piccadilly, Belzoni displayed a reconstruction of the tomb in which the sarcophagus had been discovered, alongside plaster casts of some of the contents. The sarcophagus was Soane's most expensive purchase. To install it in the crypt it was necessary to demolish a wall in the back of the house. A few days prior to this, news reached London of Belzoni's death near Timbuktu. The archaeologist's widow, Sarah, left in penury by the death of her husband, began arrangements for another exhibition of Belzoni's finds and at first wanted to re-acquire the sarcophagus. Soane resisted this and, possibly as a mediating gesture, began arrangements for a benefit event that would publicize Belzoni's exhibition. On the evenings of 23, 26 and 30 March 1825, invited guests were admitted to the ground and basement floors of Soane's house to view the sarcophagus by lamplight. The show was very carefully designed and managed by Soane. He hired a large number of candelabra, chandeliers and lamps to illuminate the façade and the interiors. In one room he temporarily installed a large mirror to manipulate the effects of light on paintings. The limestone sarcophagus was the centre of this display, glowing red from within. The distinguished guests were given coffee and cakes as well as a spectacularly theatrical experience.[26] The following month, Sarah Belzoni staged her own, financially ruinous, exhibition in the former Hunter Museum in Leicester Square, the remaining contents of which are now housed across Lincoln's Inn Fields at the Hunterian Museum.

A bust of Soane himself looks down on the interior of the sarcophagus from the east balustrade of the Dome. This suggests that the sarcophagus is not only that of Seti but also of Soane; absent only in that his actual corpse was interred in St Pancras Burial Ground alongside his family. It was impractical to build the family tomb within the house – as had been possible at Dulwich Picture Gallery[27] – so he provided a notional tomb of his own. Tucked away under the arches in the Crypt adjacent to the Sepulchral Chamber, is a scaled-down model of the aedicular structure of the Soane tomb. There are a number of mis-matches here: the huge sarcophagus, the small model of the tomb, the illustration of that tomb as an over-sized monument, set in an imaginary landscape. It is tempting to suggest that the special evening viewings were a kind of premature wake and that Soane's wake is diametrically opposed to Jeremy Bentham's appearances at meetings after his death. If Soane 'died' before his actual death, then Jeremy Bentham refused to 'die' after his.

The front of the house/museum on Lincoln's Inn Fields is its face, however, the building also has a back. This is on Whetstone Park, a small street sandwiched between the buildings on the square and the much larger ones on High Holborn. Today it is used by a number of the homeless as a quiet place to sleep. Maybe some are those who had lived in the makeshift shelters built in Lincoln's Inn Fields in the 1980s. The elevation of the house/museum to Whetstone Park is composed of a number of false windows, blank arcades and two real doors. It comes as something of a shock to realize that these doors can be related to internal doors. This exposes the thinness of the museum. Internally the spaces inter-link infinitely, as befits the labyrinth; in the depths of the interior there is no sense of a physical connection to the street. Indeed, the rear elevation could be read as a negation of the interior, were it not for the necessary flaw of the doors.

Absence is a recurring theme in all museums; whether it is in the impossibility of completing the collection or in the space vacated by an object removed for 'conservation'. In the case of the Soane house/

museum, absence takes unexpected forms. There is the absence from the tomb of the founder and the absence from the house of an occupant. On the south wall of the Breakfast Parlour there is a small glass vitrine framed by two portrait miniatures of Napoleon. The vitrine originally contained a pistol that Soane believed had belonged to Napoleon, however, the label acknowledged that the pistol was a fake. Soane bought the pistol after a pawnbroker's agent had been arrested on suspicion of theft of the item. The pistol was actually made in Turkey around 1810 and had the words 'Emperor Napoleon' engraved on its barrel in England. In 1969 the pistol was stolen from the museum and was subsequently replaced by its own photograph. For a while the vitrine itself was removed, leaving only its shadow on the wall. Now the vitrine is empty but for the two mounts that formerly held the pistol in position. On the wooden frame of the vitrine it says:

> HISTORICAL RECORD. This PISTOL was taken by PETER the GREAT, Emperor of all Russians, from the Bey Commander of the Turkish Army at Azof, 1696. And Presented by Alexander Emperor of Russia to Napoleon Bonaparte, Emperor of France, at the Treaty of Tilsit, 1807, And Presented to a Gentleman by Napoleon at St. Helena, 1820.

The back of the vitrine is a mirror.

In the hall, behind a tiny glass plate, is a real bullet-hole made during an unsuccessful attempt to rob the museum in the 1980s. But, like reflections in parallel mirrors, the false narratives and blinds seem to continue infinitely. In 1812 Soane wrote a series of notes that he called 'Crude Hints Towards an History of my House in L I Fields'. This is a hypothetical history written from an imagined future. In the text Soane examines the ruins of his own house with an archaeologist's eye. He suggests that the remains may be those of a convent and a cemetery: 'we find the ornaments with which this place is surmounted are of a kind to designate the approach to a place of sepulture, some terra santa attached to the building'.[28] Then it is as if the real author's own worries get the better of him. He proffers the alternative suggestion that the ruins are those of a house once occupied by an architect whose dreams have been frustrated by professional rivalry and family troubles.

In less than half a century – in a few years – before the founder was scarcely mouldering in the dust, no trace to be seen of the artist within its walls, the edifice presenting only a miserable picture of frightful dilapidation.[29]

Soane himself was caught in a double blind. He wanted his architecture to exist after his death, both as romantic ruin and as the legacy of his genius. He had the Bank of England depicted as if it was one of the great ruins of Imperial Rome and he designed ruins for his own house, Pitzhanger Manor. Ironically, his buildings have been subject to demolition and destruction. So the museum has to be seen as occupying ambiguous territories. Simultaneously it is tomb and house, monument and ruin, open and closed. Mirror images multiply and recede into infinity. The house/museum contains a model of the tomb he built in the churchyard at St Pancras and it is, at the same time, a model of itself.

7

THE MAUSOLEUM: WHERE DEATH ENDS

Cemetery put in of course on account of the symmetry.'
James Joyce, *Ulysses*[1]

We are talking in space, not time . . .
Conductor 71 in Michael Powell and Emeric Pressburger's 1946 film,
A Matter of Life and Death[2]

As the word 'museum' hides within 'mausoleum', so the museum conceals the mausoleum and its occupants, the dead. John Soane's relationship with deathliness extended beyond the parallels between his own home and the family tomb. In the following chapter Carlo Scarpa occupies a position in the 20th century equivalent to Soane's in the 19th, offering up parallels between the design of museums and that of tombs. The cemeteries I describe here grow like collections. Once begun they can extend infinitely, inventories and catalogues in need of constant updating. The collection itself is also a kind of memento mori *in which the objects are meant to both forestall and embrace death. The narrative of the Delirious Museum embraces death.*

The entrance to the Catacombs of Paris is via a pavilion attached to Boullée's *barrière* (tollgate) at place Denfert-Rochereau. When he was shown the designs for the *barrières* in 1784, William Beckford said: 'from their massive sepulchral character [they] look more like the entrances of a Necropolis, a city of the dead, than of a city so damnably alive as this confounded capital.'[3] The city has now engulfed Boullée's *barrière* and the building has become the entrance to a necropolis as Beckford anticipated. The Catacombs were created in 1785, when remains were removed from charnel houses and placed underground in a labyrinth of disused quarries. Philippe Ariès says: 'The charnels were exhibits . . . after the fourteenth century, under the influence of a sensibility oriented toward the macabre, there was an interest in the spectacle for its own sake.'[4] This interest in the macabre carried through into the Catacombs. From place Denfert-Rochereau there is a long walk through dimly lit passages[5] before the visitor encounters striking white obelisks painted onto black columns. Skulls and bones, mostly displaced from inner-city cemeteries, are arranged into patterns in a kind of death décor. This display is overwhelming and it rapidly becomes clear that this is more archive than museum. Instead of the selective encounter the Catacomb's decorators have had to incorporate all the exhibits in the display. Though the route is strictly controlled there are many twists and turns with only occasional attempts at orientation. Visitors eventually emerge into an anonymous street in a part of the city remote from their starting point, disorientation caused less from the encounter with the vestiges of death than with a lack of geographical information.[6] Yet there is no encounter within the Catacombs as strange as that promised by the photographs taken by Nadar in the 1860s. Nadar is best known for his portrait photography, but he also took photographs in the Catacombs, in the newly constructed sewers of Paris and from his own huge hot air balloon, 'Le Géant'. It was as if he wanted to show the whole city, not just its inhabitants or its surface but also its fabric and structure. And those who work here are literally 'down below' as de Certeau put it: 'below the threshold at which visibility begins.'[7] Some of the photographs of the Catacombs show a worker labouring amongst the bones, wheeling a barrow or building a wall of skulls. Nadar invented and patented the artificial lighting needed to take these pictures. But the exposure time was still very long, so the 'worker' is actually a mannequin, usually with his face turned from the lens of the camera. While Hitchcock used still backdrops in his 'film' of the British Museum, Nadar employed still figures to surmount the problem of low light levels. The photographs in the Catacombs show an imitation of life among the dead. And, whereas Nadar acknowledges the lifelessness of his photographed model, Breton at the Musée Grévin wanted to conjure his unphotographable wax-work into life.

In Palermo, where Carlo Scarpa stripped down and re-configured the Palazzo Abatellis[8] is that museum's doppelgänger: the Capuchin

Catacombs. These were built at the end of the 16th century to accommodate the corpses of Capuchin monks and were expanded when donors asked that they should also be given room in the vaults. Some of the bodies were dried in cells cut into the volcanic rock of the catacombs, others were dipped in lime or arsenic. In the manner of Jeremy Bentham these corpses are dressed but here, instead of occupying polite vitrines they are arranged around the walls and shown on crowded shelves. Unlike the Paris Catacombs, these corpses are those of individuals – sometimes named – and, however grizzly the exhibition is, the visitor is faced with a meeting between death and life. Clothes shroud the skeletons. Skulls are visible beneath the skin. The corpses may have been dressed out of a sense of propriety and to proclaim their social standing in life, but this also suggests a degree of respect and it preserves a morbid sense of the individual. The varied states of decay of the clothes remind the viewer that these cadavers are not in a static condition. The rotting of the clothes over the desiccated bodies stands in for the decay of the body itself. Once again the relationship between viewer and the dead is a spatial one. One body, that of a child, a pink bow in her hair, is particularly well preserved and again the mystery of preservation is evoked:

> The method of embalming little Rosalia Lombardo was invented by Dr. Solafia, a Palermitan doctor, who took the secret with him when he died. It is only known that it was based on injections of chemicals and nothing else.[9]

Bunhill Fields, on the northern edge of the City of London, may have taken their name from Bone Hill Fields; they were suggested as a site for one of London's plague pits. There is no evidence that Bunhill Fields was ever used for this, but it was the repository for the bones from the Charnel House of St Paul's. Thus it has some of the same provenance as the Paris Catacombs but here what was visible, the displayed bones of the charnel house, has become invisible. The area of Bunhill Fields is just over four acres; 123,000 registered burials took place there between 1665 and 1853. The site has gained its own resonance as much from the way it looks and from its particular location as from who is buried here. This was a dissenters' burial place. William and Sofia Blake have a stone that records that they were buried somewhere in the vicinity and Daniel Defoe has an obelisk as a monument.[10] Enclosed on two sides, Bunhill Fields has a central path that connects streets to the west and east. The path, partially made from large re-used headstones, runs between trees and railings that protect areas of chest- and table-tombs and upright slabs. The viewer here is kept at a distance, like the museum visitor excluded from the closed gallery. Behind the railings, conservators occasionally work on a stone that is laminating or tombs that are in danger of collapse. Gardeners plant bulbs and trim the grass. A central space encloses the tombs of Blake, Defoe and John Bunyan. These are the star exhibits in an otherwise defunct and melancholy museum.

These instances show the way that an encounter with death stalks the museum. This can manifest itself in a grizzly show, as in Palermo, but it is more usually in evidence in the simple display of grave goods. These are the objects deposited in the ground with the bodies of the dead. They are the objects that archaeologists tend to find, they are often the things that have been best preserved because their disposal was not due to redundancy but for the opposite reason, because they were useful and would continue to be useful to the dead. So, often, when we are looking at particular museum artefacts, we are looking into the grave trying to understand those who have preceded us; engaging with them at the moment of their death.[11] And, as in Bunhill Fields, we are subliminally recognizing our distance and our detachment from the dead.

Bunhill Fields connects back to St George's Bloomsbury in the pentacle described by Iain Sinclair.[12] The route through the burial ground runs along an east–west axis; the route through the British Museum in Chapter 6 runs north–south. That walk turns anti-clockwise around the Great Court, tracing, in reverse, the frenzied route of Hitchcock's blackmailer. By going in the other direction, travelling clockwise, the visitor passes two of the exhibits in the museum's collection of bodies. The first, in Room 64, the Gallery of Early Egypt, is an un-named man who lived in Pre-dynastic Egypt around 3400 BC. He was buried in the sand, probably at Gebelien, but the details of his discovery remain something of a mystery; he arrived at the museum in 1900. His nickname is 'Ginger' after the straggly remnants of his hair. He is thought to have died a natural death and was buried with some simple grave goods; his mummification was caused by the desiccating effect of the hot dry sand and the absence of bacteria in this environment. The second corpse along this route died a violent death: struck twice on the head, garotted, throat cut, bound, then deposited face down in a peat bog, Lindow Moss in Cheshire, at some time in the 1st century AD. The display of the two bodies[13] reflects their places of habitat and the means of their burial. Ginger is on show in a five-sided glass box. He lies on a support structure faked up in an approximation of his desert grave in the process of excavation. 'Lindow Man', as his British counterpart is known, is shown inside a box with a glass top sheltered by a canopy in the corner of the Gallery of Celtic Europe. In order to protect him from deterioration, he is barely lit and his immediate environment is carefully monitored. These are two of the museum's most famous exhibits and they are often surrounded by visitors on guided tours while the adjacent, equally 'important', exhibits remain ignored. But here, even more than with the wrapped bodies of mummies, there is an intimate engagement with the dead. We know, when we see skeletons in archaeological and medical collections, that these too are human bodies or, at least, their frameworks, but Ginger and Lindow Man are true bodies with skin enclosing their bones. They are more akin to the dressed body of Lenin, preserved so mysteriously in his mausoleum in Red Square after his death in 1924. Lenin, during his stay in London in 1902, often used the Reading Room of the British Museum under the name of Dr Jacob Richter. The Reading Room now sits at the centre of the Great Court, a few metres from Ginger and Lindow Man. Lenin's tomb is a shrine to a man who became a deity despite his philosophy, and there is something similar at work in the British Museum. Lenin, Ginger and Lindow Man are traces of the past in the present and, at the same time, survivors; a slender hope for continuity. If Lenin is the ancestor of a dying breed, the early 20th-century revolutionary communists of the Soviet Union, then Ginger represents our cultural ancestor (Egypt as the contentious 'birthplace' of Western civilization) and Lindow Man a geographical ancestor for many of the museum's visitors. The mystery of their preservation – like that of the closely guarded secret of Lenin's mummification[14] – draws us into this encounter more thoroughly. The bodies of Lenin and Ginger allow us to look at death, if not without melancholy, then, without horror. The violence of Lindow Man's demise is treated in a proper museological way that at times resembles the forensic yet is not undertaken with the same aims as a murder inquiry. His death is framed in a spirit of polite curiosity and, indeed, it is possible to look at this body without seeing the wounds and the twine still wrapped around the neck. So these real bodies do not function in the same way as the cruel images of Christ in Western art, hands and feet punctured, nailed to the cross or laid on the slab that were used to convince Christians of his suffering. Nor are they like the parallel images of corpses and wounds in the morgue photographed by the artist Andres Serrano in 1992. The visitors to the British Museum, gazing at the cadavers of Lindow Man and Ginger, are not held in time. The moments of their lives and the moments of their deaths are gone. The visitors are, instead, held in a space with Lindow Man and Ginger, a space that is between life and death. This is a unique relationship between viewer and subject; a space in which there is no room for anyone else.

The tomb of the Tradescants, the collectors and gardeners, in a graveyard by a church-turned-museum is a shrine of museology. Here there is no sign of the bodies for which the tomb was built; instead the idea of their collection is represented. The adjacent building was the Church of St Mary's, Lambeth and is now the Museum of Garden History. The monument to the Tradescants is itself a little museum. Or, rather it is the world before the Tradescants made their museum; it is the collection returned to earth along with the collectors.[15] John Tradescant the Elder (1570–1638) was a royal gardener to Charles I, and, on his plant-collecting travels, also picked up 'curiosities' from around Europe, Russia and North Africa. He brought both collections back to his home in Lambeth, London. With his son, also John, he turned this into what is considered by many to be the first museum. John the Younger subsequently made a number of visits to Virginia[16] and expanded the collection with more objects from there. Visitors were charged sixpence for entrance to what had now become known as the Ark. In 1656 as the collection grew in size and ambition, a catalogue, the *Musaeum Tradescantianum,* was written with the support of Elias Ashmole, a lawyer and scholar with an interest in alchemy. Ashmole had become fascinated with the objects assembled by the Tradescants. Some versions of the story suggest that Ashmole became obsessed by the collection and that he secured eventual ownership of it by getting Tradescant the Younger drunk, then having him sign a deed of gift to Ashmole. Tradescant had been planning to donate the contents of the Ark to a university with Ashmole as executor. On Tradescant the Younger's death, the deed was contested by his widow, Hester, but the court found in favour of Ashmole, with the condition that Hester could keep charge of it while she lived. Ashmole managed to get hold of the collection before this, however, and Hester committed suicide in 1678. Ashmole subsequently gave the contents of the Ark, plus his own collection, to Oxford University. Christopher Wren was commissioned to provide a purpose-built home for the collection and the Ashmolean Museum was opened in 1683.[17]

The catalogue for the Ark broke the collection down into 'naturalia' and 'artificialia'. This same division occurs on the carved stone sides of the Tradescant tomb. One face shows the ruins of some nondescript buildings with, in the foreground, a series of specimens: a snail, shells, a crocodile. The opposite face depicts a scene of classical ruins. Here the buildings are more recognizable: a pyramid and temples. In the foreground in this scene are capitals, column shafts and obelisks. These are seen in a kind of pre-archaeological state; scattered and lying at crazy angles. These classical fragments were not the types of things actually collected by the Tradescants. Many of their curiosities were brought back from the colonies and were closer to what later generations would call an ethnographic collection. The best-known piece, and one that still survives in the Ashmolean Museum, is 'Pohaton's Mantle', a decorated hide that has connections to Pocahontas[18] and Captain John Smith.[19] But the architectural fragments depicted on the tomb are emblems for the idea of collecting artefacts as distinct from natural specimens. On one of the short faces of the tomb there is a death's head with, hovering over it, a seven-headed hydra. Here is a conventional symbol of death combined with a portrayal of the fantastical, even unbelievable, objects contained within the Ark. Inscribed on the top of the slab is an epitaph attributed to John Aubrey, including the words: 'A world of wonders in one closet shut'; an accident of poetic invention that reinforces the way in which the collection has become inaccessible with the passing of time. The original tomb was replaced by this copy in 1853, so even this artefact is not what it was; one more in a series of contradictions around this site. The tomb is not the 'real' tomb, the collection never 'really' belonged to Ashmole, the church is not a church but a museum.[20] Even the graveyard is now a garden. The tomb has become, without being moved, a museum piece. Even in death the Tradescants, their collection prized from them, were drawn into the museum: first, through the artifice of their memorial, then through the museumization of the urban fabric of the 20th century.

The catacombs of Paris and Palermo have become museums merely by their status as tourist attractions and by their move from use to spectacle. To a certain extent this can also be said for some cemeteries. In discussing plans for the relocation of Paris cemeteries prior to the Revolution, Philippe Ariès says: '. . . the cemetery is a museum of the fine arts. The fine arts are no longer reserved for the contemplation of individual aesthetes. They have a social role; they are to be enjoyed by everyone, publicly'.[21] In the cemeteries of Montmarte, Montparnasse and, most spectacularly, Père-Lachaise, this idea of the 'museum of fine arts' is expressed to the full. The monuments were conceived as grand sculptural works and commissions were entrusted to some of the most successful artists of the day. Visiting these places today, the interest lies not so much in the individual effect of particular tombs but in the cumulative effect of repeated forms. As James Stevens Curl has pointed out, the pathways of the cemetery reproduce, in a scaled-down manner, the streets of a city.[22] Sir John Soane said in 1819:

> How wonderfully the towns of magnificent buildings in honour of the dead inspire the soul and prepare the mind for those grand effects produced by steeples, towers, spires and domes of great cities, viewed from a distance.[23]

The casual visitor passes along these streets as if walking by a series of doorways and windows. But the individual monuments also function as self-contained displays, each labelled with the family name. Many have a view into a locked and inaccessible interior: a symbolic catafalque or chapel. These chapel spaces are also scaled down, min-iaturized rooms that function both privately (to be occupied) and publicly (to be seen into). Sometimes the labels (like those in the museum) become more closely examined than the 'objects' to which they refer. Each of the large urban cemeteries of Paris issues a map showing the graves of the famous and the infamous. Père-Lachaise especially has become a kind of National Gallery of Celebrity, a mir-ror to the more august Panthéon on the Left Bank. The list of occupants of Père-Lachaise is impressive. Napoleon's generals, Sarah Bernhardt, Edith Piaf, Marcel Proust and Balzac are all buried there. Many of the tombs of the famous are ordinary or, at least, under-stated, but others are spectacular in their conception or notorious in their reputations. Oscar Wilde is commemorated with a bold struc-ture executed by Jacob Epstein. The grave of Jim Morrison has become a place of pilgrimage for the youth of Europe, Japan and America and has had to be put under police guard after the site dete-riorated into squalor. While 'Mona Lisa' gets a bullet-proof glass screen, Jim Morrison gets a museum guard.

Unlike the 19th-century cemeteries of Paris, many of those created in London to cope with the huge expansion of the city's population are in a state of decay. Abney Park Cemetery in Stoke Newington, north London, is locked into a battle with vegetation and decay. Vol-unteers work to clear paths and maintain graves, but chaos waits in the wings. There are the graves of the famous here, the founder of the Salvation Army, General William Booth and the hymn-writer Isaac Watts, but these are not people whose tombs provoke popular pilgrimage. The attraction of Abney Park lies in its romantic land-scape. This has come about as much through decay as design. The cemetery, planned in 1840, was planted with a huge range of trees that were individually labelled. If Père-Lachaise is a museum of fine art then Abney Park is, amongst other things, a museum of natural his-tory.[24] It was, therefore, built with a double use: to house the dead and to educate the living. Abney Park at the beginning of the 21st cen-tury has become a number of other overlapping museums. A Museum of Ordinary Names: names not just recorded but made material, incised in stone. Many small upright slabs have been moved from their original locations and mark out the edges of paths or stand in crowds.

Rosina Grace Pullen, Maude Louisa Dorrington, "Charlie" Charles Frederick
Job, Janice Isidore Defreitas, Emily Smith, William Smith, Ada Venetia Lud-
low. A Museum of Emblems: hands clasping, broken columns, a
shrouded beehive, limbless angels, open books. Its meandering paths
reveal surprising sights: a recent home-made headstone; an illicit burial that has gone un-noticed, a temporary marker or a spoof?[25] There
is the stone marking the burial spot of Joseph William Burdett, died
1962. In the place on the white marble headstone where once there
would have been a skull or an hourglass there is a beautifully carved
picture of a saloon car.[26] In an overgrown part near the edge of the
cemetery there is the plain headstone of John Coleman McParland
Isiah, 1939–91; 'Missed by Many; Man, Myth, Mystery, Mercurial Mon-
ster'. Even in the context of these anomalies, coming across a
headstone including a photograph of the deceased – seemingly displaced from an Italian cemetery – is a shock. The uniformity created
by stone and plant life is suddenly disrupted by this little oval portrait.
This is a way of recording death and mourning isolated from its usual
geographical context. The enclosed walled cemeteries of Italian and
other European towns double as photographic archives of the society
in which they are located. This is a language of representation that has
grown directly from a tradition of remembrance. In Northern Europe
the process and act of remembrance has taken a more abstract turn.
Susan Sontag in *On Photography* says

> To the solitary stroller, all the faces in the stereotyped photographs
> cupped behind glass and affixed to tombstones in the cemeteries of
> Latin countries seem to contain a portent of death. Photographs state
> the innocence, the vulnerability of lives heading towards their own
> destruction, and this link between photography and death haunts all
> photographs of people.[27]

So, in the context of Abney Park in its state of romantic decay, the
photograph on the headstone is a disruption to, and a heightening of,
the atmosphere of melancholy. Here is a 'contemporary' image, not
an emblem – as the saloon car must be read – but a picture of someone that brings us into the sphere of their existence. The photograph
was taken when they were alive and yet it foretold their death. Their
death was, and still is, enclosed within the photograph. In his explora-

tion of the resonances of photography, *Camera Lucida*, Roland Barthes notes: 'that rather terrible thing that is there in every photograph: the return of the dead'.[28]

The work of the French artist Christian Boltanski picks up on this use of photography as *memento mori* in many of his installations. In an interview with Georgia Marsh,[29] Boltanski says: 'The photographs and clothing that I am working with now have this in common; the [sic] are both objects and souvenirs of subjects. Exactly as a cadaver is both an object and a souvenir of a subject.' Boltanski's installations are largely responses to particular sites and their inhabitants. He often uses individually lit, historic photographs, close-ups of faces, shown covering whole walls. The spaces themselves are not lit. These installations often have the air of the communal memorial while also highlighting, literally, the individuals that make up that community. This series of works called *Leçon de ténèbres* ('Lesson of Darkness') began in 1985 with the work *Les Enfants de Dijon*. In this work Boltanski re-photographed and cropped pictures taken of Dijon schoolchildren for a work made in 1973. In the installation he made at Grand-Hornu in Belgium in 1997, *The Registers,* the identity photographs from coal-miners' pass-books are shown across a vast wall. They each have their individual lights and are mounted on rusting tins. These tins could contain the personal archives of the people on show or they could contain their ashes. Certainly there is the feeling that there is something behind this tin façade, though, of course, the contents, like the miners themselves, are missing and the tins were specially made for the installation. The re-photographed images here and in *Les Enfants de Dijon* further blur the differentiation between subject and object. The melancholy that suffuses these works is present not only in the cemeteries and columbariums of Italy, but in the single photograph on the headstone in Abney Park Cemetery.

In his labyrinthine novella 'A Gallery Portrait,'[30] Georges Perec describes a painting (*The Gallery Portrait*) showing a room full of paintings. According to Perec, this was a type of picture that originated in Antwerp at the end of the 16th century and then became popular throughout Europe into the middle of the 19th century. The 'gallery portrait' or '*cabinet d'amateur*' depicts the collector sitting in a room with one hundred of his collection of paintings. One of the pictures is of *The Gallery Portrait* itself; within this picture all the other pictures are repeated, with variations, at a smaller scale. Needless to say, that version of the gallery portrait also shows a smaller version of itself. In the story the painting (shown publicly in a room which is itself a version of the gallery shown in the painting) is vandalised by a visitor frustrated at the long wait to view it. The painting and its subjects are immediately withdrawn from the exhibition. Some years later the collector dies, leaving instructions in his will that he should be entombed in yet another version of the room in which the painting was originally made.

> His body was mounted by the finest taxidermist of the day, brought in especially from Mexico, . . . then positioned in the same armchair in which he had posed. The armchair and corpse were then taken down to a cellar which faithfully reproduced, though on a much smaller scale, the room where Raffke [the collector] had hung his favourite paintings. Heinrich Kürz's vast canvas [*The Gallery Portrait*] took up the entire far wall. The deceased was placed in front of the picture in a position which exactly matched the one he occupied within it.[31]

In a series of blinds and feints the story drifts into lengthy quotations from essays and catalogues dealing with both *The Gallery Portrait* and the pictures shown within it. Perec, in effect, creates a complete world around this single work – a work which disappears into death with its owner. The fictional collection has gone from public exhibition to private tomb and has only re-emerged through narrative.

In the Picture Room at Sir John Soane's house/museum the walls are hung with the works of William Hogarth. But that is not all the room contains; the walls are not really walls at all, but a series of shutters that open to reveal more pictures. On the south side of the room, inside the first left-hand opening plane is a painting by Soane's long-time collaborator J. M. Gandy. This picture is described in the museum's *Description* as: 'buildings erected or designed by Sir John Soane shown as an exhibition of models and drawings in an expanded and fantastical version of the Picture Room (drawn c. 1824)'.[32] Of course, Soane himself is missing from this picture as he is missing from the Picture Room itself. Unlike Jeremy Bentham, Soane received a conventional burial and, unlike the fictional Raffke, did not have his mortal remains preserved and sealed into a room of endlessly receding planes.

He must have toyed with some version of this idea though. John Summerson recounted how the word 'mausoleum' occured on Soane's drawings for his work on the basement of his house at 12 Lincoln's Inn Fields in 1808, only for it to disappear in subsequent designs.[33] In 1824 when Soane's wife Eliza died, he decided on a family tomb in St Pancras Churchyard. Did he consider then the possibility of a mausoleum within the house/museum? The precedents for this overlap between collecting, display and death had already been made by the time that Soane had designed his own country house, Pitzhanger Manor in 1804. Summerson has pointed out the extensive use of sepulchral motifs in the entrance gates to the house. At around the same time some of these motifs appeared in Soane's work at the Bank of England.[34] The front parlour of Pitzhanger Manor had a shallow domed ceiling and niches set within the walls. These niches were filled with various antique urns and vases bought by Soane over a number of years. The overall effect was that of a columbarium. The design for this was probably influenced by the house of Thomas Hope in Duchess Street, London. This house, while not exactly a model for Soane's own Lincoln's Inn Fields home must have made an impact on Soane. Unlike Soane, Hope was not a trained architect, but in converting his own Robert Adam-designed mansion in 1800, he created a house that was also a museum and a piece of theatre.[35] On the first floor of the house Hope made a series of set-pieces intended either to house parts of his collection in suitable surroundings or to evoke historical periods and places. Three interconnected 'vase rooms' have the most obvious parallels to Soane's work, the first of these being an even more direct evocation of a columbarium than that at Pitzhanger. Hope, after all, had the luxury of not having to consider use and functionality in the making of his sepulchral/domestic interior. Soane's front parlour was a working family room. Other influences on Soane were only to emerge when he developed plans for his Lincoln's Inn Fields house later. In Hope's Duchess Street mansion there was an Egyptian Room with, sitting at its centre, a vitrine containing a mummy. This anticipated Soane's own acquisition and display of the sarcophagus of Seti I. There were sculpture and picture galleries, an Indian room and a staircase with Turkish decoration. The Flaxman Room contained not only works by the sculptor of that name but a supposed fragment of the Parthenon frieze displayed on a velvet cushion. In Senate House, near Jeremy Bentham's auto-icon, there is a Flaxman Gallery where plaster models of his work are arranged around the walls of an octagonal gallery. Adjacent to Hope's Flaxman Room was the 'Lararium' a kind of pan-theistic shrine displaying figures from Indian and Chinese temples alongside a statue of Marcus Aurelius and busts of Dante and Napoleon.[36]

But it was eventually left to another set of collectors, real, not imagined, to work the trick described by Georges Perec, though in reverse, making the private collection both the public museum and the public tomb. The collectors were Noel Desenfans and Sir Francis Bourgeois, and the architect they employed to effect the trick was Soane. The work had two stages. The first of these was a tomb in the house of the art-dealer Desenfans in what was Charlotte Street (now Hallam Street), London. In partnership with the artist Sir Francis Bourgeois, Desenfans had amassed a collection of paintings in his house. These had been acquired for King Stanislas of Poland, but on the abdication of the king the two found themselves in possession of the collection. When Desenfans died in 1807 Soane designed a domed interior space, the chapel, and a vaulted burial chamber that was intended to hold the deceased, his wife and Bourgeois, his business partner. John Summerson remarked on the curiosity of the household at Charlotte Street;[37] the Desenfans had no children but Bourgeois, younger than Noel Desenfans by ten years, lived with them. This co-operative triumvirate is in marked contrast to that of the Tradescants and Elias Ashmole. The scheme designed by Soane was built, though the house was not even owned outright by its tenants. Bourgeois explored the possibilities of buying the freehold from the landowner, the Duke of Portland, but this idea was dismissed by the duke. It continued to be a publicly accessible gallery, but before long Bourgeois and Mrs Desenfans decided that the collection should be placed in the hands of a worthy institution as had been Desenfans' intention. Here, the second stage of transformation began. In Bourgeois' will he stated that the pictures should go to Dulwich College in South London and be displayed in a purpose-built gallery that would include a new mausoleum for the three intended occupants of the Charlotte Street tomb. In 1811 Soane was commissioned by the trustees of the college to design the new gallery. The scheme was intended to form the second side of a new quadrangle with the exist-ing gothic structure as a starting point. But Soane had to convince the college of the wisdom of building a new gallery before he could win them over on the subject of a huge expansion plan. The quadrangle remained un-built. The status of the mausoleum within the plan became another stumbling block to progress with the trustees. Soane produced eight designs for the layout, most of which proposed a much larger building than that which was completed. At an early stage Soane established the essential relationship of the mausoleum to the gallery though up until the point of building, the mausoleum and the entrance were switched on the plan. He chose to put the burial cham-ber of the collection's founder not only on axis but also only one room back from the entrance. As Giles Waterfield has pointed out, this had its own precedents. Elias Ashmole's portrait hung over the entrance to 'his' museum in Oxford. More strikingly there was the precedent of an artist being buried among his work in the sumptuous Tempio in Possagno occupied by Canova.[38]

The visitor to Dulwich Picture Gallery is drawn first to the mausoleum, though in making the short journey towards it the cross axis of the galleries becomes visible and new vistas are opened up. But the mausoleum is central to the museum and something of its atmos-phere pervades the whole building. Contemporary reactions to the new gallery commented on the dimness of the lighting. What Soane did was to put an emphasis on indirect forms of lighting, bouncing nat-ural light around within lanterns. This technique was highly influential in the late 20th century: Robert Venturi's extension to the National Gallery, London (1991) and James Stirling's Clore Wing (1987) for the paintings of Soane's friend Turner at the Tate both bear the stamp of Dulwich Picture Gallery. Today, the natural light is supplemented by sensitively installed electric fittings and the difference between the crepuscular mausoleum and the evenly lit galleries has been height-ened. Dulwich Picture Gallery is small compared to most public collections and so the visitor is never very far from this reminder of mortality. The short axis that runs through the mausoleum must be crossed each time the visitor moves from one wing to the other and there at the periphery of one's vision is the suffused yellow light of the tomb, creating a kind of persistent cerebral after-image. Soane used a version of the plan he had created for the earlier mausoleum: a circular 'chapel' leading to a rectilinear burial chamber. The chapel is surrounded by over-scaled Tuscan columns. Black 'porphyry' sarcophagi sit on the three sides of the burial chamber. There are no Christian symbols within the mausoleum, but on the lantern above are depictions of Oroburos – the snake eternally swallowing its own tail.

The extension to the gallery in 2000 by the architect Rick Mather sits discretely back from the austere blank wall of Soane's entrance front. At the same time, it negates Soane's hoped-for quadrangle by suggesting an enclosed space on the entrance side rather than that of the mausoleum as was Soane's intention. Whereas the mausoleum is inescapable inside the building, it now seems almost hidden on the outside. The necessary link to the other existing buildings on the site made by the extension stops the gallery being seen as a free-standing structure. In fact, Dulwich Picture Gallery is already such a conglomeration of additions and amendments that this hardly matters, but it serves to distance the exterior of the mausoleum even further from the entrance. The part of the mausoleum that extends from what is now unequivocally the rear façade of the building is the burial chamber; the 'chapel' being embedded in what were alms-houses and are now a run of small galleries. On each of the three faces of the mausoleum there is a false door inside a stone aedicule set into a brick arch. As if to emphasise the theatricality of these doors they are not only visibly immovable but they are also detached from the real wall behind them. It is as if Soane wants us to believe first that these doors were sealed after the remains were deposited and then wants to reveal that there must, after all, be another way in. Above the arches sits one more blind: small, false sarcophagi for each occupant.

Very little of Dulwich Picture Gallery is real. Its various extensions have obscured the core of the building as Soane made it and then, in 1944, a V2 flying bomb landed in Gallery Road, adjacent to the mausoleum façade. The pictures had been removed, but large portions of the gallery, including the mausoleum, were effectively destroyed. More than for any other of his buildings, Soane recorded the construction phases of the Picture Gallery, but these illustrations have

14. Dulwich Picture Gallery mausoleum. South wall, prior to Second World War damage, 1944.

15. Dulwich Picture Gallery mausoleum. North wall, showing bomb damage, 1944.
(facing page) 16. Dulwich Picture Gallery. Coffin of Noel Desenfans uncovered by bomb damage, 1944.

something of the ruin about them too. The photographs of the bomb damage rewind this process. From ruin to building to ruin. In the explosion the iron coffins were exposed but, unlike the gallery itself, they were left intact.[39]

Usually when I visit Dulwich, I take the train from London Bridge to North Dulwich Station. At this point of arrival the experience of visiting the gallery begins for me. The platforms of the station sit within sloping brick retaining walls, into which are set vaulted alcoves. The effect is of ruinous catacombs that have been converted for use as a railway line. The walk to the gallery passes a small, locked burial ground, with chest tombs older than the gallery itself. So even before arrival at the front door there are these melancholic pre-echoes of Soane's obsessions that are only made relevant by that particular walk to that destination. This melancholy lies at the heart of the museum. Soane has built Dulwich Picture Gallery's doppelgänger into its fabric in the form of the Mausoleum. In her introduction to Walter Benjamin's *One Way Street*, Susan Sontag says: 'If this melancholy temperament is faithless to people, it has good reason to be faithful to things. Fidelity lies in accumulating things – which appear, mostly, in the form of fragments or ruins'.[40]

The Glyptothek in Munich has one of the most important collections of Greek and Roman statuary in Europe. At its heart is a display of figures from two pediments. These are incomplete, yet the overall form of the pediment is visible. Individual figures are also missing pieces; legs have no torsos or torsos seem to float above the ground. The missing pieces, the bits that are not there, become the most memorable exhibits. Near the end of the route around the galleries is a display of Roman heads. Visitors approach this display on a raised level above that on which the plinths for the heads sit. It is momentarily like looking out over a crowd. Moving through the 'crowd' on the same level a different feeling is conveyed. This is a series of monuments to the lost: those we shall never know. In his book *Grave Matters* Mark C. Taylor says: 'The graveyard is where we keep the dead *alive as dead*',[41] Ginger, Lindow Man, John Soane, the Tradescants, the Desenfans and Francis Bourgeois are all kept 'alive as dead' in museums.

8

CARLO SCARPA: THE LABYRINTH IN TIME

I thought of a labyrinth of labyrinths, of one sinuous spreading labyrinth
that would encompass the past and the future and in some way involve
the stars.

Jorge Luis Borges[1]

*This section of the book (Chapters 8, 9 and 10 especially) moves back into
museum building, concentrating on the work of certain architects: Carlo
Scarpa, Le Corbusier, James Stirling, Frank Gehry and Daniel Libeskind.
Here I am in pursuit of the Delirious Museum hidden within the secular
temples of modernity. The search here is for the back-story, the narrative
that lurks behind the chronological development of architectural history. The
museums that I will look at can be read as moments of high-modernism,
post-modernism and deconstructionism but these stylistic/philosophical
categories are secondary to my investigation. As was the case with the work
of John Soane it is necessary to unearth the delirium within the built work.*

Ariadne unemployed

At one sole glance, one can discern the Cartesian layout of the so-
called 'labyrinth' at the Botanical Gardens and the following warning
sign:

NO PLAYING IN THE LABYRINTH

There could be no more succinct summary of the spirit of an entire
civilization. The very one that we will, in the end, pull down.

From *Potlatch*[2]

The Situationists wanted to retrieve the labyrinth as a revolutionary
tool, one that would undermine the work ethic. The Italian architect

and designer Carlo Scarpa had no such ambition. His engagement
with the city was at the level of architectural detail rather than as a
fluctuating utopia. Yet his buildings, especially his museum works,
contained within them the delirium of a labyrinth constructed of
materials, narratives and history.

Scarpa was born in Venice in 1906. He died whilst on a visit to
Japan in 1978. He studied architectural drawing and spent years
teaching this and designing glassware. Up to the end of the Second
World War most of his other design work involved interiors and
exhibitions. When he gained some larger commissions in the 1950s
he was taken to court by the Association of Venice Architects for
practising without a proper licence. Though he was acquitted, Scarpa
remained outside the mainstream architectural establishment in his
home city. Yet he was successful in Venice and in the wider world.
From around 1942 he began to build a reputation through a series of
exhibitions in Venice, such as Paul Klee (1948), Giovanni Bellini (1949)
and Tiepolo (1951). In 1953 he designed an exhibition of the work of
Sicilian masters in Messina, Sicily. This led to his first major commission for re-building a museum in an existing space: the Museo
Nazionale de Sicilia in Palermo.

Scarpa's exhibition work was characterised by the detail he
devoted to the individual works to be displayed. Often the placing of
works was done in unconventional ways. In the Messina exhibition,
the central room contained a display of the work of Antonello da
Messina. The paintings were shown on panels and easels against
draped semi-transparent hangings. Behind these, pink insets were let
into the windows facing north and blue insets let into the windows
facing south. The colours were diffused and projected onto the new
drapery walls of the exhibition space. Other exhibition designs show
the works displayed on cloth-covered panels, appearing to float free
of the walls, and groups of pictures running edge-to-edge around corners. Looking back at these relatively early works it is now clear that
the exhibitions were experiments for the permanent museum installations to come. Scarpa continued to undertake exhibition
commissions throughout his life.

Scarpa's other design 'laboratory' was in drawing. His sketch drawings were not finished depictions of design intentions but they

explored the development of his meticulous involvement with subject and object. When it came to the work on the renovation and conversion of historic buildings into museums these drawings became an inherent part of the exploratory process of designing. Scarpa wrote: 'I want to see things, that's all I really trust. I want to see, and that's why I draw. I can see an image only if I draw it'.[3]

In 1951, Scarpa met one of his heroes, the American architect Frank Lloyd Wright. Many of Scarpa's new buildings bear the stamp of Wright's influence. There are striking visual parallels in their work: an interest in the decorative possibilities of geometry and the spatial potential of stretched planes and free plans. But these stylistic similarities all but disappeared when Scarpa dealt with existing buildings. Maybe the constraints of 'history' negated Wright's influence. After all, Wright in his own work did not have to contend with the historical context to any extent, nor would he have wanted to.[4] What remains from Wright in the museum work is an interest in decoration. The obsessive details of fixings, finishes and colours of materials transcend the functional into a kind of theatrical (if understated), decorative luxury. Scarpa took the language that he evolved in his museum work onto a level that transcends straightforward relationships between object and environment. The restless narratives that he created can be appreciated both as installations carried out with exemplary wit and poetry and as fragments of delirious, built psychogeography.

Palermo

Anthony Vidler has spoken of the urban uncanny as 'the spatial incursions of modernity' into the fabric of the formerly 'walled and intimate' city.[5] Palermo is still of a type described by Walter Benjamin and Asja Lakis in their essay 'Naples':

> The stamp of the definitive is avoided. No situation appears intended forever, no figure asserts its 'thus and not otherwise'. This is how architecture, the most binding part of the communal rhythm, comes into being here: . . . anarchical, embroiled, village-like . . .[6]

The churches of Palermo are full of emblems and the relics of saints. At night the streets are illuminated by fairy lights and are rocked by the parading of the relics on their holy days. Corporeality once removed is represented not only in the mummified bodies of the Capuchin monks but also in traditional Sicilian wooden marionettes and in popular associations with the Mafia. The 'urban uncanny' of Palermo in Sicily is diverse and evasive. However, in places around the old port area of La Kalsa and Via Alloro it is more easily pinned down. In 1943 the waterfront and the area immediately beyond it was the target of saturation bombing by the Allies. The street where Goethe lived during his stay in Palermo, and where Garibaldi stopped on his way north, trails off into hinterland. There are still large blank areas on the city map. Many former palaces remain as shells and some streets are walled off as if a siege had only recently been broken.

The entrance to the 15th-century Palazzo Abatellis, the Galleria Nazionale di Sicilia, is easy to miss – a tiny opening in a huge, otherwise closed, door. Stepping through the opening there is an instant change of atmosphere; from stone to stucco, from dark into light, from restraint to release and, momentarily, from Palermo's uncanny chaos to calm. But the experience of the Palazzo Abatellis is one of continuity with the city in which it is located. The impact of Carlo Scarpa's work on the Palazzo, carried out in 1954, is not, at first, obvious. Beyond the street door there is a large archway and beyond that is a courtyard, its green floor criss-crossed with stone. The right-hand side of this courtyard connects to a two-storey loggia. The other three sides are stuccoed walls. Openings in these walls have stone surrounds. It is these walls that give the first clue to a complex architectural intervention which undermines that immediate sense of calm. The stucco is applied in large sections that are carefully delineated with a rebate. These seem not to refer to the pre-existing elevation. Instead, they look as if they might be the marks of a proportional system. These sections of wall are also like large mending plates and this has a direct implication for how the rest of the building is seen: as an object in need of repair. This is like the crumbling city of Palermo: a piece of (urban) fabric which needs to be stitched together and patched. Benjamin and Lacis said of Naples: '. . . within the tenement blocks, it [the city] seems held together at the corners, as if by iron clamps, by the murals of the Madonna'.[7] Scarpa intended that these 'plates', which actually marked the daily progress of the work, should be read as separate elements; each is of a slightly different hue.[8] In reality the differences between the plates are illegible but the break lines remain visible.

Unlike Sir John Soane's Museum, for instance, there is a defined, though complex, route around the building. Scarpa has already constructed his own psychogeographic itinerary; the *dérive* is preordained. The labyrinth here is one of reading, not of space. This tour starts by crossing the open courtyard on an oblique diagonal. Scarpa re-configured the pattern of the pavement in the courtyard to suggest movement across it, replacing the static focal point of a fountain in the centre. The diagonal leads to a door in the largest uninterrupted wall. The door out of this first gallery is positioned on line with the entrance, leaving an area in which Scarpa composes the first elements in the chronological displays of sculpture. The next two rooms reorientate the visitor to face their long axis. Dominating these spaces is a large mural of the *Triumph of Death* by an anonymous 15th-century painter. The third room, in which the mural is placed, is much higher, with daylight coming in from a domed ceiling. The ensuing series of spaces follow the edge of the courtyard but the relationship between them is complex rather than being organized along a classical enfilade. Where Scarpa uses something like the enfilade, it is to one side of the rooms so that larger areas for display are created and there are more opportunities to manipulate the compositional effects. Along the route there are views out (and even one possible way out) into the courtyard that locate the parts in terms of the whole. The small rooms containing sculpture are elaborate compositions. Sculptures in white marble are displayed against polished, coloured plaster panels and horizontal timber strips. These panels serve to focus the view onto particular objects and particular 'settings'. So, instead of just getting an impression of a group of sculptures in a room, the visitor is encouraged to look at the composition, the object and then the object in its immediate context. The last of these might include a curtain and the materials used for the object mount, but equally it could include daylight as a defined component. The existing elements of the room also come into play; in places the

otherwise rectangular panels break in order to accommodate projecting stone details. The obsessive control of detail is tempered by a
pragmatism defined by pre-existing conditions. These related 'events'
take place in three-dimensional space and in movement.

When Scarpa's route begins its ascent to the first-floor painting galleries he draws attention to this change of level by extending the first
step into a floating plain of stone the size of a landing. As the stair,
after twisting and re-joining the original staircase, reaches the loggia,
there is a slice taken out of the wall of the adjacent gallery, giving a
glimpse of the interior. Emerging onto the loggia itself there is a view
down onto the entrance to the galleries and the imperfect geometry
of the courtyard. The upper galleries then run in another series
around the perimeter of the courtyard. The first room here has
within it a discreet smaller room with two entrances. An exhibit (a
large crucifix) sits diagonally in plan in front of one of these openings,
acting like a half-closed door.

Along the street side of the building is the largest gallery in the
museum that connects, in turn, to one of the smallest. These two galleries are in contrast, not only in scale, but in material (stone to wood
panelling) and in focus. The large room contains a number of freestanding Renaissance crucifixes and wall-mounted altar-pieces. It is a
space intended to be seen in movement and there is no fixed route
around it. The small room is dominated by a freestanding screen holding the tiny 15th-century *Virgin Annunciate* by Antonello da Messina.
Though there is no doubt that the picture is meant to command the
space, the other paintings in the room are also orientated towards a
person moving into the room by being placed on screens set at an
angle from the wall. These screens can be shifted slightly to take advan-
tage of the daylight in the room. The effect of the angled screens is to
make the other objects in the room gather around the central painting.

The following room again introduces an axis and once again this is
orientated to the *Triumph of Death* mural. The viewer is now at first-
floor level looking towards the edge of a floor with no railing. Beyond
this edge, revealing itself as one approaches the low rope barrier, is
the mural, which is now central to the viewer's eye line. There is no
hint at ground level that the mural will make this dramatic reprise. On
the lower level there is no reason to look back along the axis and the

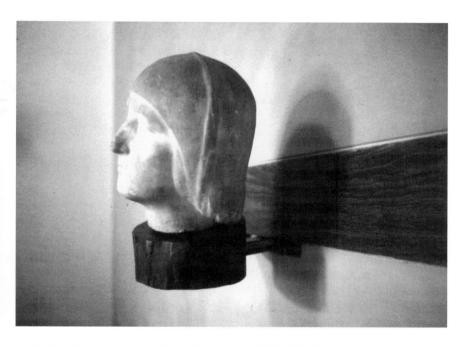

17. Carlo Scarpa, Palazzo Abatellis, Parlemo (1953–54). Head of Francesco
Laurana.

only clue to the higher space is the occasional disembodied voice coming from beyond (it turns out) the rope barrier. This sequence
constructs a narrative moving from death to life to death. Scarpa
exploits the coincidence of the collection to dramatic ends. The Triumph of Death is a large and impressive work when seen from ground
level. By altering the viewpoint, using changes of scale and playing on
a feeling of vertigo with an object placed beyond the precipice, Scarpa
heightens the impact of the work. This dramatic engagement runs
contrary to notions of neutrality in museum design. It is as if Scarpa
was using the language of the 'spectacle' and, in opposition, the
'situation' to unsettle the predominant system of museological interpretation. Without the intervention of the architect/curator the
objects in the Palazzo Abatellis would not engage in this disjointed narrative. Scarpa acknowledges this, but instead of taking a simple attitude
to their display, he complicates their message. While apparently giving
the objects their own space in which to be read, what he is actually
doing is manipulating the objects and the spaces into a dialogue with
the other objects and spaces of the museum. Scarpa said of this work:

> . . . the architecture of the Palazzo should not constrain the museum
> that will be housed in it, but nor should the latter suffocate the
> architecture: the two elements must live one inside the other in mutual
> harmony . . .[9]

Richard Murphy has spoken about how 'by his [Scarpa's] invitation
to discover objects and paintings [he] transforms the visitor from
observer to participant'.[10] This echoes Marcel Duchamp's belief that
it is the viewer who completes the work of art.[11] Another view of this
involvement with the display is suggested by Georges Bataille: '. . . the
galleries and objects of art are no more than a container, the contents
of which is formed by the visitors: it is the contents which distinguish
a museum from a private collection.'[12] The Palazzo Abatellis immediately sets up this dialogue with its 'contents'. None of the effects that
Scarpa creates have any meaning without the movement, even interaction, of the individual visitor. This was a theme that Scarpa was to
develop in much of his museum work.

In my description of the sequence of spaces I have identified details
that seemed to be part of the dialogue between object, architecture
and viewer. But I am aware that the complexity of the design leaves

other readings open. Within the larger discussion about the way that the new interacts with the historical there are other conversations to be engaged in. Some of these are straightforward, for example, the hierarchy of information or attention to detail: others are harder to pin down: the movement of light around a room or the glance of a sculpture. Delirium is the shadow of the collection and its architecture.

Possagno

In 1955, Scarpa was commissioned to design an extension to the 'Gipsoteca Canoviana' in Possagno in the foothills of the Dolomites in northern Italy. This building houses Antonio Canova's collection of working plaster models for his sculptures. The site for the extension was a narrow strip running parallel to the existing symmetrical, neoclassical galleries. Scarpa's intervention consisted of two rooms opening off the existing display spaces. The first of these is a cube with top daylighting where most of the sculptures sit on plinths on the floor or on skeletal brackets on the wall. The position of the natural lighting gives the first clue to Scarpa's intent. Let into the four top corners of the cube are three-sided windows. Two of these actually invert the corner, eating into the purity of the cube. In this way Scarpa sets up the de-materialization of the gallery. By removing what should be the most stable elements of the structure – the corners – he suggests that the container here should not be taken for granted. He called these missing corners 'fragments of sky'; the outside breaking into the room physically and extending into shafts of light. The second space, a long tapering gallery, adjoins the cube. It begins with a small loggia to one side, interrupted by a series of stepped full height windows. The other wall has a kink defined by the site plan that emphasizes the funnel effect of the gallery. A single step down marks the edge of the first gallery; a recumbent sculpture sits on a simple low metal plinth spanning this step so that two of the legs of the plinth are longer than the others. There then follows a series of single and double steps descending towards the end of the gallery. The final piece of sculpture in the gallery, a plaster version of Canova's *Three Graces*, dominates

18. Carlo Scarpa, Gypsoteca Canova, Possagno (1955–57).

the end of the space. Both the viewer and the sculpture sit in a small, framed glass box in which the viewer is drawn into an intimate, spatial relationship with the work. The wall behind the sculpture is pierced by a series of small randomly placed openings so that once again the immediate context of the work is made active rather than passive. The combination of effects that Scarpa brings to bear on these two galleries is in extreme contrast to the axiality of the neo-classical galleries. But it is as if this is not enough; the two new galleries almost disintegrate in their brief progression. The cube gallery loses its corners, then, with each step, the plan becomes more unsettling and more open-ended.

Venice

The effects in Possagno are a result of the manipulation of space and light. In Scarpa's work on the re-modelling of the Querini-Stampalia Foundation in Venice carried out between 1961 and 1963, his repertoire extends into the realms of lavish materials. The entrance here, like so many in Venice, is over a bridge. This is a delicate construction of teak, brass and steel, referring both to Venetian boat-building and to Japanese precedents. The interior arrangement of the rooms to accommodate new galleries returns the space to its original layout, clearing away 19th-century accretions. To solve the recurring problem of flooding, Scarpa inserted a number of overlaid planes and surfaces. The floor becomes a complex raft (a motif that was to be repeated in Castelvecchio, Verona, without the functional rationale), gutters are formed in the spaces between floor and wall. Interior walls are clad in travertine with a polished brass hanging rail and lighting recessed flush in its face. The surface of the floor is divided as if it were a courtyard, polished stone marking out the grid between smooth shuttered concrete. This overlay of material onto existing space leads to tiny, unstable mismatches, points at which the floor grid has to re-align in order to accommodate the shifts in the 16th-century building, stone-cladding wrapped around a column with its gold-tiled edges crumbling away with geometrical composure. This

refers to the construction of the cladding but at the same time it
evokes its decay.

Verona

The work that was to benefit most from the early experiments in the
Palazzo Abatellis is the Castelvecchio Museum in Verona.[13] This was
begun in 1957 and was to occupy Scarpa sporadically until 1973. The
medieval castle had been turned into a barracks in the 19th century
by Napoleonic troops. In the 1920s it was converted into a museum
with the rooms re-imagined as a Renaissance palace. Like the Palermo
museum, the Castelvecchio was severely damaged by bombing during
the Second World War. Scarpa's work, then, involved the same sort
of stitching together as at the Palazzo Abatellis. But this work was not
just on a much larger scale, it also involved Scarpa in both archaeology
and demolition.

The Castelvecchio is in fact a number of buildings: the major portion is grouped around a large, informal courtyard. There is also a
tower that acts as a hinge connecting a roadway, a bridge (neither of
which are actually part of the building) and the Reggia. The bulk of the
painting galleries are contained within the building that sits beyond the
courtyard and the roadway to the west. The re-planning of this collection of spaces became, in effect, a piece of small-scale urban planning.
As in Palermo, the ground-floor rooms of the main building are
devoted to sculpture. Scarpa took the entrance from the courtyard off
the façade's axis to the end of the building, thereby creating a unified
series of galleries. The galleries are in fact a building within a building.
This is visible from outside as well as in; the windows of the new work
slide past just behind the old masonry as if they were disconnected.
Similarly the interior floors appear to float away from the walls, creating a defined break between the old and the new. This relationship is
not always straightforward and is not merely a case of reverence for
history. In the very first gallery, Scarpa pushes a room – the Sacello –
out into the courtyard; an immediate alteration to the scale of the
interior. This room forms one side of the entrance area from the outside (the other edge is marked by the administrative wing to the east)

without referring to any of the conventional architectural symbols of entrance. There is no canopy, no projecting walls; the entrance itself is an absence of wall. Internally, the Sacello is marked by a change in scale and materials. The floor here is of terracotta tiles and the walls are dark green plaster. Object mounts are connected directly to steel bands running horizontally at floor and ceiling level. This disrupts the conventional museological separation between architecture and display. Daylight makes shafts of light from the slot at the top of the wall. Again, this runs contrary to the goal of uniformity in museum lighting. It is as if this little room acts as a statement of intent for Scarpa: the nature of the experience of visiting the Castelvecchio will be fragmentary and discontinuous. Francesco Dal Co has said of Scarpa:

> The incompleteness that is the typical mode of his research reveals his concept of the work in relation to time. It thus becomes possible to see the architectural fragment as the favoured embodiment of Scarpa's work . . .[14]

As at the Palazzo Abatellis, Scarpa sets up a route through the building but here it is much more complex, involving overlapping paths and dead-ends. So, although he differentiates the Sacello from the main gallery to which it is attached, Scarpa is also saying: 'do not expect uniformity, be on your guard'.

Scarpa's work is often characterized by commentators by the clarity with which he distinguishes the old from the new[15] but this is not always the case; there is often a more complex relationship between these two elements. The archways between the rooms in the sculpture galleries' enfilade are marked by large rough stone slabs standing upright within the door reveals. These came about when Scarpa saw a threshold slab temporarily propped up in the archway with its unfinished underside showing. He then instructed that this slab should be reproduced and repeated down the length of the gallery. This is not pastiche. Instead, it takes a component, the meaning of which has already been altered: the threshold inverted, stood on end and built into the wall, and further skews its use by repetition. The implication of placing these stones in archways is that the walls have been cut. Past and present are blurred in the creation of this effect.

At the end of the sculpture gallery there is a glass-covered hole cut in the floor to reveal the excavation of an older building's foundations below. This device has become a commonplace of the renovation of historic buildings, but Scarpa's treatment of it, apart from being an early example of the type, is given little emphasis; this is, after all, just another effect in an armoury of uncanny responses to history and display. In the course of the route round the Castelvecchio, Scarpa employs a huge vocabulary of de-stabilizing effects. The route, after the sculpture galleries, runs under the roadway and rises to first-floor level within the tower, emerging at first-floor level into the painting galleries in the Reggia. In these rooms Scarpa plays with the ideas of hiding and revelation experimented with in his exhibition designs and developed in Palermo. One gallery has paintings displayed on skeletal easels, originally designed for the Museo Correr in Venice, with their backs turned to the doorway. This draws viewers into the room, forces them to look at the paintings from the relatively constricted viewpoint of the corner. As in the final room of the Possagno gallery, visitors are forced into an intimate, if difficult and even over-heated, relationship with the work. It is as if Scarpa is himself turning his back on the norm of museological display and inviting the visitor to do the same. In the same room fragments of historic frescos have been uncovered but Scarpa does not take the usual polite route of avoiding the display of pictures on the wall. Instead, he mixes the use of the walls as 'archaeological' surface and display surface. As in Possagno and the Sacello, display lighting is minimal with daylight providing most of the rather unpredictable illumination. Some smaller pictures are mounted on panels with the horizontal centre line marked out as a joint in the fabric. Scarpa, rather than attempting to create a historical or a 'neutral' background in which the picture sits, makes a point of emphasizing the fact that this is an object taken out of context and displayed in a museum. In one of the larger painting galleries, pictures are shown at right-angles to the plane of the wall, supported at their ends by insubstantial looking metal rods. This leaves the form of the room intact but draws attention to the artifice involved in the making of a (Delirious) museum.

The complexity of Scarpa's position regarding the relationship between the past and the intention of design is nowhere more extreme than in the splintering that occurs as the building reaches the hinge of the tower and the surrounding battlements. Within this fractured joint is placed the large equestrian statue of Cangrande della Scala.

19. Carlo Scarpa, Castelvecchio Museum, Verona (1958–73).
Statue of Cangrande.

Manfredo Tafuri has written: 'the surreal placement of the equestrian statue . . . is typical of [Scarpa's] simultaneously humorous and
pensive rapport with the past'.[16] Views of the statue recur throughout
the visitor's progress through the museum. It is visible from the
courtyard, sitting on a tall concrete plinth amongst the built ruins
made by the removal of the 19th-century grand staircase that rose up
in this corner. Below it the ground falls away into the vestigial moat
excavated as part of Scarpa's exploration of the site. Above the statue
is the jagged profile of the roof, terracotta tiles giving way to a new
copper cladding that terminates unevenly. The structural roof beams
sail on into space beyond functional necessity and even further than
would be required to 'express' this element of structure. The statue
is visible from underneath, as the route moves from ground floor
through the tower to the Reggia. Here the emblematic wings of the
horseman's armour are seen in silhouette against the sky.

Scarpa worked on the position of this iconic sculpture (it is often
considered to be the symbol of Verona) over a number of years. He
first placed it on a tall, freestanding, tapering plinth slightly in front of
the building line so that it was visible from the museum's entrance
along the façade. He went on considering both the position and the
design of the plinth in many drawings after this temporary solution
was arrived at. The continual process of exploration of the building
eventually suggested to Scarpa that the statue had to be moved
behind the old building line so that it took its place within the wound
made by demolition. Though Cangrande is glimpsed and can be
viewed from various places before the route actually reaches the
statue, its most dramatic exposition takes place after the visitor
leaves the Reggia and is crossing to the second series of painting galleries on the first floor of the barracks building. After passing through
the tower the route breaches the old wall of the castle with a staircase descending through a narrow slot. To the left a view opens out
to the river and the abutments of the bridge. At the bottom of the
stairs another step juts out, inviting a walk along the exposed battlements high above the river. But before this point is reached there is
a view off to the right revealing the statue from above, and at the bottom of the stairs the route over a diagonal bridge becomes clear. This
bridge leads to both the picture galleries and the statue. A jagged spi-

ral walkway descends round and underneath the horse and its rider, offering a series of shifting viewpoints with the courtyard, the rough castle wall and the roof as changing backgrounds. This descending route culminates in a steel platform that juts out into space. The cantilevered platform flexes with the weight of visitors. As with the earlier encounter with the *Triumph of Death* in Palermo, Scarpa is playing with theatrical effects and with the feeling of vertigo.

The statue is placed on a cantilevered podium projecting along the same axis as the main building. The statue itself is skewed on its plinth in order, as Scarpa put it, 'to emphasise its independence from the structure supporting it; it is a part of the whole, yet it still lives its own separate life'.[17]

It is doubtful if the design of this rich and complex experience could have been arrived at in any way other than over time and as part of a series of explorations and experiments. The effects that Scarpa creates are not tamed within a rigorous system. Instead, they fly off at tangents and are open-ended. Speaking of his work on Castelvecchio, Scarpa said in a lecture in 1978:

> I decided to adopt certain vertical values, to break up the unnatural symmetry: Gothic, especially Venetian Gothic, isn't very symmetrical. This called for something more, but then I got tired . . . yes because I never finish my works . . . .If there are any original parts they have to be preserved.[18]

Even this statement is open to interpretation. Elsewhere in the essay, referring to another project, he says: 'I even had to violate things . . .'.[19] At Castelvecchio he had to both 'violate things' and preserve the 'original parts'. The incorporation of these two contradictory aims is what makes Castelvecchio so important. In the end this contradiction is left unresolved, in ruins, like the splintered space in which Cangrande sits. It is as if the demolition and excavation programme is still going on – as if Scarpa is still in the process of drawing.

The shifts that Scarpa accomplishes in his museum work add up to a subversion of traditional display. Scarpa was not part of an identifiable stylistic movement.[20] However, he used strategies similar to both the Surrealists and the Situationists (albeit to different ends). He was interested both in juxtaposition of objects and architecture and in the disruption of narrative by spatial means. His work appears at first fixed in its 'meaning', but beyond the obsession of detailing and control there is the delirium of fluidity.

San Vito d'Altivole

In 1969 Scarpa was asked to design a tomb for the Brion family in Treviso in Northern Italy. This was not the first piece of funereal architecture with which Scarpa had been involved but it was by far the largest. In some ways it could be considered the equivalent in his work to the family tomb of John Soane – when Scarpa died in 1978, his son designed a simple slab that marked the burial spot of the architect within this extensive complex. What began as a tomb actually became the design of a whole cemetery. The narrative elements that Scarpa had developed in his museum designs over the preceding decades reappeared here in an explicit way. This was space re-arranged to mark a journey from life into death. The plot for the cemetery wraps around two sides of an existing town cemetery and accommodates a funerary chapel common to both layouts. The L-shaped plot is dominated at its corner by a bridge structure sheltering the two Brion tombs. This relates through a series of waterways and pathways to the rest of the site. As in Scarpa's museums there is the use of certain effects to heighten the sensation of the journey on which the visitor has embarked: particular views are created by introducing slots and the orientation of the buildings is complex rather than straightforward. The corners of the sloping walls enclosing the cemetery are broken so that the view out to the countryside is clear, while there is no view in. Like the corners of the cube room at Possagno, this dematerializes an otherwise solid structure. There is no physical trace of the museum here. Scarpa, unlike Soane, was not asked to incorporate a mausoleum into a gallery nor did he create a museum within the cemetery. What is at play is a parallel proposal. Scarpa's tomb and Scarpa's museums operate using the same language. This is a language of theatre, of disruption and even of *détournement*. It is a language that resists resolution. Speaking in 1978 of the Brion Tomb and its relationship to the architecture of the past, Scarpa said: '. . . We lack certainties – everything is debatable, architecture is a shambles . . .'.[21]

9

THE SPIRAL IN RUINS

> . . . already a fictitious past occupies in our memories the place of
> another, a past of which we know nothing with certainty – not even that
> it is false.
>
> Jorge Luis Borges, *Tlon, Uqbar, Orbis Tertius*[1]

*The desire to destroy the museum is a thread running through Modernist
artistic and architectural practice. Chris Burden wanted Samson to push
down the walls of the gallery.[2] In 1968 the American artist Edward Ruscha
showed his painting* The Los Angeles County Museum on Fire. *The
museum is shown from a high viewpoint, isolated as if it is an architectural
model. Smoke billows from the roof while flames emerge from the back of
the building. The painting shows the ideal at its moment of destruction. In
1975 the Guggenheim Museum in New York was to receive similar
treatment from two separate sources. One is a painting by the Russian
emigrés Komar and Melamid, called* Scenes from the Future: The
Guggenheim Museum. *This shows the museum in an advanced state of
decay, set in a pastoral landscape, the rest of Manhattan wiped out. The shell
of the building has collapsed and a tree grows from the centre of the void.
The second response to the museum came from the Czech artist Jiří Kolář.
He took a photograph of the Guggenheim and crumpled the image, fixing it
at a moment of implosion. In 1909 Marinetti in Italy called for the flooding
of the museums. Carlo Scarpa re-assembled the museum as if from found
objects, accepting the inbuilt flaws (and delirium) of the original material. In
contrast, many pioneering Modernist architects were only really interested in
the museum if it could be started from scratch. Le Corbusier invented a
museum 'type' that he adapted to various sites and circumstances. Frank
Lloyd Wright used his museum commission, the aforementioned*

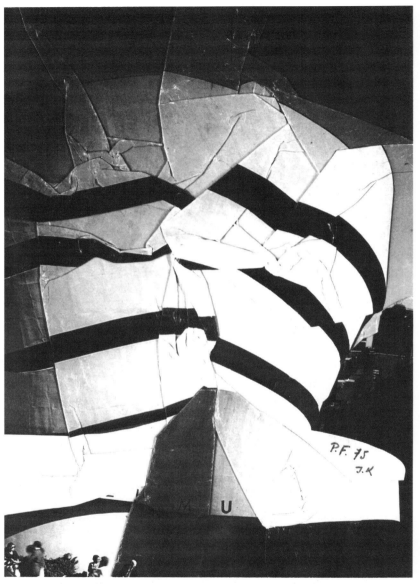

20. Jiři Kolář, *Guggenheim Museum*, crumplage (1975).

Guggenheim, to express his differences with the 'idea' of Manhattan and the gridded street pattern. Mies van der Rohe went further than both, reversing Le Corbusier's process by adapting his museum commissions from building types he had developed for other projects. But even in these buildings delirium lies, waiting to be unearthed, just below the surface.

The spiral

For Le Corbusier the museum was, like much of his design, a utopian project. In order to see another possible version of the Delirious Museum it is necessary to demolish the museum that Le Corbusier desired. Le Corbusier proclaimed the failure of the museum, as he saw it, in an essay of 1925; 'Other Icons; The Museums'. In this, he attributed the failure of museums to their incompleteness: 'THE MUSEUM IS BAD BECAUSE IT DOES NOT TELL THE WHOLE STORY. IT MISLEADS, IT DISSIMULATES, IT DELUDES, IT IS A LIAR'.[3] Le Corbusier contrasts the deceitful 19th-century museum full of 'decorative art' with his vision of the ideal museum's contents: 'A plain jacket, a bowler hat, a well-made shoe. An electric light bulb with bayonet fixing; a radiator, a table cloth of fine white linen . . . A number of bentwood chairs with cained seats like those invented by Thonet of Vienna . . .'.[4] 'THE MUSEUM REVEALS THE FULL STORY, AND IT IS THEREFORE GOOD: IT ALLOWS ONE TO CHOOSE, TO ACCEPT OR TO REJECT'.[5] Without acknowledging it, Le Corbusier is here evoking that commercial encyclopedia: the department store. And, without knowing it, he is proposing a collecting department of the Delirious Museum.

While Le Corbusier made this unwitting connection, he did not refer to the form of the department store when working on his museum proposals. The glass atrium, a space common to museums, stores and arcades, stems from the 19th century; this, to Le Corbusier, must have already seemed like a dead idea. Instead, he took as his starting point the 'transcendental geometry'[6] of the spiral. Le Corbusier's first version of the form was in his Musée Mondial proposal for the Mundaneum, Geneva (1929), a project linked to the site for the

League of Nations headquarters. The idea behind the Mundaneum was that:

> In one place on the globe the total image and significance of the world should be visible and understood; that this place should become a holy place, as an inspiration and stimulation of great ideas and noble activities; that there should be installed there a treasure, made of the sum total of intellectual works, like a contribution from science to universal organization . . .[7]

The plan of the Mundaneum has similarities to Aztec ritual sites, while the Musée Mondial takes its form from the Tower of Babel transposed onto a square plan. Le Corbusier referred to the museum as a 'shrine'. In this scheme external and internal spirals descend to earth around an open space. Given the name, the Musée Mondial, and the aspirations of the Mundaneum, it is tempting to interpret this building as a microcosm of the whole world. However the Musée Mondial proposal had definite limitations for Le Corbusier. Its finite plan obviously could not cater for the 'complete' collection, what Le Corbusier called 'the whole story'. For this he proposed the Museum of Unlimited Growth of 1939. The original unexecuted scheme was for Phillipeville, North Africa. It tackled the problem of incompleteness by making an entrance at the centre of a rectilinear 'spiral' raised on pilotis. The visitor's route and development of the building was then outwards. The building could, therefore, expand infinitely to accommodate the expansion of the collection. Given Le Corbusier's disappointment with the traditional museum, it is difficult to imagine a building big enough to contain all that would need to be collected over time. He came closest to realizing his ideal in the Museum at Ahmedabad, India (1958), where the square spiral form reappears. But here, it is contained within a closed blank box, as if it were a coiled spring. Maybe Le Corbusier for once doubted the wisdom of his proposals.

The unlikely, utopian project of the Museum of Unlimited Growth is the continuation of a tradition running from the Encyclopaedia of Diderot and d'Alembert to the Victoria & Albert Museum and beyond. Its delirious impossibility is echoed in fiction. Flaubert, in his story *Bouvard and Pecuchet*, (1880) documents the attempts of two

Parisians to re-make their lives in Normandy.[8] They embark on numerous projects, failing at each, guided as they are by contradictory manuals and technical instructions. Douglas Crimp has made the case for the novel as a critique of the idea of museums.[9] He points out Flaubert's belief that the museum is embarked on an impossible project: to render all objects alike by classification and systemisation. He quotes Eugenio Donato:

> The fiction is that a repeated metonymic displacement of fragments for totality, object to label, series of objects to series of labels, can still produce a representation which is somehow adequate to a nonlinguistic

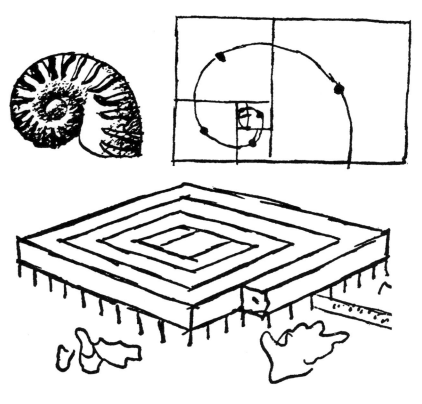

21. Le Corbusier, Museum of Unlimited Growth (1939).

universe. Such a fiction is a result of an uncritical belief in the notion that ordering and classifying, that is to say, the spatial juxtaposition of fragments, can produce a representational understanding of the world.[10]

In the short story 'The Man Who Collected the First of September, 1973', Tor Åge Bringsvaerd describes an attempt to document the events of just one day in a central archive, an attempt to face the 'everyday' reality in which Ptk, the protagonist, is stranded.[11] He collects news stories from around the world and invents elaborate filing systems so that information can be retrieved, but the enterprise can never be completed because even when time and space have been contained there is an infinite number of narratives. The apparently rational enterprises of Bouvard, Pecuchet and Ptk prove to be not only futile, but also ruinous. The first ends in bankruptcy, the other in fire, madness and death. Le Corbusier's infinite encyclopedia is here turned into human folly.

In unearthing the Delirious Museum, the utopian museum projects of Le Corbusier are included precisely because they are ultimately tragic. Le Corbusier tried to replace history with an impossible rationalism based on taxonomy, a clean sheet that would replace the museum as he knew it.

By inverting the elevation of Le Corbusier's Musée Mondial it is possible to recognize the form of another icon of both modern architecture and museum design. The spiral of the Guggenheim Museum, New York, by Frank Lloyd Wright (1943–59), imagined in ruins by Komar and Melamid and crumpled by Kolář, not only descends earthwards (or spirals out of control into the sky) but also closes in on itself like Dante's Hell. In the mythology of modern architecture this wayward sculptural form is seen as Wright's rebuff to the Manhattan grid. The Guggenheim was influential; a series of buildings refer to it, from Richard Meier's High Museum, Atlanta (1980–84), to Hans Hollein's scheme for the Guggenheim in Salzburg (1988), where the conical 'building' was to be carved out of a mountainside. This leads to another route into the labyrinthine Delirious Museum. The model for Wright's Guggenheim is the Panopticon prison proposed by Jeremy Bentham: the void surrounded by galleries, the act of seeing made concrete.[12]

If Le Corbusier's desire was to re-make the museum, Mies van der Rohe, his contemporary, wanted to deny its existence. The Constructivist designer Alexander Rodchenko wrote in 1920:

> Work for life and not for palaces, cathedrals, cemeteries and museums. Work in the midst of everything and with everybody; down with monasteries, institutions, studios, ateliers and islands.[13]

This comes close to Mies' implicit attitude to the museum. In 1943, five years after his arrival in the USA, Mies was invited by the magazine *Architectural Forum* to make a proposal for a theoretical project. He submitted a design for 'a museum for a small city'. The best-known collage for this design shows the artworks, Picasso's *Guernica* and two sculptures by Maillol, floating in space against backgrounds of foliage and water. The architecture itself is invisible, like a pre-echo of Scarpa's de-materializing cube at Possagno, though with a different intention. The other collage created for the scheme has only faint lines showing the floor and ceiling patterns. There is no 'museum' there. The plan shows a series of objects: auditorium, offices, print room, walls for display, arranged on a rectangular structural grid. The context established by Mies for the artworks is, therefore, the infinity of the grid and the landscape. Were it not so utopian and anti-urban, this proposal would correspond with more delirious intentions. In the text accompanying the illustrations, Mies says:

> In this project the barrier between the artwork and the living community is erased by a garden approach for the display of sculpture. Interior sculptures enjoy an equal spatial freedom, because the open plan permits them to be seen against the surrounding hills. The architectural space thus achieved becomes a defining rather than confining space.[14]

His single completed stand-alone museum project was for the resolutely urban Neue Nationalgalerie in Berlin (1962–68). This is a schizophrenic building divided into two clear parts. The visible part is a black steel and glass pavilion sitting on a podium above street level. The museum's galleries are situated in the buried part of the museum under the podium adjoining a walled, sunken garden. The pavilion acts as a sign, an entrance and as an exhibition space for the museum. In this last capacity, until fairly recently, it has been spectacularly unsuccessful. Most exhibitions mounted in the space merely served to fill it up – making what was always intended as a void or, at least as free space, a solid. The glass box created a museum without walls, a museum with nowhere to display the artworks. It has emerged that the pavilion is an excellent site for large-scale installation works and for sculpture.[15] Maybe Mies was considering his own early exhibition designs when he made this proposal. He and Lilly Reich designed a series of trade and propaganda exhibitions in the late 1920s and early 1930s while Mies was still in charge of the Bauhaus. The most striking of these is the exhibition Material Show. In the exhibit *Wood; the Dwelling in Our Time*, roughly cut logs are arranged stacked and gridded on the floor, boards stand like menhirs in space.[16] The exhibition has something of the look of one of Donald Judd's installations created for his studios at Marfa, Texas, or an elemental Carl Andre arrangement. This has parallels in the development of 'found' spaces (converted warehouses and factories), not only as suitable locations for large-scale sculpture and installation art, but also as generators for it. And in a way the pavilion of the Neue Nationalgalerie is also found space. Mies developed the idea of the building on a podium throughout his years in America. In the project for an office building in Cuba for the Bacardi company he extended this notion by sinking ancillary accommodation into the podium itself. It was this idea that Mies developed and carried through for Berlin rather than a notion particular to the museum. When the museum was completed the only other building in the immediate vicinity was the Matthiakirche. In photographs this red brick church appears to occupy a space on the plinth of the museum alongside the sculptures. Mies created a space from which the city could be viewed, in effect detaching the museum from its context. Looking at the city from inside the glass box is like looking at a projected image in a camera obscura. The museum here has become a viewing device. The building, or at least its visible tip, when seen from the street has to compete with all the clutter that cities generate and here the delirium of detachment and the purity of the structural ideal break down. Reading further against the grain of Mies' intention, the buried part of the museum can be read as the archaeological space. Here is the exposed excavation of Scarpa but this time it is the artworks themselves that are held in suspension, exposed then preserved and displayed like the bodies preserved in the ashes of Vesuvius at Pompeii. This accident of design connects the Neue Nationalgalerie to the projects of the town planner Patrick Geddes (1854–1932) who believed that the healthy development of urban life depended on detailed examination of the city fabric.[17] His most visible manifestation of this is in his work in Edinburgh's Old Town. Here he made a museum of urban life with, at its top, the Outlook Tower where he put to use an existing camera obscura.[18] Making this visual connection between city and museum in, for example, the works of Geddes, Mies van der Rohe and Frederick Kiesler, is one of the central principles of the Delirious Museum.

The spiral demolished

Mies' Neue Nationalgalerie can be compared to Karl Friedrich Schinkel's Altes Museum in Berlin of 1823–30 on a number of levels. The two share raised podiums and severe rectilinear forms. Mies, typically without referring to the specificity of the building's use, acknowledged a debt:

> The Altes Museum in Berlin – you could learn everything from it – and I tried to do that. In the Altes Museum [Schinkel] has separated the windows very clearly, he separated the elements, the columns and the walls and the ceilings, and I think that is still visible in my later buildings.[19]

Anthony Vidler makes the case for a connection between the Altes Museum and Le Corbusier's Musée Mondial. Both are based on interconnecting galleries in a square plan wrapped around a central void.[20] The same precedent, though with very different intentions, is picked up by James Stirling with his designs for the Neue Staatsgalerie in Stuttgart (1977–84). This project was the last (and only successful entry) in a trio of competitions for museums in German cities. These projects mark a development of Stirling's work hinted at in an earlier, much smaller scheme for St Andrews University in Scotland in 1972. This was for an arts centre based around a Georgian house and courtyard. Stirling left existing elements while creating a new formality and even monumentality with sweeping side wings more reminiscent of Robert Adam than small, domestic-scale architecture. It threw into this mix more conventionally 'modern' concerns like a technologically advanced system of movable walls and outdoor film projection. In the scheme for the Nordrhein-Westfalen Museum, Düsseldorf, 1975, Stirling expanded both his exploration of the neo-classical and his ideas of bringing the particular urban context to bear on design solutions. In Berlin Mies made a pavilion to act as a sign for a buried museum, in Dusseldorf Stirling proposed a similar strategy, here the museum is not buried underground but within a city block. Unlike Mies, the intention is pragmatically urban rather than utopian. This scheme acknowledges the haphazard nature of the city fabric and exploits the juxtapositions that the city throws up. Stirling borrowed the central open drum of Schinkel's Altes Museum and took its roof off to open up a space in the middle of the dense infill block of his proposal. This is only one of a whole repertoire of effects that Stirling put to use to make connections to historical precedents and local context. In Dusseldorf there are obvious references to Le Corbusier as well as Schinkel and there is the appearance of the pedestrian route snaking through the block and through the central rotunda. Vidler compares this device to Le Corbusier's use of pilotti in the Musée Mondial to make a continuous pedestrian plane under the building.[21] The site for the Wallraf Richartz Museum, Cologne called for a more monumental approach, spanning the railway-bridge over the Rhine. But the monument is chipped away at by Stirling as he responds to the pressures of the immediate environment. Stirling's proposal was for, in effect, a small city of buildings of differing forms with complex joints and links.

The third scheme, that for Stuttgart, is the most complex. Here there is not only the built evidence of Stirling's design thinking but the feeling that this was a work that developed in its intentions as it progressed. The precedents for the Stuttgart scheme are manifold. The plan alone refers to that of the existing museum to which Stirling's building joins, to Schinkel, to Le Corbusier and to the stylized eagle of the German flag. Other elements show the influence of De Stijl, Constructivism, Stirling's own housing designs for Runcorn, and

Stuttgart's railway station. These references, reflections and echoes all contribute to the Staatsgalerie's inclusion as a Delirious Museum.

As in Düsseldorf, the brief called for a pedestrian route linking the two open sides of the site. Stirling took this as one of the governing principles of the design, once again integrating the form of the rotunda from the Altes Museum.

Thomas Muirhead in his essay 'Modernism and the Urban Tradition',[22] referring to Düsseldorf, calls this 'the museum invaded by the city'. Douglas Crimp in more critical mode says regarding Stuttgart:

> One can ascend a ramp in front of the museum, enter the space of the rotunda, circle around one side of it, and exit on the street above without ever having entered the museum proper, whereas to enter the space from inside the museum, one must always weave one's way to it as if to the center of a labyrinth. At no point does the rotunda give directly onto the art galleries.[23]

Crimp avoids the ambiguity of this space. Stirling meant it as a democratization of the monumental. It is both of the city and of the museum. As a space at the centre of a labyrinth it is a point of orientation while it is also a piece of (free) urban theatre. Vidler expresses the view that it is also a 'cemetery at the [museum's] heart'[24] without explicitly making the connection to either Soane's Dulwich Picture Gallery or the painting *The Island of the Dead* by Arnold Böcklin.[25] In the latter, a figure dressed in white robes approaches a circular island with fragments of neo-classical architecture emerging from the raw stone; tall cypress trees occupy the centre of a natural rotunda. Stirling uses this form to develop other ambiguities. Schinkel's rotunda was enclosed for functional reasons but Stirling transforms his into an outdoor room by making a simple, over-scaled cornice around its edge. Stirling said:

> And it's no longer enough to do classicism straight, in this building the central pantheon, instead of being the culmination, is but a void – a room like a non-space instead of a dome – open to the sky.[26]

This migration of exterior and interior elements continues elsewhere. The gallery doorways are based on an existing example on the outside of the adjacent opera house.

The doorway out from the galleries into the 'museum space' of the rotunda is set below the floor level so that visitors ascend into the rotunda through a freestanding aedicule. From the interior of the rotunda these stumpy columns and lintel are, therefore, partially buried. Stirling is here suggesting a built archaeology. He is at once unearthing some imagined history of the museum and designing a ruin. Indeed the idea of the 'ruin', as much as some of the totalitarian associations of neo-classical architecture, caused much consternation at the time of the building's completion. Anthony Vidler commented:

> Certainly the building of a 'ruin' by a British architect in the center of a city itself devastated by war seems to have overdetermined its negative reception, especially as the ruin refers to a museum that was indeed ruined by the bombing.[27]

There are parallels here to the controversy surrounding the renovation of the neo-classical Munich's Alte Pinakothek by Leo von Klenze (1836), partially destroyed by bombing in the Second World War. In its renovation by Hans Döllgast in 1957 the central section of the building had to be rebuilt. He chose to make this wound in the fabric visible by changing the colour of brickwork and simplifying the fenestration. This visible scar is still a matter for discussion: should the building be restored to its original form or left with the visible signs of trauma forever exposed? The same question arises in the adjacent Glyptothek Building, also by Klenze, where the destroyed interiors have been re-instated in a stripped-down form – the bare brick exposed, contrasting with the stone of the classical sculptures. The physical trauma of this difficult past is made manifest in both buildings. Stirling addresses the same traumatic events in his project in Stuttgart. It is no coincidence that this drama should be played out in museum buildings whether new or existing. Museums have the potential to be the collective houses of memory.

Crimp also notes the preponderance of symbols of ruin in Stirling's building. Referring to the blocks pulled out from the carpark wall, he acknowledges that this is a reference to the historical tradition of building picturesque ruins while claiming that it is also Stirling's witty response to Crimp's essay of 1980, *On the Museum's Ruins*.[28] Of course, as Crimp also points out, it is Stirling's way of stating his antagonism to the high Modernist position of 'truth to materials'. These stone blocks, removed from function – a mere joke – are 'real' while the stone of the wall itself is a veneer. Elsewhere, Stirling goes against the grain of another Modernist dictum, not to say cliché, coined by Mies himself: 'God is in the details'. In detailing the stone-cladding, Stirling deliberately left some features unresolved in such a way that the stone would eventually stain. This was not meant to reproduce the 'old' but it can be seen, like so many of the techniques used by Stirling, as an act of subversion.

Like Scarpa's museums (but with no stylistic similarities) Stirling's Neue Staatsgalerie is an architecture of fragments: pre-existing elements in a new ensemble. Scarpa's vocabulary is that of display, Stirling's is that of the city:

> The new building may be a collage of old and new elements, Egyptian cornices and Romanesque windows but also Constructivist canopies, ramps and flowing forms – a union of elements from the past and present. We are trying to evoke an association with museum and I find examples from the 19th century more convincing than examples from the 20th.[29]

In fact, Stirling's building could be read as a collection of quotations, an anthology, with as its unifying concept, a desperate engagement with the city. For Stirling the only model available for dismantling and re-use was the 19th-century museum, because the 20th-century version had no recognizable form. The unbuilt Musée Mondial had no meaning for the public, Mies' museums were interchangeable with office buildings and the beautiful and quiet museums of Louis Kahn were, as Vidler has pointed out, 'faceless'.[30] The galleries of the Neue Staatsgalerie are also of a type recognizable from the 19th century and here Stirling's conservative streak operates without irony. These rooms are straightforward spaces with flat walls, laylights and two doors on axis. Stirling was, at best, not much interested in the contents of these galleries and so they become, like so many museum rooms from the 19th century, 'found' spaces for contemporary art. This points out the perversity of Stirling's position. The exterior of the building made a connection to the traumatic condition of the 20th-century city while the interior display spaces retreated from a similar engagement with 20th-century art.

Before his death in 1992, Stirling completed three other museum projects: the Sackler Museum, Harvard (1979), the Clore Gallery

22. James Stirling. Staatsgalerie, Stuttgart (1977–84). Opening to underground carpark.

extension to the Tate, London (1980), and the Tate in the North, Liverpool (1984). The last of these was an un-characteristic conversion of a Victorian dockside warehouse building. It therefore fits one of the archetypes of late 20th-century museum architecture stretching from Donald Judd's galleries in Marfa through the Andy Warhol Museum in Pittsburg to Tate Modern, London: the re-used industrial space. The other two projects by Stirling jettison the idea of the ruin inherent to the Staatsgalerie but are equally layered with historical and architectural references. The Sackler Museum is an L-shaped corner building on the Harvard campus, separated from Le Corbusier's Carpenter Centre for the Arts by the adjacent Fogg Museum. A striped wall punctuated by apparently random windows wraps around the corner of the site with the monumental entrance tucked into the short return of the plan. From here a long staircase ascends through the building to the galleries and offices. This staircase has its predecessors in those of Klenze's Alte Pinakothek in Munich and in Bernini's Scala Reggia in the Vatican, both in terms of scale and in the way that Stirling's staircase is not part of a grand, governing axis. In Munich the staircase leads to a blank wall at which visitors have to turn 90 degrees to enter the galleries, in Harvard the staircase leads ultimately to a gallery; whose axis runs at right-angles. Stirling said: '. . . I think of the staircase as an event in itself . . . as a steeply inclined bazaar with overlooking windows'.[31] Once again, as in the Stuttgart rotunda, Stirling uses the relationship between inside and outside to introduce ambiguity to the programme. Another connection to Stuttgart is Stirling's use of the idea of archaeology. Referring to the small flight of descending stairs before the entrance, Stirling said: 'Maybe it's like stepping into an archaeological dig; here the up flight of steps associated with a monumental building is reversed'.[32]

The clarity of the Sackler plan (a staircase dividing galleries and offices) could not be repeated in Stirling's commission to design a new wing for the collection of Turner's paintings to be housed at the Tate Gallery. The Clore Gallery is a graft on a strongly axial building that, like Stuttgart, aims to exploit its context. Stirling wraps his building around a small open courtyard anchoring its ends on the existing Tate and a freestanding lodge on the corner of the site. The elevations adjacent to these two 'anchors' use a stone grid to contain plaster and brick-facing according to context. This potentially endless grid is contained by a cornice line picked up from the Tate building and interrupted by Stirling's massive, Boullée-like, entrance façade. The gridded elevations are well-mannered and recessive, having something of the air of a garden building, but the entrance is the point at which the Clore Gallery makes its presence felt as a separate entity from the Tate itself. The door sits within a large negative open pediment surmounted by a lunette window. This refers back to the facing elevation of the Tate while inverting the elements. Stirling also acknowledged other implications of this composition: 'Yes, the association of a tomb and then a memorial; also you go down into those sorts of places. Maybe all museums are like tombs – secure vaults containing things of great value.'[33] The entrance sequence following on from this doorway is twisting and dis-orientating. Stirling again refers to the Scala Reggia, but his staircase is more convoluted. As Stirling put it:

> We wanted to exploit the promenade through the entrance hall as a prelude to the galleries and bring people through on a zig-zag path backwards and forwards across the central axis from the sunken garden.[34]

Echoing some of the discordant colours used by Stirling in Stuttgart, the temperature of this sequence is heightened by his use of bright green, ultramarine, peach, turquoise, pink and apricot. This device is one of Stirling's most problematic characteristics – a kind of spoiling that disrupts the spatial reading of his architecture.

These two relatively small buildings continue and develop the themes explored by Stirling in the German museum projects of the 1970s. In his fixation on an architectural language based in history, Stirling was able to re-define the possibilities of museums as delirious memory houses. He used the play of movement, especially in entrance sequences, stairs and ramps, to extend these possibilities. He took the logical, infinite and impossible museum proposed by Le Corbusier and turned it on its head making a series of complex and pragmatic urban buildings both open-ended in their possible meanings and imbued with a sense of troubled historical continuity.

A similar motivation, though using yet another language, seems to have been at work in the designs of a number of Deconstructionist architects in the late 1980s and 1990s. The Deconstructionist project is obviously not concerned primarily with the idea of the museum, though with the tremendous expansion internationally of museum building these concerns have, inevitably, overlapped. This expansion of building has run in parallel to the growth of the architectural star system that has brought the avant-garde into the mainstream.

In discussing the Co-op Himmelb(l)au component at Groninger Museum in Groningen, the Netherlands (1995), it is necessary to put it into its immediate architectural and social context. Groningen's local authority anticipated the so-called Bilbao effect in the early 1980s by initiating a number of high-profile architectural projects. One of these was a project to mark the boundaries of the city with various towers and monuments; another was the commissioning of various architects to design pavilions in which the annual video festival would take place. Each of these projects was aimed at designers who had built little previously but were influential academically, such as Zaha Hadid and Daniel Libeskind. The master-planner appointed for the new museum was Alessandro Mendini, the Italian architect who is closely associated with the 1980s design group Memphis. At inception he chose a number of collaborators for the project. These were Philippe Starck, Michele de Lucchi and the artist Frank Stella. Each, with Mendini, was given a section of the new museum to design. The site is an island in the canal, connecting to the main pedestrian bridge joining the station with the city centre. The position of the building, perpendicular to the bridge, sets up an axis with a series of pavilions strung out along the canal. The scheme by Frank Stella for an 'Old Master' pavilion was rejected early in the design process after client and artist disagreed on the relative merits of different versions of his scheme.[35] Co-op Himmelb(l)au were then appointed to design this component. The pavilions as built are of a stylistically uniform character with one notable exception. In some ways there are obvious parallels with Stirling's knowing historical approach to design here. The tower that marks the entrance is storage space and is covered in gold mosaic reflecting the idea of the treasure within. The doorways in Mendini's contemporary art galleries refer directly to those of the

Thorvaldsen Museum in Copenhagen. But the overall effect is recognizably Memphis and distinctly cartoon-like. Mendini acknowledges that he has taken his inspiration from the picturesque pastiche of Disneyland.

The exception to this stylistic rule is the building by Co-op Himmelb(l)au. Their pavilion was designed using a number of formal strategies involving chopped-up cardboard forms, photocopied enlargements and drawings sent to the local shipyard by fax machine. The main structure of the building was then fabricated in parts by the shipyard and transported by canal to the site. The surrealist device of chance is as pertinent here as it is in Breton's *Nadja*, as is the notion of 'drift' or *dérive*. This detachment from the brief and the emphasis on a formal, poetic process of production might seem to belie my assertion that this can be associated with Stirling's project of redefining the architecture of museums. After all, this is a long way from Stirling's referential approach to the museum, carefully analysing, interpreting and re-assembling historical precedents into a cohesive whole. However, the Old Master Pavilion, in the context of Mendini's banal and relentless axis, has an open-ness and uncertainty of 'meaning' in common with Stirling's work. The plan devised by Co-op Himmelb(l)au is straightforward: an open gallery space (crossed by a transversal bridge) attached to a smaller more enclosed room. But the overall effect is one in which the space disintegrates. The walls fall away, the floor seems to gently slide into the canal (pieces of it have already dropped off leaving gaping apertures covered in glass) and the roof has all but disappeared. This is the museum caught at the moment of destruction by Chris Burden's *Samson*. The superimposed diagrams etched onto the steel plates suggest some previous life, maybe as components discarded in the shipyard. Rather than 'found space' this seems to be 'found construction'. The space itself is fugitive, leaking out through the joints that have opened up in this exploding box. Amongst the wreckage something like conventional white display walls float in the space. These walls stand vertically and, in comparison to the restlessness of the disintegrating box, are fairly static. The picture-hang nods towards the condition of the building by 'skying' some paintings in the tradition of 18th-century galleries. This has the opposite effect from that intended. Instead of challenging the viewers' perception of the pictures, they are turned into décor. So, in the end, the 'Old Masters' disappear along with the coherence of the building: they have, in effect, stopped being art.

In the exhibition Frank Gehry; Architect, which travelled from New York to his own Guggenheim Museum Bilbao in 2001 there was a map showing the architect's preferred site for the new museum. Super-imposed on the map are three red arrows. These point to the place in which the Guggenheim now stands. Gehry has made some notes on the map: 'Strong visual connection from Museo. Important to have visual connection from City Hall Bridge. Visual presence of new building exterior and interior from across the river . . .'.[36] This points to the notion of visibility that is the motivation behind the Bilbao Guggenheim project. In this the new museum fits in with the globalization of the Guggenheim brand where each building has its own identity within the overarching corporate structure of a cultural multinational. As more than one commentator has pointed out, the new museum is a symbol and even a logo for Bilbao.[37] The Guggenheim occupies a spectacular site – not overlooking the city – but on one of the bends of the twisting River Nervion. Driving in on one of the winding roads descending into the city from the surrounding mountains, the building is the first distinguishable feature of the urban network spreading out below. Getting closer, it is clear that the museum is piled up around a nucleus with its pinwheel or 'flower' plan reaching out to the surrounding city. A tower is located on the far side of the adjacent bridge, connecting the pedestrian walkway to the museum; another walkway, instead of just running past the building along the riverside, sweeps out in a wide arc apparently taking in the river itself. But these elements of connection are a blind. The building's dis-connectedness is a stronger feature than any contextual approach that the architect or his publicists might aspire to. More than anything, this is architecture as shiny, hard object. Its architectural intentions belong within a utopian tradition. In photographs the shiny titanium skin stands out from the dull masonry of nearby buildings. In certain views it looks like an alternative city, improbably shaped and forever, impossibly new. But the dis-connectedness is also about scale. The Guggenheim Bilbao is a big structure meant to show big art. Ironically this is a building in which the wayward and unfeasibly large-scale art of the 1960s and 1970s is finally tamed. Talking about recent and anticipated future art in 1967, the performance artist Allan Kaprow could say: 'the concept of the museum is completely irrelevant'.[38] His discussion with Robert Smithson goes on to explore ways that the 'useless' museum could be emptied: 'I am attracted to the idea of clearing out the museums and letting better designed ones like the Guggenheim [New York] exist as sculptures, as works, as such, almost closed to people. It would be a positive commitment to their function as mausolea'.[39] But the Guggenheim fights against this 'function' and asserts its own position as ideal urban object, unsullied by the slow decay of the surrounding city whilst simultaneously parcelling up art as commodity for the consumption of the cultural tourist. Richard Serra's huge sculpture *Snake* created for the largest gallery in the building, seems like the artist's own bitter riposte to those who engineered the removal of his outdoor piece *Tilted Arc* from Federal Plaza, New York, in 1989.[40]

The programme for the Guggenheim Bilbao comes from the architect's obsessions as well as from art marketing and curatorial ambition. It is this personal approach that suggests a continuity to Gehry's early work and particularly to his domestic projects. These were, on the whole, inward looking, befitting their edgy socio-geographical location in Los Angeles. Gehry's particular version of 'taking apart', or deconstruction, as it has come to be called, is based on the reconfiguration of form. Gehry himself has called this an interest in the gestural in architecture. The Guggenheim Bilbao clearly works on this level, it is instantly recognizable and spectacular and even seems to defy logic. How it differs from much of Gehry's earlier work is in its ostentatious display of expense. The early work was based on cheap and everyday materials such as steel mesh, corrugated metal and clapboard. One of Gehry's obsessions is with fish. The form of a twisting fish has been used by him in various projects both as skeletal shading and as sign.[41] The titanium sheets that clad the Guggenheim have been compared to fish scales; they look more like money, silver coinage pressed into building material. Here we have echoes of Mendini's golden storage tower at Groningen, but in Bilbao the whole building has been transformed into a treasure chest of precious metal.

Gehry, like Stirling, drops the entrance to the museum below street level. Here the change in level is not the tentative, archaeological and anti-monumental device of Stirling's Sackler Gallery but a sweeping amphitheatre that places the entrance to the museum on centre stage. Beyond this space, the entrance atrium that marks the centre of the plan re-directs the gaze vertically as in a cathedral. Thomas Krens, director of the Guggenheim Foundation, in discussing how the atrium should be developed, said to Gehry: 'This atrium is yours, you're the artist here. This is your sculpture . . . you then make perfect exhibition spaces around it.'[42] But this seems to deny that the rest of the building is sculpture too. Indeed, it is a sculpture meant to contain sculpture; a giant piece of consuming public art.

Where Co-op Himmelb(l)au superimposed a system of drawing and communication (cut-ups and the fax machine) onto the programme for the Old Master Pavilion at Groningen, Gehry's version of this detachment is the computer software programme 'Catia'. Originally developed for the aerospace industry, this programme allowed the Gehry office to turn the wild forms of Gehry's sketches into a realizable structure. But the software's capabilities also became an end in itself. The building is the shape it is because it is possible to build in that shape. This is the museum as spectacle; 'The spectacle is the existing order's uninterrupted discourse about itself, its laudatory monologue'.[43]

Anthony Vidler said: 'Bilbao remains *in the process of its conception* profoundly indifferent to our presence'.[44] Le Corbusier proposed an impossible, ever-expanding spiral for the museum, while Mies not only ignored the spiral, but ignored the museum too. James Stirling took the spiral apart and in the process began dismantling the museum, mixing it into the city. Frank Gehry has re-assembled the museum in the form of a luxurious object, as untouchable as an icon. In discussing the museum at the beginning of the 21st century it is virtually impossible to ignore the effect of the Guggenheim in Bilbao, but its model remains that of the impermeable institution holding the delirium of the city at bay.

10

AFTER THE WALL: STUDIO LIBESKIND

This is how space begins, with words only, signs traced on the blank
page. To describe space: to name it, to trace it, like those portolano-
makers who saturated the coastlines with the names of harbours, the
names of capes, the names of inlets, until in the end the land was only
separated from the sea by a continuous ribbon of text.

Georges Perec[1]

The Beginning is: the letter – ancient initials that tie together traces
and erasures.

Daniel Libeskind[2]

Berlin (*Between the Lines*)

*Like those of Paris and London, I have inscribed the map of Berlin with a
line marking the place of the Delirious Museum. I walked this route,
inventing it as I went along, getting lost, crossing forgotten borders and half-
remembered barriers in February 2003. Walter Benjamin, in his childhood
reminiscence 'A Berlin Chronicle', wrote: 'Not to find one's way in a city may
be uninteresting and banal. It requires ignorance – nothing more. But to lose
oneself in a city – as one loses oneself in a forest – that calls for quite a
different schooling.'[3] The trail does not end in Berlin. It weaves through
Osnabrück, Manchester, Rotterdam and London and it will extend beyond
this book. It begins in Berlin, not just because this city has such a tragic
history, but also because the first major work of Daniel Libeskind confronted
this history in the form of a museum building. But somewhere along the
ensuing route the Delirious Museum is lost and the buildings of Studio
Libeskind seem to shift into signature works, trophies exhibited as prizes of
urban regeneration.*

The route starts with Marx and Engels, their bronze backs turned dis-
consolately on the crumbling people's palace named in their honour
on the Spree. They look out at the vandalized peace monument and
the radio tower, the Fernsehturm, and Alexanderplatz beyond. On
Museuminsel many of the pink glass panels of the Marx-Engels Forum
are broken or gone, some are replaced by plywood, eyeless like the
statues. Across the street are the Prussian cultural showpieces of the
Altes Museum and the cathedral. The Altes Museum is one of a complex of five museums clustered on the end of the island. At the time
of writing two of these are closed for refurbishment and, despite the
straightforward confidence of Schinkel's façade to the Altes Museum,
the site looks unresolved and incomplete. The S-Bahn line cutting
through the site at high level seems to disappear into the buildings.
Unter den Linden runs west from here through Bebelplatz (formerly
the Opernplatz) where, in May 1933, the first burning of books by
authors considered undesirable by the Nazis took place. Borges, in his
short essay 'The Wall and the Books',[4] talks about the Chinese
Emperor Shih Huang Ti who is credited with the construction of the
Great Wall. He was also responsible for the burning of all books in
existence from before his reign so that his detractors could no longer
compare his own achievements to those of his predecessors. Those
who were found to be hiding books were punished by being branded
and set to work on the construction of the Great Wall. Borges wrote:
'Perhaps the burning of the libraries and the building of the wall are
operations that secretly nullify each other'.[5] In London in 1966
Latham's burning of book towers outside the British Museum had
been a challenge to the authority of institutions. The burning of the
books in Opernplatz was part of a series of events that led inevitably,
through holocaust and war, to the construction of the Berlin Wall.
Further west, along Unter den Linden, is the Brandenburg Gate. This
once stood in the 'death strip' of the Wall and its fortifications; the
gate is now surrounded by banks and embassy buildings. To the north
from here is the Reichstag, ostentatiously returned to use as a seat of
government by Norman Foster. A spiral rises in the glass dome
where, on 27 February 1933, another fire raged, destroying the interior of the Reichstag.[6] The route to the south skirts the Tiergarten
and passes the site for the Peter Eisenmann-designed memorial to the

Jews of Europe that also clings to the line of the Wall. Near here, marked only on a few maps but not on the ground, is the site of Hitler's infamous bunker. Spectacularly visible is Potsdamerplatz, replanned as the commercial hub of the city by Renzo Piano and with buildings by a roll-call of internationally recognized architects. A metre-long fragment of the Wall sits on a plinth and, stretching away from it, a subtle change in the surface of the pavement marks the line of the Wall. Following this vestigial split in the city a longer section of the Wall has been preserved on Niederkirchnerstrasse, balanced precariously above another relic of trauma, the basement vaults of the Gestapo headquarters. This is the site of The Topography of Terror, an outdoor exhibition that will be moved to a new building on an adjacent site by the architect Peter Zumthor. The Wall is protected by a fence; its surface on the western side is, of course, covered in graffiti. During its functional lifetime the Wall had already been transformed into text, in its death throes this process accelerated. Near this site is Checkpoint Charlie, now an almost inexplicable border post inserted into the seamless fabric of the new old Berlin.

> That is why one has to tread carefully in Berlin streets; without thinking the walker could tread on someone's roof. The asphalt is only a thin crust covering human bones. Yellow stars, black swastikas, red hammers and sickles crunch like cockroaches under the walker's feet.[7]

Not far from here, in the former West Berlin on Lindenstrasse, is a building that, between conception and construction, straddles the convulsive moment that was the final breaching of the Wall that would lead to the obliteration of East Germany. When Daniel Libeskind won the competition for the extension to the Berlin Museum with the Jewish Museum in 1989, the Wall was intact. After the historic events in November of that year when the crossing points between east and west were opened up, all major building projects in Berlin were put on hold. It took much lobbying to resuscitate the project and the museum was not completed until 1999.

Up until 1989 Libeskind had been an architect committed to teaching and writing, while making drawings and sculpture that deliberately avoided the possibility of habitable building. In 1987, one of these sculptures, called Three Lessons in Architecture: The Machines, was destroyed in an accidental fire in Geneva. Maybe *this* destruction opened up the possibility of building for Libeskind. The three primitive-looking, yet complex machines that made up the work were called the 'Reading Machine', the 'Memory Machine' and the 'Writing Machine'. In 1985 Libeskind wrote:

> The three machines propose a fundamental recollection of the historical vicissitude, in particular of Western architecture. They constitute a single piece of equipment and are mutually inter-dependent. Each is a starting point for the other . . . I think the objects in architecture are only residues of something that is truly important: the participatory experience . . . It is this experience that I would like to retrieve, not the object.[8]

In Libeskind's competition entry for the Jewish Museum a number of experiences are summoned up in order to construct the building's emotional narrative. He describes his starting points for the design as follows:

> Its first aspect is the invisible and irrationally connected star which shines with an absent light stemming from specific locations. The second one is the cut-off of Act 2 of Moses and Aron [by Schoenberg] that culminates in the non-musical fulfilment of the word. Its third is the ever-present dimension of the deported and missing Berliners. Its fourth is Walter Benjamin's urban apocalypse along the 'One Way Street'.[9]

The presentation site diagram for the scheme shows the building occupying a junction in an elongated Star of David cut from an historical map of Berlin. Superimposed on this are the vectors joining the significant places identified by Libeskind, an aerial view of the project model and the lines of the canal to the south and the Wall to the north. The Wall is a heavy black line that turns negative as it cuts through the missing urban fabric depicted on the old map. But, unlike the twisting and broken line of the canal, the Wall is shown in its geometrical solidity. The black line is picked up at a smaller scale in the plan of the Jewish Museum and its extension. In this Libeskind seems to be acknowledging the importance of this artificial barrier that for decades divided the life of the city. The brief for the building did not make this connection but Libeskind proposes a memorial not just to the past trauma of the Jewish community but to the then-present division of the city. Though the Wall had, to all purposes, disappeared by the time the museum was completed, there is still a sense in which Libeskind's building is a broken fragment of it and, as such, has been appropriated to the cause of memory rather than that of forgetting.

Other fragments of the competition proposal reinforce the idea of the building as an instrument of memory. On one model the base on which the building is presented is papered with the names of Jewish inhabitants of Berlin prior to the Holocaust. This echoes Libeskind's unbuilt plans for *City Edge*, Berlin (1987). In this Libeskind posited a city constructed of texts and references: 'A voyage into the substance of a city and its architecture entails a realignment of arbitrary points, disconnected lines, and names out of place . . .'. [10] In the presentation various objects (a hammer, books, the proposed buildings) spring from the model's base wrapped in text at once bound by words and trying to emerge from the ground. In another part of the model is a monograph on Mies van der Rohe, his frontispiece photograph is visible. The book is screwed and bolted onto the model, a constructivist red bar flies across the portrait, its legs pinioning the pages; Mies is here forever linked to Berlin, like the other refugees of the 1930s.

The project for the Jewish Museum was named *Between the Lines* by Libeskind and these two lines in plan remain the most visible manifestation of his self-imposed programme. One line is a continuous zig-zag and gives the building its external form. The second is a broken straight line containing a single disrupted void and is the defining structural element of the interior.

As my own jagged path through the amnesiac city led me to the museum, the museum itself generates a series of radiating lines in the surrounding pavement, pointing into the distance, suggesting both the 'irrationally connected star' and the routes of deportation and escape. Though the building is an 'extension' it seems at first not to be connected to the original Berlin Museum. Visitors enter the original Baroque building and then descend underground to reach the Jewish Museum. In a literal manner the way into the Jewish museum is through history and it becomes, in effect, a building with no entrance.

23. Studio Libeskind, Jewish Museum, Berlin (1999).

At the foot of the staircase Libeskind then introduces another of his narrative devices: the road of continuity. This sloping path leads up towards the main staircase, connecting the exhibition galleries grouped around the void. Intersecting with this road are two others: the road of exile and the road of the Holocaust. The first of these leads visitors out into an enclosed garden, dedicated by Libeskind to the writer E. T. A. Hoffman, author of *The Sandman*, who worked in the adjacent Baroque building, comprised of a grid of tall concrete pillars with trees growing from their tops. The base of the garden slopes, juxtaposing with the regularity of the columns. This leads to a feeling of disorientation and despite the massive quality of the architectural elements, instability. Even more dramatic is the culmination of the road of the Holocaust. Here a heavy steel door opens into a tall empty tower faintly lit through a slot at high level. The door closes with a thud and there is a sudden change in temperature. If at times the device of narrative layers seems abstract and distant from the experience of actually being in this building, at this point the narrative reads with horrifying clarity. Libeskind, echoing Theodore Adorno's phrase 'to write poetry after Auschwitz is barbaric', described this space as 'the end of the Museum. The end of all museums',[11] as if the possibility of a museum was negated in the face of the Holocaust.

The Jewish Museum was first opened to the public without a display of the collections. This exposed a programme for the building that can now only be recovered through text or by a kind of archaeology. The exhibitions installed in the galleries could be nothing but inadequate in the circumstances. Libeskind acknowledges that these spaces were always intended for displays. Speaking of the discontinuous 'structural' void running through the building, Libeskind said:

> The void is a physical space which is part of the city, and it is also a reminder that however many objects you bring to the Museum, essentially the only way to connect with Berlin is across the Void.[12]

Nevertheless, the greater emotional narrative of the building is, at times, lost amongst the cacophony of stories being told by objects, graphics and audio-visual material. This comes about, not just because the architecture of the building has within it its own story, but because this integral story is one of tragedy. Libeskind is right to assert that the Holocaust tower 'ends the Museum'. The experience of the tower points out the absence at the heart of this strand of history. The exhibitions in the Jewish Museum fill that absence. The exhibits negate Libeskind's proposition that this is 'the end of the Museum', and they turn the museum back into a problem: how do objects relate history and where is the line between interpretation and truth? All of Libeskind's attention is directed towards absences, whether physical or conceptual: the discontinuous void, the empty tower, the routes of exile and deportation,

> What I have tried to say is that the Jewish history of Berlin is not separable from the history of Modernity, from the destiny of this incineration of history; they are bound together. But bound not through any obvious forms, but rather through a negativity; through an absence of meaning of history and an absence of artifacts.[13]

The building has, by definition, a physical presence but it looks unfixed and restless. The Jewish Museum is comprised of texts: the walls are in the process of dematerialization; a commentary on the burning of the books and the building of the Wall. Next to the solid rectilinear form of its Baroque neighbour it is like a building in flight, as if it is taking a complex route to avoid detection and capture.

The Jewish Museum can never represent everything that Libeskind has put into it. Jacques Derrida described it as 'a ghostly gift to the people of Berlin'[14] as if it is the spectre of history and maybe even the spectre of Libeskind's own design. The Star of David is not physically inscribed onto the form of the city; the pavement on which the building is constructed is not papered with the names of exiles and the dead. Inevitably, some of the names given to the spaces by Libeskind have been replaced. The E. T. A. Hoffmann Garden is now the Garden of Exiles, the project has passed from idea to building and is no longer known as *Between the Lines*. So the building takes its place as another archaeological site with meanings to be unearthed in the future. On my first visit, a guide told me that the number of steps between the basement and the exhibition space was significant in that they corresponded to the number of layers of understanding (49) for each verse of the Torah. I have found no other reference to this but the guide's observation serves to highlight the impossible complexity of the process of moving from idea to form, bound up, as this process is, in history, text, the personal associations of the designer and the associations brought to the space by the visitor. Libeskind often prefaces talks on the Jewish Museum with a slide showing his passport bearing the inscription of a German immigration official that his entrance was allowed so that he could work on the commission to design the Jewish Museum. This is yet another text buried under the fabric of the museum.

Osnabrück (*Museum Without Exit*)

While working on the Jewish Museum, Libeskind won a commission for a smaller building in the western German city of Osnabrück. The programme for this museum, like the Berlin project, has its roots in Jewish history and in the Holocaust. The Jewish painter Felix Nussbaum was born in Osnabrück in 1904. He left Germany in 1932 to study in Rome and was never to return. Instead, he and his wife, the painter Felka Platek, travelled around Europe staying in Monte Carlo, Paris, Ostend and Brussels where, in 1940, Nussbaum was arrested by the invading German army. He then escaped from an internment camp in the south of France and re-joined his wife in Brussels. They were to remain in hiding until their discovery by the Wehrmacht in 1944. They were then deported, eventually being sent to Auschwitz where they were both killed. In his years of exile and flight Nussbaum continued to paint and is especially famous for a series of stark self-portraits that reflect the fate of the Jews under the Nazis.

In this project Libeskind was presented with a microcosm of his concerns in the Jewish Museum. Here was the story of one man's flight and murder to be told through the meeting of his paintings and the building that was to house them. There was the possibility here to make a linear narrative: a tragic story with a beginning, a middle and an end. Instead, Libeskind opens up the telling of Nussbaum's personal story and places it in a number of contexts that transcend the strictly chronological: the urban (Osnabrück), the historical (the Nazis and the Holocaust) and the social (collective memory).

> These [existing] buildings are treated as the familiar, yet solitary, everyday figures, while the entire site is reorganised around the nexus of a new topography that connects the town back onto itself. The

Nussbaum Museum becomes the link to a lost history. It acts as a transformer transmitting the mysterious irreversibility of time and destiny.[15]

Unlike the Jewish Museum, the Osnabrück building has an identifiable entrance of its own. This is at the end of a bridge that sails over the remains of an arched Roman structure. The door opens into a narrow space so that visitors' expectations are immediately undermined. There is no grand foyer here, no space for orientation. The entrance is aligned with one of three distinct elements of the building's composition: the 'Nussbaum-Gang' a long, enclosed, concrete box. From here the route leads into the beginning of the exhibition within the 'Nussbaum-Haus'. This contains the painter's work from his Berlin years. This, in turn, connects back to the enclosed space of the Nussbaum-Gang in which the paintings from the years of exile are shown. The last element of the composition is the 'Nussbaum-Bruck' in which his last works are shown. There is, therefore, a straightforward chronological breakdown of the museum's narrative. But each of the three elements works in other ways too. The materials for each component are different, going from timber cladding for the 'house', to concrete for the 'road' to steel for the 'bridge'. The alignments of the various parts are also dictated by other influences. The house points to the site of a synagogue burnt on *Kristalnacht*, the Nussbaum-Gang splits the site like a compass point making spaces looking towards Berlin and Hamburg and towards the locations of Nussbaum's exiles and eventual death in Auschwitz. The bridge building connects the other to the original museum that has its own tragic associations: it was once the headquarters of the local Nazi party.

The works of Nussbaum and of Libeskind reach a synthesis in this building. The architecture does not distance itself from the work of the painter but becomes engaged with it in a complex dialogue. At times one or the other dominates but there is never a sense of them reading as separate projects. In the Nussbaum-Gang the space is much narrower than a conventional display area would dictate. Libeskind explains that this reflects Nussbaum's working methods at the time the paintings were created, in attics and small rooms with no distance to stand back. Libeskind talks about the experience that he wants to make accessible:

I tried not to be sentimental about Nussbaum. But one could really look into those days and see a message which is like the message lost in a bottle and coincidentally found somewhere. Who can possibly know what that message is and what can be passed on: what statement, which code? I thought that one should pass on everything in that message, including the darkness, the inarticulateness, the opacity and that which cannot become analysis.[16]

But of course, Libeskind in his unsentimental approach to Nussbaum retains a personal response and it is this that makes the Osnabrück building and the Jewish Museum so affecting. These were also buildings whose designs were generated by years of architectural research in a period in which Libeskind built very little. Subsequently Libeskind chose to operate within the architectural system of commissions, competitions and built projects such as in the projects discussed below for Manchester and London. The Jewish Museum and the Nussbaum-Haus contain tragic and delirious narratives of events that are inherent to their conception. The Delirious Museum is characterized by its complexity and by its ability to balance opposites. 'Both and' rather than 'either or'. The narratives contained within these two museums are personal *and* historical as well as subjective *and* objective. The layouts of the buildings and the reference points of the designs can be seen ranging across a spectrum from clarity (surface) to obscurity (archaeology). In later works, whatever the merits of the designs, delirium becomes no more than an architectural style.

Manchester (*Earth/Time*)

The area of Manchester and Salford, England, around the Ship Canal is one of those urban developments that look as if they come out of a brochure. There is a large mall, a designer bridge, mirror-glass office blocks and a spectacular cultural centre – the Lowry. This last was designed by Michael Wilford and contains theatres, restaurants and galleries devoted to the faux-naif painter T. S. Lowry. It is a striking composition of forms clad in glass and the titanium with which the Guggenheim Bilbao is also covered. Across the canal and across the bridge is the Imperial War Museum North (1997–2001) by Studio

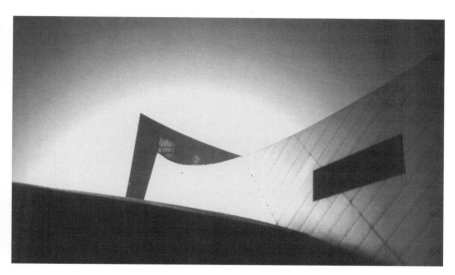

24. Studio Libeskind, Imperial War Museum North, Manchester (1997), Water, Earth and Air Shards.

Libeskind. This too has a metal skin but here there is none of the visual relief that comes with the transparency of glass walls. The three forms, which Libeskind calls 'shards', that make up the building sit on a solid black socle that gives nothing away to the surrounding environment. The shards represent air, earth and water and are curved as if torn from the earth's crust. The simple diagram that explains this concept is reproduced in the museum for visitors' information. It shows the globe with lines of latitude and longitude, then the globe with the shards splitting away from it followed by the shards floating in space then coming together in the basic form of the building. For Libeskind, the violence of this gesture is mirrored by the museum's subject matter. The immediate site does not allow for much development of context. Behind the building sits the large block of a flour-mill, the rest of the immediate surroundings are carpark and the flat impassive expanse of the waterway. In acknowledgement of this (and the peculiarly difficult nature of the subject) Libeskind sites the entrance in a discreet corner facing the road, turned away from the waterway and the spectacular Lowry Centre. The straight path marked out in the tarmac cuts across a zig-zagging pattern as if in memory of the Jewish Museum, but here the straight line is continuous and the zig-zag is like a shadow traced on the ground.

The 'entrance' sits at the junction of the Air and Earth Shards but turns out to be a bluff. The Air Shard is a tower and is, in fact, open to the elements. The skin here is broken and so the connection to air is real. The tower is a deliberately ambiguous outside/inside space. The pathway twists round to a set of doors marking the entrance to the Earth Shard and this time it is clear that the visitor is really entering a museum space. Continuing the theme of the ambiguous entrance door, the route, taking visitors up to the first floor, is twisting and unresolved. The front desk, shop and café sit awkwardly in a series of spaces on the ground floor. These, in turn, connect to a staircase that starts wide but narrows down as it rises. The main exhibits are housed on the first floor, sitting under the roof of the Earth Shard. The floor of the main space is curved – sloping away from the entrance door. Just beyond this point a small metal cross is let into the surface of the floor marking a notional North Pole in the shattered crust. The lines of longitude and latitude are also represented in the asphalt floor. This floor slopes down past a series of exhibits built on and around tall 'silos' made to contain the bulk of the exhibits and large-scale artefacts, like a Harrier Jump Jet and an eerily lit Trabant car. The effects of these two approaches to exhibition, the conceptual and the object-based, sit uneasily together. The feeling of disquiet brought on by the sloping floor bumps into the brutal solidity of the artefacts and the more bluntly didactic audio-visual presentations that occur at timed intervals throughout the day. There is some of the same sensation here as at the Jewish Museum in that the programme for an exhibition can never synchronize with the deliberate complexity of the building. In some ways, the main exhibition space of the Imperial War Museum is nothing more than a shed but it is a shed tuned to an awkward philosophical relationship to its programme.

The Water Shard contains the restaurant and has views out to the Ship Canal. But the most dramatic narrative element of the building is that of the Air Shard. This contains no exhibition and has no function other than that applied by the architect. Here the shard is turned on its end and within the void there is a staircase and lift. The lift travels up through the void attached to the side of the structure. Inside this void the steel structure criss-crosses the space. Arriving at the viewing area, the walkway leads through a tunnel and out into an open space. From here the city can be seen apparently sliding away to the east, an optical illusion caused by the irregularly shaped opening in the wall. Views out through the vertical cladding of the tower further distort the panorama. Here is the city seen in stop-frame, fractured in space and time. But as the museum sits on the edge of a site for urban regeneration there is almost no city there; only its ruins. Turning back towards the tunnel, the optical illusions continue with the concrete enclosure of the staircase and the floor appearing to slope at wild angles. The floor exaggerates the sense of disorientation as the angled grid now looks as if it is falling away and there is a clear view down to the ground. While the Earth Shard is self-contained and inward looking, the Air Shard connects to the city, its immediate context, in a direct and unsettling way.

The composition of the building mimics then distorts an unlikely typological precedent: in its most basic reading it resembles one of the big sheds of the city edge. The Earth Shard (exhibition space) and

Water Shard (ancillary accommodation) act as the mother and baby form of out-of-town retail warehouses. The Air Shard is a marker – the sign to be seen from the road. Onto this programme Libeskind has overlaid his own concerns and those generated by the building type. Compared to the spectacular architectural compositions and juxtaposed materials of the adjacent Lowry Centre, the Imperial War Museum is a difficult, even ugly and broken, object. If the Jewish Museum and the Felix Nussbaum Museum are tragic in their conception, then this building comes out of sudden, earth-shattering trauma.[17] The building shares certain stylistic tropes (such as the scattered ceiling pattern with lighting built into slots and the acutely angled walls) with the Berlin and Osnabrück projects. The IWM North's 'subject' is equally complex, but here the narrative is much simpler: the earth shattered by conflict, the disorientation of war. In this it is not just a scaled-down version of the Jewish Museum but is a different kind of design, one less personal and also less resonant. The meaning of Libeskind's passport has been diluted: he is now an international architect with studios in various countries with their own impetus. With each step of this undertaking there is the feeling that Libeskind is moving away from the archaeological complexity of his first built works. He is still deeply engaged with both memorials and with memory. But what kind of memory is more likely to come into play here: the individual, the collective or the institutional?

London/Rotterdam
(*The Spiral*/Beyond the Wall 26.36°)

In both Berlin and Manchester, Libeskind's spaces are ultimately diminished by their exhibits. In his exhibition Beyond the Wall 26.36°, at the Netherlands Architecture Institute in Rotterdam in 1997, Libeskind was able to plan the spaces and the exhibits in parallel. This exhibition was a review of Libeskind's work to-date, governed by his then most recent but now defunct project, the *Spiral* for the Victoria & Albert Museum in London.[18] Models and drawings were built into a series of plinths and walls that emerged from the floor, sailing in a progression of folding plates up into the large exhibition hall. The display structure was, in effect, a prototype of the V&A proposal. The 'catalogue' box accompanying the show contained a variety of objects relating to the project: reproductions of Libeskind's sketchbooks and those of the engineer Cecil Balmond, a cut-out card model of the basic structure, a file of working drawings and a flicker book of the *Spiral*'s fractal growth. The exhibition and the box together represented a delirious celebration of the project that almost served to render the notion of completing the building void. What emerged from each of these projects (exhibition and catalogue) was a building with a structural impetus obliquely responding to the programme for the museum extension. The *Spiral* proposal was on the verge of being a building with no purpose other than being 'itself'. Libeskind, in conversation in 1996, talked about the V&A as 'an enigma, an incredible system of accretion, a secret city'.[19] This echoes Robert Harbison's description of the V&A:

> The four floors are not 1, 2, 3, 4 but 1, A, 2, B – as it were two systems present in the same place ... Two-things-in-the-same-place of the scheme is echoed by a bifurcation of the displays into galleries which show all kinds of object of a certain period and galleries containing a certain class of objects in all periods.[20]

The *Spiral* conspired in this overlaying of systems especially as it turned its back so resolutely on conventional gallery space. Libeskind saw the spaces as rooms for: 'projections, laser shows, video presentation and hands-on experience . . .'.[21] Apart from an entrance foyer, the most recognizable type of space was the observation floor at the top, where visitors would have been able to look out over London and the museum's roofscape and, hence, its own history. The fragments that piled up to make the *Spiral* are an accretion of both the 'secret city' of the V&A and what Borges called 'the red and peaceful maze of London'.[22] Here was a coming-together of two labyrinths in a structure ostensibly intended as an organizational tool but that was actually an instrument of further chaos.

Libeskind called the *Spiral* a 'Gateway to the twenty-first century'[23] and said of the Victoria & Albert: 'The V&A was not conceived as a repository for objects or a container for passivity and nostalgia.'[24] This sets out Libeskind's concerns clearly, but omits to consider the subversive power of the object. The meanings attached to the things in the collections of the V&A are transitory and open in the same way that the meaning of Libeskind's architecture aspires to open-ness. So long as he denies the importance of objects, his relationship with museums (and, especially, the Delirious Museum) remains compromised. The Osnabrück museum is a synthesis between objects (painting and building) and subject that is not resolved in his other museum work. The intense emotional, historical and personal narrative of the Jewish Museum's architecture is reduced by the imposition of displays. In Manchester the most effective component of the building is the visceral experience of the Air Shard, a space devoid of exhibits. The problem of the *Spiral* was that it would become a glorified foyer that, like the Great Court of the British Museum, would create an imbalance between showpiece architecture and the difficult territory of museum displays. In 1979 Libeskind made a set of drawings called *Micromegas* with the subtitle 'The Architecture of End Space'. Writing in the catalogue of an exhibition of these drawings and recent building models at the Soane Museum in 2001, Libeskind wrote:

> The Micromega drawings, unlike the fragmented ruins collected by Soane at the end of an era, are constructed lineaments of my project in architecture. A project that continues across ruins of buildings, yet itself can never be ruined because it is wholly spiritual and thoroughly precise in its anticipatory hope.[25]

The exhibition at the Soane, unlike many similar shows in this labyrinthine space that spread virus-like throughout the museum, occupied only the purpose-built display gallery and the Breakfast Room. Libeskind acknowledged the complexity of this latter space in his catalogue essay referring to it as 'a model of a model and a projection for us today of a non-existent building'[26] and making allusions to *Alice Through the Looking Glass*. But there is a sense in which he distances his own project from that of the Soane Museum and, by implication, all museums. Libeskind's business is with architecture and its direct relationship with people. In his project there is no room for the intermediary that is the delirious reading of the object. His architecture is complex and vital and yet it is about the redeeming possibilities of architecture as pure form unsullied by the ambiguous detritus of the past. It is as if he wants to replace objects with the idea of architecture and negate the narratives held within these objects through the production of built form. But in this he is replacing melancholy with tragedy.

11

LOS ANGELES: THE HIDDEN MUSEUM

A long time before I visited Los Angeles, I knew a version of it from a guidebook.[1] I could never quite believe the juxtapositions and oddity, the delirium, of the city's attractions. I read the guidebook as if it was a novel, not knowing what would happen next. I read about the Max Factor Museum with its gothic devices for the 'measurement' of beauty, the fantastic themed architecture of the movie houses and the object buildings, like the famous hat-shaped Brown Derby Restaurant. Fifteen years elapsed before I got to know the real Los Angeles and, in the meantime, different versions of Los Angeles had come and gone.

Los Angeles is unlike the other cities described up to this point in the book. It is not that it has no history or that it has no regard for its history. Rather it is a city whose history is short and one where the past is often effaced as if in a caricature of capitalist consumption in the pursuit of the new. These, in themselves, are reasons to compare Los Angeles to the 'old' cities of Europe. Another significant factor in this equation is that LA's past is celluloid-thin. Its visible history consists largely of light passing through film rather than as a collection of architectural relics. Scarpa, Stirling and Libeskind have all produced work within a long historical tradition and, like Soane before them, have made use of the palimpsest in the form of history, memory and place. If the Delirious Museum can be made and not just evolve, then it is important to track it down in 'new' places where the palimpsest, if it exists at all, is certainly not apparent.

In his book, *Circus Americanus*,[2] Ralph Rugoff has explored Los Angeles as a series of vitrines. These are not just the vitrines of the museum but are also those other glass screens between viewer and 'object': the car windscreen, the television or the lens of the movie camera. This is reminiscent of the window in Edgar Allan Poe's story 'The Man of the

Crowd' discussed in Chapter 2 and of Baudelaire's statement: 'to feel oneself everywhere at home; to see the world and yet to remain hidden from the world'. These screens are for looking through as well as looking at and for hiding behind. In Rugoff's version of the city, all experience is mediated by at least one layer of glass. This sense of being remote from 'real' life is not, of course, entirely positive but it forms a basis for understanding the American urban condition at the start of the 21st century. Rugoff says 'in Southern California . . . we seemed to be heading towards a future in which we would become the curators of our own lives'.[3] This has echoes of both Andy Warhol and the Situationists. Does Rugoff's statement mean that the museum has no 'function' in this context? In Los Angeles, is the museum entirely redundant or has it, instead, expanded into everyday life, beyond the built space within which it is more usually contained?

The single most visited tourist attraction in LA is the Getty Center, located high above the Santa Monica Freeway. It has its own past – a kind of invented pre-history in the form of the J. Paul Getty Museum. This was in Malibu, up a wooded canyon off the Pacific Coast Highway and was the second home of the collection.[4] It had begun its life in John Paul Getty's own ranch-style house at the top of this canyon. When the collection moved down to the new building, strict rules were introduced regarding access to the museum. Visitors by car had to pre-book to ensure a parking place. Those who arrived by bus had to show a validated ticket at the entrance. Needless to say most visitors did come by car but these cars were made to disappear before visitors encountered the museum itself. The long driveway lead to a wall with an open colonnade on top. This wall formed the entrance to the semi-submerged carpark and on top of the carpark sat a huge peristyle garden. In 1955 Getty, the oil baron, published a novella called 'A Journey to Corinth'[5] in which he describes in some detail the construction of a villa in Herculaneum, near Neapolis, the ancient Naples. The owner of the villa, a wealthy Roman, makes a collection of Greek statuary from the sale of works looted in the sack of Corinth. The villa described by Getty in his story is one that existed, the Villa dei Papiri, and there is considerable archaeological evidence of its form, as it was buried in the eruption of Vesuvius in AD 79. When, in the late 1960s, Getty had to find a new home for his expanding collection he turned to this source to provide his model museum. The parallels between the sites and the functions of the villa and the museum are numerous. There are similarities of climate and light between southern California and the Bay of Naples and both live under the threat of imminent destruction, one from a volcano, the other from earthquake. The Roman villa was a place of refuge for its owner and it was a place in which great art (often of Greek origin or Roman copies from Greek models) could be contemplated. As the 'Guide' to the museum says: '. . . the reborn villa embodies Mr. Getty's fantasies about the men he thought of as his antecedents in Imperial Rome . . .'.[6] There is even a justification for the parking garage as a levelling device similar to Roman vaulting. The museum is a pleasant, if unnerving, hyper-real environment. There is, however, nothing ersatz about this building; this is not the stuff of clip-on portico Beverly Hills. Yet, despite all the positive aspects of the choice of building for the museum, there was still something of the uncanny about the place. Reyner Banham said of it:

> The erudition and workmanship are as impeccable, and absolutely deathly, as this kind of pluperfect reconstruction must always be . . . no blood was spilled here, nor sperm, nor wine, nor other vital juice.[7]

The justification for the choice of architectural environment was, in effect, a smoke screen. What the Getty Villa achieves, first by seclusion, then by control of access, and ultimately through the architecture, is a sense of detachment from its immediate environment. The villa, prior to the construction of the Getty Center, was the 'front of house' for an organization with such huge resources that it has been accused in the past of upsetting the balance of acquisitions in the art and antiquities market. Their policy of acquisition has expanded from ancient art and 'Old Masters' to important works by the Impressionists and photography. Many museums are notorious for the amount of material in storage and not on show but the Getty is an institution famous, respected and, even, distrusted not just for what it has but for what it can acquire. This sense of wealth pervaded the museum. No expense was spared; the objects were individually considered and placed, the environment was, in Banham's word, 'pluperfect'. The location, the building and the collection conspired to create what the Surrealists called an *objet deluxe*, something to be appreciated in purely aesthetic terms, an artefact with almost no attachment to the everyday: the Principality of Getty.

As if to reinforce the naturalness of the situation, the museum produced an activity box for children called 'Make Your Own Museum'. This consisted of a series of fold-out galleries and floor patterns, some punch-out museum objects and a small didactic book. This was the *Boîte-en-valise* for hobbyists. It was made into a literal portable museum with its own walls, floors, objects and two-dimensional visitors. The accompanying book went from a fairly sober analysis of the origin of museums, through some suggestions for laying out the cardboard museum with the objects provided, to a double-page spread illustrating less orthodox forms of display. One showed an over-sized bendi-toy woman presiding over a cage of tiny wild animals; another had a parade of toy cows on their way in to view an exhibition of coloured pencils. The museum structure around which this was based and which the children could work within was, of course, the J. Paul Getty Museum. The idea here was not, after all, to 'make your own museum' but to act as a guest curator within the Getty institution.

The J. Paul Getty Museum was clearly outgrowing its home. A perfect evocation of a Roman villa has limits to how it can be extended. So the museum acquired a new site where it could be re-united with the other parts of the Getty cultural organization. The chosen site for the Getty Center is on top of a hill some miles inland. After a competition in 1983, Richard Meier was chosen as the architect. The group of buildings designed by Meier bears a close resemblance to an acropolis. As the Getty had a history of being housed in a version of domestic, though undoubtedly grand, classical architecture, clearly the next step was to call upon the monumental side of that tradition. Unlike the villa, Meier's buildings do not engage in games of classical stylistic verisimilitude. Individually, they are recognizable as Meier's work:[8] complex geometric forms composed of curves and grids with the museum buildings clad in marble, as opposed to the enamel panels usually associated with his work. The parallels with the Acropolis of Athens are, though, inescapable. Here is a symbol of the power of culture as a political force. The new Getty Center is of the city yet rises above it, the acropolis presenting itself to the landscape in a gesture not of integration but of separation. Unlike the original museum, it is not a discreet separation but one which announces its difference to the thousands passing below on the freeways every day. This is the museum invoking the city through its design. However, the city invoked is not the Los Angeles of crime, riot and pollution. Nor is it the two-dimensional Tinseltown Los Angeles. If the old Getty Museum sat at the heart of a benign principality, then the Getty Center is the citadel of a city-state. The old villa/museum, despite its recreation of a domestic setting, had something still of the Soane's house/museum. On its hill above the Santa Monica Freeway the Getty declares itself to be part of an international movement of museum super-buildings.

The car-parking is off-site and the journey up the mountainside is undertaken by monorail. This is the kind of 'ride' singularly absent from the public transportation system, but which is available elsewhere in the theme park version of Los Angeles. At the same time, it is reminiscent of the external 'free-show' Centre Pompidou escalator. In common with the over-the-top, pseudo-environments of LA shopping malls such as Universal CityWalk[9] and 2 Rodeo Drive and the 'gated communities' of Beverly Hills, the Getty Center is a protected secure place, but, unlike them, the Getty has the bonus of cultural cachet.

Meier's plan sets a number of linked pavilions (or temples) around a linear plaza on the hilltop. The pavilions are characterized by the play of geometric forms and overt references to shapes reminiscent of the early modernism of Le Corbusier, in particular the relationship between the grid and the curve seen in the plan of Villa Savoye.[10] Meier has developed this language over many projects with the difference that here this game can be undertaken with little reference to urban context and is on a grand scale. From the central space the gardens and promenades spill out on to the surrounding hillside with views to the distant ocean.

The apparent generosity of the Getty Center is countered by relentless corporate branding. So there remains the lingering impression that this is generosity originating in a detachment from the civic sphere rather than from within it. This impression is ultimately reinforced by the plaza, which is a controlled 'urban' space where spontaneity is unimaginable. And, unlike the camera obscura where the viewer seems to be brought closer to the city, the grandeur of the panoramic vista from the South Promontory effectively detaches the viewer from Los Angeles.

This sense of detachment works into the buildings too. The conviction with which the external architecture fulfils its aims is broken by the interiors of a number of the galleries where a historicist approach to décor and display has been taken. While technical considerations are still at work to provide the best possible environmental conditions for the artworks, many rooms are dressed up in a luxurious pastiche of traditional gallery interiors that sit awkwardly with their immediate surroundings. No doubt the precedent for this was seen as the villa, but here the emphasis has shifted towards the ersatz. Once again the lingering impression is one of money spent.

In J. Paul Getty's story 'A Journey from Corinth', the 'Lansdowne Herakles', one of the statues now in the Getty collection, is acquired by Piso, the patrician, Roman owner of the villa. The statue is later given to the Emperor Nero and then to Hadrian, the builder of the villa at Tivoli outside Rome, and is subsequently taken to England and ultimately the 'New World'. Hadrian's Villa at Tivoli became one of the tropes of post-modern architecture. It is a large complex containing a palace, temples and various water features, each evoking some significant place in the emperor's memory. The villa sits in a valley looking inward at what is, if not a microcosm of the world, at least an artificial miniature city. The Getty Center takes this model and inverts it, the fortress perched on the hilltop, declaring its difference from, and even its superiority to its surroundings. What form would the Getty Center have taken to remain, like the Getty Museum, in the realm of the delirious? This was clearly not the project of the Getty administrators, but it would have had to drop the idea of and the word 'Center' and move out into the city, broken up between canyon, beach, neighbourhood and street.

In 1999 the architects Robert Mangurian and Mary-Ann Ray published a book of proposals for the façade of a small museum in Culver City, Los Angeles.[11] They called the project 'Wrapper' and the museum for which they had made their proposals was the Museum of Jurassic Technology (MJT) at 9341 Venice Boulevard. They proposed 40 different 'possible city surfaces' for the museum, the first of which is called 'Ark (1:1)'. In the notes accompanying the collages and drawings that make up the façade proposals, David Wilson, the museum's director, writes about the importance of the image of the Ark for the collection. He makes reference to Noah's Ark, to 'Tradescant's Ark' in Lambeth and to the MJT's own founding collection: that of the Thums, two gardeners from Nebraska.[12]

Wilson and his dedicated team have built up a series of ambiguous displays of life on the forgotten margins that present an alternative to the icy detachment of other Los Angeles museums. If the point of transition (or, indeed, suspension of disbelief) at the Getty Museum was the parking garage wall across the canyon, then at the MJT that point is in the area immediately adjacent to the entrance in the unremarkable storefront on Venice Boulevard. Next door to the museum is Coast Real Estate – a frozen interior that is often mistaken for one of the museum's exhibits.[13] At the threshold of the museum itself the visitor goes from light into dark, from the unfocused space of Los Angeles to a controlled, if labyrinthine, interior world. In an introductory audio-visual display, the Museum of Jurassic Technology is set within a tradition running from cabinets of curiosity through the great collecting and educational institutions of the 19th century. Images that appear in 'Make Your Own Museum' are used here. The first showcase has a model of the box-like and un-seaworthy Ark as it is described in the Bible, rather than the recognizable vessel usually seen in illustrations:

> The length of the ark *shall be* three hundred cubits, the breadth of it fifty cubits, and the height of it thirty cubits . . . A window shalt thou make to the ark, and in a cubit shalt thou finish it above; and the door of the ark shalt thou set in the side thereof; *with* lower, second, and third *stories* shalt thou make it.[14]

The model is carefully constructed with a bite taken out of its side to show the internal compartments for the animals/exhibits. It rocks gently on an invisible flood.

The surrounding exhibits display the origins of the museum in natural history collecting. In an alcove there is the display dealing with

25. The Museum of Jurassic Technology, Culver City, California.

the 'Deprong Mori', a bat found in South America that is able to fly through solid objects. Small showcases contain exhibits dealing with 'Protective Audio Mimicry', 'Corundum by the Verneul Method' and the 'European Mole'. An adjacent gallery contains the exhibition 'Tell the Bees; Belief Knowledge and Hypersymbolic Cognition' with rec-reations of various folk remedies such as 'mouse cures' for bed-wetting and 'duck's breath' for mouth infections. The exhibits here are models displayed in vitrines, glowing in the darkened room in which they are placed. This kind of environment is, of course, the common currency of museums, but David Wilson has recognized the de-stabilizing component of this condition:

> A darkened room full of intensely lit display cases provides a tangle of reflection. We have greatly framed ourselves to see objects and not their reflections, however if we allow ourselves to see what is actually there, the environment is far more complex. Objects float in space while others exist in vitrines from one perspective and disappear from another – two or more objects can share the same physical space and their numbers can be multiplied infinitely. From the prospect of the Museum's patron each of these objects, unverifiable by physical contact, is as real as the next.[15]

This over-laying of meaning lies at the heart of the Museum of Jurassic Technology. In its mixture of the credible and the implausible it asks the viewer to consider the legitimacy of both. At the same time it is both critical of, and enmeshed in, standard museological practice.

In one corner of the museum there is a model of the Iguassú Falls on the border of Paraguay and Brazil. Peering through a peep-hole at this model, visitors can see the proposed, but unbuilt, suspension bridge spanning the falls, neatly encapsulating the idea that two things can exist in a single space at the same time, as the bridge in the exhibit is invisible from all but one viewpoint. This is one of the displays in the Delani/Sonnabend Halls. These rooms contain a series of objects and models detailing the lives of two extraordinary individuals: Madalena Delani, 'a singer of art songs and operatic arias' and Geof-frey Sonnabend, 'a memory researcher and neurophysiologist'. The display and the accompanying publication could be treated as a mani-festo for the museum. The rhetorical tool of the theatre of memory where arguments and salient points are arranged along a route through a series of interconnecting rooms like a collection in a domestic interior pre-dates the founding of museums.[16] However it is relevant by extension to many public displays. It can, for instance, be applied to the Soane Museum, a private collection turned public. Here was an attempt to consolidate the memory of an individual through the display of his collection and work. In fact, the complexity of the thought process (the argument) that created the Soane Museum, for instance, makes the subject (the text) almost impenetrable. In contrast, what the MJT's exhibit explores is the shifting nature of memory.

> Sonnabend believed that long term or 'distant' memory was illusion, but similarly he questioned short term or 'immediate' memory. On a number of occasions Sonnabend wrote, 'there is only experience and its decay' by which he meant to suggest that what we typically call short-term memory is, in fact, our experiencing the decay of an experience.[17]

To back these theories up there are a number of diagrams of 'the cone of obliscence' and 'the plane of experience' intersecting. This could almost be seen as obfuscation, but in the context of the MJT it reads more as a discreet clue to the foundation of the museum.

> 'We, amnesiacs all, condemned to live in an eternally fleeting present, have created the most elaborate of human constructions, memory, to buffer ourselves against the intolerable knowledge of the irreversible passage of time and the irretrieveability of its moments and events.' Geoffrey Sonnabend, *Obliscence: Theories of Forgetting and the Problem of Matter* (Chicago, Northwestern University Press, 1946), pp. 16.[18]

Other exhibits turn abstract notions of memory into three-dimensional displays: one on the 'Proustian' model contains a cup of tea and a petrified 'petite madeleine' biscuit, the taste of which allowed Marcel Proust to travel back in his mind to his childhood. A tiny valve in the display releases the aroma of the biscuit.

The exhibit 'Garden of Eden on Wheels' has as its sub-title 'Selected Collections from Los Angeles Area Mobile Home and Trailer Parks'. These collections are, as one might expect of those living in restricted spaces, minimal. Many collections are made extraordinary through multiplication, profusion and scale. The display in 'Garden of Eden on Wheels' does deal with the collections but the real emphasis of the exhibit lies in the models ranged around the walls of the room showing the trailers themselves. These have been made at about one-twentieth scale and show the trailers in the context in which they were recorded, so they are seen by the highway or under a flyover. And, instead of sitting on the bases of their vitrines, the trailers sit on patches of ground ripped from the earth. The accompanying essay makes much of associations between the Ark and the mobile home as refuge in the face of impending apocalypse and the models reflect this. Like the gently rocking Ark these are floating islands with their plant roots, service cables and sewage pipes trailing in space. But this scaled-down and uprooted piece of context simultaneously deals with detachment and with a connected-ness to the city of Los Angeles. The trailer-home models are like fragments of the city models of Paris and London. They are prototypes for the Los Angeles city model and pre-echoes of that city's much-anticipated destruction. At the same time they refer to archaeology. The particular archaeological imagination of Los Angeles is based on the tar pits of La Brea, adjacent to the Los Angeles County Museum of Art. Here the bones of prehistoric creatures have been discovered in fine states of preservation and full-scale models of the animals have been placed around the rim of the pits. The trailer home models are an alternative to this view of archaeology as something that deals with ancient history. This display highlights an archaeology of the present and of the everyday. There is nothing here that stretches credibility, instead the display itself is the vehicle for putting (at least) two things – in this case ideas – in one place.

Athanasius Kircher was a Jesuit scholar who lived between 1602 and 1680. His biography reads like a fiction but is not.[19] He was born in Geisa in Germany where he escaped death on a number of occasions: he was swept into a mill wheel and emerged unscathed, he fell under the feet of on-coming horses in a race and was once again left unharmed, he got lost in a forest and had to spend the night in a tree to avoid robbers and bears, and he cured himself from gangrenous chillblains, reputedly through prayer. In 1618 he was admitted as a novice to the Jesuit College at Paderborn. In his subsequent travels, many of which were made necessary due to religious strife, he was stranded on an ice floe, fell into the machinery of yet another water wheel and was captured by Protestant troops who wanted to hang him. One soldier spoke up for him and he was spared. Along the way he became interested in science and linguistics and in 1633 he was summoned to Vienna to take the place of Johannes Kepler as mathematician to the Habsburg Court. The trip from Avignon was, once again, full of incident and it led him by a convoluted route to Rome. When he arrived there he discovered that his orders had been changed and he was no longer to go to Vienna but was to stay in Rome at the Collegio Romano, the heart of the Jesuit Order. Apart from one more trip, to Sicily, Malta and Naples, Kircher was to spend the rest of his life there developing his studies in, amongst other subjects, magnetism, hieroglyphs, music, the Tower of Babel, China and subterranean fires.

In the course of his work, Kircher also began to build up a huge collection of artefacts that came together as the Musaeum Kircherianum. This became one of the most important sites for visitors to Rome in the middle of the 17th century. Kircher drew on his own collection assembled on his final trip and on objects returned to Rome by Jesuit missionaries from around the world. Alongside these 'real' artefacts were facsimiles of obelisks executed in wood and Kircher's own inventions such as perpetual motion machines, a magic lantern and catoptric (reflected light) cameras. In 1770, 90 years after Kircher's death, Charles Burney visited the museum: 'The curiosities which I chiefly went to see were Father Kircher's musical instruments and machines, described in his *Musurgia*: they are now almost all out of order . . .'.[20] Kircher's ideas on the translation of hieroglyphs were later discredited when a definitive reading was obtained through Jean François Champollion's work on the Rosetta Stone, and the rest of Kircher's reputation seems to have been swept away at the same time. Many of his theories were overtaken by those of Newton and Boyle and their followers but what is left is an entire system of possible science running in parallel to prevailing scientific beliefs.

At the Museum of Jurassic Technology there is a display dealing with Kircher and it seeks to re-introduce the Jesuit scholar's work into a real space, rather than an imaginary one.[21] The 'impossible'

Magnetic Oracle invented by Kircher is made manifest in the exhibition, as are a 'botanical clock', a 'bell wheel' and his Baroque vision of Egyptian pyramids. In the frontispiece to the catalogue of the Musæum Kircherianum published in 1678, the collection is called a 'theatre of nature and art' in an acknowledgement of the mix of the found and the made that is also visible in the accompanying illustration. The viewpoint in the illustration is an artificial one, above the heads of the three visitors to the museum and shows a high, domed room with a long vaulted space opening off it down one side. In the foreground there are two wooden obelisks and above them are cosmological scenes painted onto the domes. Shelves full of archaeological artefacts line one wall and portrait busts are displayed on plinths running down the side of the long gallery. Nature is represented by shells, a hanging crocodile and by a skeleton standing on top of a table.

In discussing the Musæum Kircherianum, Paula Findlen has said:

> . . . the Collegio Romano museum was the central axis through which all accounts of Rome, and of Rome's unique relationship to the world, intersected. For this reason, Kircher and his disciples constantly praised his museum as a 'theatre of the city and the world'.[22]

The Museum of Jurassic Technology in its position on the edge of museum culture cannot occupy an equivalent position for Los Angeles, but it is certainly a delirious 'theatre of the city and the world'.

Los Angeles is a city with a relatively short history and therefore a relatively short memory.[23] All the more reason, perhaps, that the examination of the past should be such an urgent concern. It would be a mistake to confuse this relative 'newness' with insubstantiality. As the Museum of Jurasssic Technology proves, it is possible to engage with the past at the personal level of human memory – in the form of its exhibits, or on the level of an institution – the (delirious) museum itself and its relationship to its predecessors. However, by removing itself by one degree from the rational narratives of most museums, the MJT ultimately challenges the preconceptions both of its predecessors and of its, much larger, neighbours.

12

LAS VEGAS: THE PAST SURE IS TENSE[1]

And you, forgotten, your memories ravaged by all the consternations of two hemispheres, stranded in the Red Cellars of Pali-Kao, without music and without geography, no longer setting out for the haçienda where the roots think of the child and where the wine is finished off with fables from an old almanac. Now that's finished. You'll never see the haçienda. It doesn't exist.

The haçienda must be built.

Ivan Chtcheglov[2]

One of the first responses I had coming to Nevada was whether this was really part of the United States.

Joe Yablonsky, former FBI chief[3]

This is a final itinerary, a last drift governed by spectacle, situation and history. It takes place in the assemblage of absurd spaces that is Las Vegas. In the spirit of the city itself, this drift is characterized by loss and unfulfilled dreams. Some of the strategies I use are stolen from the Situationists. Subtitles are taken from 'Formulary for a New Urbanism' by Ivan Chtcheglov.[4] This text is the most complete description of a Situationist city, one that is structured around human need and desire rather than capitalist contingency. Several writers on post-modernism have used Las Vegas as a paradigm.[5] My aim, by contrast, is to reclaim it from both capitalism and post-modernism for the Delirious Museum. So what follows is a collection of architecture, proto-museums, wayward stories and connections. Las Vegas shares a technique with many contemporary museums in the way that it attempts to contain narrative. The project of the Delirious Museum is to subvert this position and to take narrative apart using certain urban strategies. In examining one of the most 'scripted' cities, I want to find the cracks in the surface so that I can unearth more 'exhibits' for my Delirious Museum.

The Bizarre Quarter

On 27 January 1951, the walls of Las Vegas shook, windows broke and people were thrown out of their beds. The first in a series of A-bomb tests had just occurred in the desert about 65 miles north-west of the city. This was a long-anticipated event – it had been under discussion for some years previously. Anxiety in Las Vegas soon gave way to an air of excitement over the blasts. Even before the end of the first run of tests, called Operation Ranger, visitors had started to indulge in dawn parties to watch the mushroom cloud rising over the horizon. A favourite spot for these was the rooftop restaurant of the Desert Inn. In 1955 a local celebrity, the stripper Lili St Cyr, timed her wedding at El Rancho Casino to coincide with a nuclear test. Vegas had turned destruction into mass spectacle.

El Rancho was converted from a motel to a resort casino in 1941 – the first casino to be built outside the city limits – and it began the rapid development of the Strip out along the old Highway 91.[6] Up to then the centre of the gambling industry had been Fremont Street. The 'old' view of Las Vegas is based on Fremont – flickering walls of light, eternal day outside, eternal night inside. In 1995 the street underwent a renewal by the Jerde Partnership, the architects responsible for Universal CityWalk in Los Angeles. CityWalk is an entirely constructed environment; a 'virgin' site within a part of the Universal Movie Studios lot. Its connection to the city exists solely by road and by association. There are fountains and a 'street' which is open to the sky; it is an urban spectacle composed as if from a checklist. It has been described as a 'trailer' for the city[7] and as the 'scripted space *par excellence*'.[8] Ralph Rugoff describes it as 'a funeral monument to the idea of public space . . . an embalmed street that's been prettied up for an open casket viewing'.[9] In Las Vegas Jerde had to work with some existing bits of city. Over Fremont, a vaulted structure has been built covering a new pedestrianized zone. Here the architects didn't need to make a new street – merely re-invent it. This being Vegas, the vault is composed of thousands of lights which are programmed to run a show at half-hour intervals. Among its many variations this *son et lumière* reproduces an aerobatic flypast and a stampede of buffalo. This is the Passage de l'Opéra documented by Aragon in *Paris Peasant* and demolished in 1929, rebuilt in 1995 as flashy spectacle. It is the arcade celebrated by Benjamin, where Modernism was born, taken to its absurd, Disneyfied conclusion. The transformations take place, not in the enclosed, hermetic world of the wax museum, as they did for Breton at the Musée Grévin, but in the space of the city itself.

The expansion of Las Vegas that El Rancho heralded was taken up next by the Last Frontier Resort in 1942, a mile down Highway 91. As part of this development there was a 'Frontier Village' that included a number of buildings rescued from older towns. The 'Little Church of the West', that was also included in the Frontier Village is said to be a copy of one from a Californian mining town. It was first moved in 1944, from one side of the Strip to the other. In 1979 it was moved in order make way for the Fashion Mall to the opposite end of the Strip, into the grounds of the Hacienda Casino.

The Hacienda and the Red Cellars of Pali-Kao

Immediately after the demise of the Situationist International, Debord, writing in a modest publication documenting the garden of fellow Situationist Asger Jorn, said:

> ... could one not have appeased the Situationists around 1960 by means of a few lucidly conceived recuperative reforms, that is, by giving them two or three cities to construct instead of pushing them to the edge and forcing them to unleash into the world the most dangerous subversion there ever was?[10]

Of the 'two or three cities' that the Situationists should have been given, one of them would have been Las Vegas, if not the whole city, then at least a casino. Instead there is only the coincidence of a name. Architecturally, the Hacienda, which should have been the Situationists' own casino, was unlike many of its neighbours in its simple curved façade and plain tower marking the entrance. The owners had, in a small way, begun the popularization of Las Vegas by attracting family visitors through building several swimming pools and a go-kart track in the casino's early days in 1956. In addition, the Hacienda was close to the airport from which it flew its own fleet of planes for the tourists of Chicago and New York. On 1 January 1996, after a display of fireworks, the Hacienda was detonated for public entertainment. Fire tore through rooms behind glass-less windows. There was a dramatic explosion at the base of the building, but when the dust had cleared, the central tower of the casino was still largely intact, standing at a wild angle. The following morning the tower was finally demolished by wrecking ball. Its place in Las Vegas mythology has been secured by its refusal to go quietly in demolition. The Hacienda was destroyed to make way for a new casino hotel called, at its inception, 'Project Paradise'. But, like projects named by Daniel Libeskind, buildings here change their titles over time. 'Project Paradise' eventually metamorphosed into the less ambitious sounding 'Mandalay Bay', a vast complex of hotel, casino and leisure facilities catering for the new family visitors to Las Vegas. Nothing is as it seems here, even the theme (some vague geographic space that refers to Borneo) is unstable. So there are various 'modern'-looking eateries, including the Red Square Restaurant, its colossal statue of Lenin decapitated in a farcical echo of the real trauma that was the fall of eastern bloc Europe; the end of history in a place that could not exist without history. It is as if the Hacienda has already been replaced by the Red Cellars of Pali-Kao; a place without geography and with piped soft-rock instead of music. Even the street name Hacienda Avenue has been excised from the vicinity of the Strip. It still exists, but only as a continuation of Mandalay Bay Road a block away on the other side of the freeway. So even in this town of permanent renewal, names exist as palimpsests pushed out to the edges.

The Little Church of the West had, meanwhile, been put on the National Register of Historic Places. This building is as 'authentic' as Las Vegas gets so, in order to avoid destruction, it was moved once more to its fourth location on the other side of the Strip.

26. Hacienda Avenue, Las Vegas.

The hotel of the epoch

To the north of the Hacienda/Project Paradise/Mandalay Bay, the immediate next-door neighbour is the Great Pyramid of Cheops – reconstituted in negative in black glass and displaced from Egypt via Lincoln's Inn Fields and the Louvre. It is formally called 'The Luxor. The Next Wonder of the World'. This, as the publicity says, is 'the only 30-storey pyramid shaped hotel in the world'. On its 'attraction floor' there is a reproduction of King Tutankhamun's Tomb as discovered by Howard Carter in 1922. In a display case at the start of the exhibition is an undistinguished lump of stone from the pyramid at Giza, a gift of the Egyptian government. Visitors are guided round the exhibition by 'Howard Carter' speaking on an audio tour. As Mark C. Taylor has pointed out,[11] the display, by showing a reproduction of the outer of three coffins of Tut's sarcophagus, draws attention to the absence of the body at the heart of the pyramid. All that was solid becomes void. Needless to say the Egyptian theme is carried on elsewhere in the casino: there is the Pharoah's Pheast Buffet, the Nile Deli and the Ra Nightclub. The pyramid is guarded by a huge cartoon sphinx that doubles as the monorail station. The dead eyes of the sphinx stare out at an obelisk in the carpark. When the hotel opened it was possible to take a tour along the 'Nile' – 'a 15 minute guided boat tour of Luxor filled with Egyptian History'.[12]

This has echoes of Des Essientes' imagined and aborted travels in J.-K. Huysmans' novel *A Rebours* (1884). First, he reproduces a ship's cabin within his dining room in order to recreate the effect of travel without actually having to go anywhere. 'Travel, indeed, struck him as being a waste of time, since he believed that the imagination could provide a more-than-adequate substitute for the vulgar reality of actual experience.'[13] When Des Essientes' desires get the better of him, he sets out on a real trip to England. On his way to the train terminus he transforms in his mind, a wet Paris into the London of literature and, especially, Dickens. Stopping at an 'English tavern' he drinks and eats then decides that, in fact, he should return home. 'I've been steeped in English life ever since I left home, and it would be madness to risk spoiling such unforgettable experiences by a clumsy change of locality'.[14] The Bizarre Quarter that is Las Vegas allows for many such experiences: the Forum shopping mall with its animatronic Roman Gods and accelerated dawn-to-sunset sky-effect vaulted roof; Siegfried and Roy's white Siberian tigers in the Mirage; and a permanent circus. Certainly going to Las Vegas might be classed as 'travel' but once one has arrived it is possible to 'visit' Egypt, New Orleans or medieval England without any 'clumsy change of locality'. Robert Venturi, Denise Scott Brown and Steven Izenour in their book *Learning from Las Vegas: The Forgotten Symbolism of Architectural Form*[15] identified this tendency:

> ... for three days one may imagine oneself a centurion at Caesar's Palace, a ranger at the Frontier, or a jetsetter at the Riviera rather than a salesperson from Des Moines, Iowa, or an architect from Haddonfield, New Jersey[16]

But Vegas stops short of the immersive experience characterized by the film *Westworld*[17] (where fantasies are realized in a series of historic reconstructions and where the robots who make this environment possible eventually flip into malevolence). It does, though, preserve the inevitable by-product of tourism – alienation – while keeping the tourist safe and the uneasiness engendered by this alienation contributes to delirium.

The Historical Quarter

On the crossroads of the Strip and Tropicana Avenue stand four sentinel hotel/casinos. Next to the Luxor is the Excalibur (a cartoon Camelot) then, going clockwise around the intersection, there is New York New York, rising out of the water spray from the fire boats, the MGM Grand (the largest hotel in the world) and on the next corner, the Tropicana. Embedded deep within this building is the Las Vegas Gambling Hall of Fame – 'the World's Largest Gambling Museum' – with over 15,000 exhibits. Numbers, especially large ones, are important in Las Vegas. Most of the display is taken up with old postcards, ashtrays and other mementoes of casinos, but there is also a video presentation of the demise of some of these casinos, including that of the Hacienda. For Vegas this is a real museum, unlike the Frontier Village's rescued historic buildings or, indeed, the city itself, and at its heart is this blunt reminder of transience disguised as spectacle among the preserved, melancholic memorabilia.

On the diagonally opposite corner is New York New York, hysterical capitalist psycho-geography in built form in which the situation is recuperated by the spectacle on a huge scale. At the apex of the site is the Statue of Liberty with, immediately behind it, the waters of the Hudson River. Towering above this is a Coney Island roller coaster, then the hotel itself, an evocation of classic 1930s New York. Here, then, is the city (a 'real' city) recreated and sanitized in the name of capital. There is no need, after all, to go to New York when you can go to New York New York. An advertising slogan proclaims New York New York as 'the best city in Las Vegas'.

Las Vegas shadows Los Angeles, but not all shadows are behind the object that creates them. Sometimes Vegas seems like LA's doppelgänger. It knows where it has been and can second-guess what it is about to do. Las Vegas has learnt tricks from Hollywood and from Disneyland and can apply them to the city. It has the past to plunder as freely as it desires, because none of it has to be the real thing. The simulacra that Las Vegas presents are, of course, versions of the 'recognized' past, 'authentic' cities and, even, 'real' movies. The pervasiveness of Las Vegas culture could be seen as a threat to the value of museums. One might think that Las Vegas would have no need for museums; the image of the city is, after all, composed of hyper-real, imagined and distorted pasts.

The Noble and Tragic Quarter

The city does have its own archives, such as that of the Gambling Hall of Fame at the Tropicana. Unfortunately, the Debbie Reynolds Casino and the Debbie Reynolds Hollywood Movie Museum with it have gone.[18] On display there was a collection of 'real' costumes from movies, displayed in a series of tableaux. In the context of Las Vegas this turned the prop into the authentic object. On East Tropicana Boulevard, slowly overtaking a suburban shopping mall, is the Liberace Museum, where a similar process is taking place. This may be high kitsch but the museum's collection of genuine artefacts (a mirror-tiled Rolls Royce, a 260-diamond piano-shaped ring) are displayed with as much commitment to immortality as the objects in the Soane Museum. The artist Jeffrey Vallance, who for some time lived in Vegas, has made this connection, installing his exhibition 'A Visual Tribute to Mr. Showmanship' there in 1995.[19]

These museums help keep in check the anxiety that comes with the threat of destruction, a threat that is never far away. The 'volcano' that performs each hour adjacent to the street outside the Mirage resort is a faint echo of the shaking that resulted from the A-bomb tests and is a pre-echo of the inevitable demolition of the Mirage itself. The journalist Marc Cooper identified another association:

> . . . it was the Big Vig who, gazing out at the gas flames and the burping steam, put it best. 'It makes me nostalgic for my childhood,' he said, remembering lazy summers spent collecting industrial artifacts in the shadow of chemical refineries and cracking plants. 'It looks just like Elizabeth, New Jersey'.[20]

This, in turn, evokes the ordinary transformed into a delirious dream world. In this case it is the specific ordinary of industrial America that Robert Smithson, the sculptor, turned his attention to in *A Tour of the Monuments in Passaic, New Jersey*.[21] He lists and photographs the monuments he passes on a walk around this city: 'The Bridge Monument Showing Wooden Sidewalks', 'Monument with Pontoons: The Pumping Derrick', 'The Great Pipe Monument', 'The Fountain Monument', 'The Sand-Box Monument (also called The Desert)' – all found fragments of urban landscape. So Las Vegas conjures up both a mythical, glamorous New York and, inadvertently, its real, everyday hinterland. The spectacle of the volcano and the images of industrial dereliction that it evokes are simultaneously inviting ruin while keeping it at bay. Reyner Banham in his book *Scenes in America Deserta*[22] wrote, 'It won't blow away in the night, but you begin to wish it might, because it will never make noble ruins, and it will never discover how to fade away gracefully'.[23] If Vegas does not meet its end through violent destruction, then the alternative is that it will be buried by the desert. This is the starting point of a CD-ROM, *The Réal* by Mark C. Taylor and José Márquez[24] in which a lost laptop is discovered in 2003 in a

Las Vegas now one mile beneath the sands. The 'game' is to unearth the secrets of the Motel Réal buried within the computer's hard-drive; two archaeological processes in one. The story told in this electronic book is one of connections with Pharaonic Egypt and the architecture of light. Banham also identified the desert as the ultimate threat to Vegas:

> Las Vegas is a symbol, above all else, of the impermanence of man in the desert, and not least because one is never *not* aware of the desert's presence; wherever man has not built over the desert grimly endures – even on some of the pedestrian islands down the centre of the Strip.[25]

The Square of the Appalling Mobile

In *Learning from Las Vegas*, Venturi, Brown and Izenour celebrated the automobile's impact on the built environment exemplified by the Strip. Today the emphasis on the car has shifted and there is now a significant element of 'pedestrianism' in Sin City. Indeed, it could be argued that Vegas has now generated a new, if awkward, kind of *flânerie*. Everyone here is a 'man [or woman or child] of the crowd'. There is a strange symbiotic relationship between automobile and pedestrian in this situation. The car's cruise down the Strip is tempered by the volume of traffic, while the stroll of the walker is constantly thwarted by the circuitous routes imposed on the sidewalk by the casinos. In this relationship cars (from absurdly stretched limos to vintage T-birds) become as much a part of the spectacle as architecture. Like Venturi, Reyner Banham revelled in the spectacle of Las Vegas, comparing it to mannerist art. More recently, Ralph Rugoff has referred to this, and taken Banham's comparison further, calling it the 'aesthetic labyrinth of the moment'.[26] The casinos themselves are, of course, designed as labyrinths; people are not meant to find their way out. Even the symmetrical form of the Luxor gives way to an intentional chaos of forking paths. The interiors of the casinos hardly differ: they have the same myriad lights, the same foreground aural overload of fruit machines and the same patterned carpets. The linearity of the Strip, like the axiality of the pyramid, implies some kind of ease of movement, but there is so much control of the environment and sensory overload in evidence that disorientation is the norm. Las Vegas is a linear labyrinth, a system that appears to be legible but is, not unlike my London walk, full of blinds and dead ends. Mark C. Taylor's take extends this to include the constant barrage of information that assaults visitors:

> The bright lights of the Strip stage a virtual potlatch of meaning. Instead of communicating meaning, which can be read at a distance, proliferating signs immerse us in a superficial flux that never ends. Monuments built to stop the flux turn out to be glass pyramids . . .[27]

. . . endless walls . . . mammoth caverns, casino mirrors . . .

In 1998 Las Vegas had another shift of a gear when the Bellagio was opened by the owner of the Mirage, Steve Wynn. This, with its Gallery of Fine Art, was meant to re-define the culture of Las Vegas for the 21st century. Jeffrey Vallance described the effect of the paintings in this luxurious gallery: 'In a town where fake is the name of the game, seeing something truly authentic seems all the more unreal.'[28] When he eventually sold the Bellagio, Wynn secured the art collection for himself. What started at the Bellagio has now become currency in the new Vegas. By far the most visible of the new cultural enterprises is the 'Guggenheim at the Venetian' that has been linked onto the ever-growing global brand. The chain now extends from New York through Berlin, Bilbao and Venice to Las Vegas. And Guggenheim Vegas has been designed by that most paradoxical of architects, Rem Koolhaas. *The Delirious Museum* comes full circle and overlaps with the architect's manifesto of 1978 in his book *Delirious New York*. Koolhaas, like Le Corbusier, was disappointed by the obvious reality of Manhattan but responded by repositioning New York as the birthplace of his own delirious modernism. Where Le Corbusier thought the skyscrapers should be white and were too small, Koolhaas, in *Delirious New York* re-wrote the city's script. One of his early completed buildings, the Kunsthal in Rotterdam of 1992, was a riposte to the fossilizing effect of the museum and was a homage to both Mies van der Rohe and Le Corbusier. This is a building that celebrates the transience of the art exhibition. To emphasize this, Koolhaas placed the figure of an Arab, a nomad, leading his camel, striding along the roofline of the building above the entrance (a similar scene can be witnessed in the landscaped grounds of the Sahara Casino on the Las Vegas Strip). In the 1990s it was a badge of architectural super-stardom to build an important museum but Koolhaas cemented his international reputation by building other public structures and by designing striking private houses. At the same time he was working through a series of ideas about scale (which he called 'bigness') and the porosity of both buildings and texts. In 1995 Koolhaas published *S,M,L,XL* in collaboration with Bruce Mau. [29] In the lexicon made up of diary fragments that runs through the book he reveals a moment similar to Nadja's non-encounter with the Louvre:

> MUSEUM 1   What should a museum look like, a museum in Manhattan?
> MUSEUM 2   The measliness of myself and humanity struck me to the core. But luckily the museum was open that evening until six, which made matters a little better. For I believed that museums should be open twenty-four hours a day, and should not cost anything, as was the case in England, so that I might roam about the African Plains Hallway at four in the morning with thoughts of the African veldt deep in my head.
> MUSEUM 3   Then a funny thing happened. When I got to the museum, all of a sudden I wouldn't have gone inside for a million bucks. It just didn't appeal to me – and here I'd walked through the whole goddam park and looked forward to it and all. [30]

In 2001, Koolhaas published his collaboration with the Harvard Graduate School at which he taught, the two-volume *Project on the City*. The first of these, *Great Leap Forward*, looks at the development of the Pearl River Delta, the second *Harvard Design School Guide to Shopping*, [31] has an ambiguous relationship to its subject. It is at once a criticism and a celebration of the importance of consumerism. On the inside cover of Volume 2 is this statement:

> SHOPPING is arguably the last remaining form of public activity . . .
> Town centres, suburbs, streets, and now airports, train stations,

museums, hospitals, schools, the Internet and the military are shaped by mechanisms and spaces of shopping.[32]

One chapter is a re-analysis of Las Vegas based on an interview with Robert Venturi and Denise Scott-Brown: 'To simplify, the main thing is that it [Las Vegas] went from the archetype of strip and sprawl to the scenography of Disneyland'.[33] In the same section is a series of photographs taken on a walk along the north side of the Strip between Mandalay Bay and Treasure Island with a map showing the route taken, weaving in and out of car-parks, getting on and off moving sidewalks. In *Learning from Las Vegas*, this journey would have taken place in a car. In its vast array of statistics and documentation and the book's glossy presentation, Koolhaas' work cannot entirely disguise some residual distaste for the activity it describes. A more straightforward relationship to shopping is exhibited in another of his books, also published in 2001, detailing the research his office had undertaken for the Prada chain.[34] As if feeling the need to respond immediately to the ideas floating around in his published work, the books appeared at almost exactly the same time as two major projects were opened, the Prada shop in New York and the Guggenheim Las Vegas. The former is a huge and expensive stage set where there happen to be a few clothes for sale. The latter is much less showy and engages with its context in a rather tentative way. First, it would be unfair to describe the Guggenheim Las Vegas as a museum (though all the publicity uses the caché of that word to give the enterprise the requisite tone). What have been created are two exhibition halls, so in that respect the Guggenheim project is not so very different to the nomadic intention behind the Kunsthal in Rotterdam. However, the context of the Guggenheim spaces is very different from the exposed urban site of the Kunsthal. The Venetian sits firmly within the new Las Vegas (for at least as long as the new lasts). Where many of the casinos use the long avenues that connect them to the Strip to make a space for a mall, the Venetian's shopping experience is given a whole floor to itself above the gambling floor. The 'canals' that form the public spectacle on street level are continued inside the building 'upstairs' in the shopping mall. This is the architectural equivalent of conspicuous consumption – consider both the absurdity and engineering difficulties involved in putting canals upstairs. The Venetian is also a reminder of the way that Las Vegas is a place where money is visibly spent and invisibly lost. The larger of the two Guggenheim spaces has no exterior to speak of. Its vast blank walls blend into the bland back of the adjacent casino. Koolhas has made a big, well-finished, interiorized shed, the external face of which is its publicity. This space is dedicated to touring shows generated by Guggenheim central (its opening show was the Art of the Motorcycle, a no-expense-spared spectacle designed by Frank Gehry). In fact this space has since 'temporarily' closed down, abandoned at the same time as Gehry's downtown waterfront scheme for another Guggenheim in New York. The other element of the project, which is still, so far, open, is called the 'Guggenheim Hermitage Museum'. This is seen as a way of extending the St Petersburg museum's presence in the west (they have also opened a more modest branch in London's Somerset House and have launched the *Hermitage* magazine). This building does have an exterior of sorts. It is a steel box covered in supergraphics inserted into the elaborate pastiche Venetian surroundings, visible adjacent to the entrance to the Venetian Hotel and as an alien wall taking up one side of a baroque arcade linking the hotel and the casino. It could be the only steel visible in this city of tiny lights (unless one counts the structure of the one-third-scale Eiffel Tower in the Paris casino). The internal walls are also made up of steel plates, the paintings 'hung' on them with the aid of magnets. Here is Koolhaas once again stating his opposition to the museum. These walls can play host to any number of exhibits without ever leaving traces – the exhibits will pass on, leaving the exhibition space intact. There is something here that evokes goods passing across supermarket shelves, leaving them untouched, ready for the next consignment. There is also something 'industrial' about the museum as an object, like a piece of derelict equipment in one of the wastelands of Smithson's Passaic or the Big Vig's Elizabeth, New Jersey.

. . . modern science . . . new myths . . .

But Koolhaas was, it seems, worn down by the system of architectural competitions and commissions. At the same time as entering

into a devil's pact with shopping he relented and took a museum commission on board with his winning entry to the Los Angeles County
Museum of Art redevelopment. Koolhaas proposed complete demolition of the buildings on the site on Wilshire Boulevard, sparing only
one notable structure. The existing site is an unresolved collection of
buildings and semi-public spaces. Previous re-developments have
merely served to reinforce the sense of confusion in the place. The
pavilion for Japanese art by Bruce Goff (1988) is the exception to this.
This structure is freestanding, linked only by a swirling ramp to the
central plaza of LACMA. The Koolhaas competition proposal, while
deliberately avoiding any strong architectural definition, integrated
this pavilion into the plan. Instead of defining the architectural form
Koolhaas concentrated on a way of organizing the collections that
would evolve into an architectural strategy. His proposal was that the
collections should be organized and displayed within parallel spaces.
This avoided a purely linear view of (art) history and it allowed a dialogue to be created between separate cultures.[35] This was a system
of organization that Koolhaas explored in his proposal for Parc de la
Vilette, Paris, in 1983 and it challenged linear progression, or, to put
it in imperialist terms, 'the progress of civilization'. This was in
marked contrast to the shop and warehouse approach of his Las
Vegas work. LACMA was a fundamental re-evaluation of museum
architecture with huge implications for curatorial practice. But bene-
factors to the museum refused to back the extensive demolition
proposed by Koolhaas and have, instead, commissioned a scheme by
Renzo Piano that will unify existing elements into a cohesive architectural whole, thereby avoiding the difficult issue of a confrontation
with traditional curatorial practice.

New, changeable decors . . .

In 2002 the exhibition at the Las Vegas Guggenheim Hermitage was a
collection of 'masterpieces'. There were 45 pictures in the show,
admission price to the gallery was $15, which works out at around 33
cents per picture. In order to reach the gallery visitors enter either
through the lush hotel lobby or through the jangling cacophony of the

gambling hall. At the Steve Wynn Collection the atmosphere is very different. If the Koolhaas project exhibits an element of reluctance to engage with the mystique of the museum, the same cannot be said of the exquisitely anal staging of the Wynn Collection. This is in the remnants of the Desert Inn, located in the no-mans land of mid-Strip, south of the Stratosphere and north of Circus Circus. The Desert Inn is the hotel where Howard Hughes holed up in the 1970s and from where he began his own assault on the old Las Vegas.[36] The tiny gallery is contained, almost concealed, within what is now a business centre and golf club that could easily be the dead neutral space of a Middle Eastern hotel lobby – the décor exhibits a kind of vacant luxury. Here the admission price is $10 and there are only 12 pictures, working out at 83 cents per picture. The display technique could hardly be more different from the cool self-conscious design of the Guggenheim. Each visitor is personally shown in to the gallery by a uniformed guard and presented with a hand-held audio guide. On this the collection is introduced and explained by the multi-millionaire Wynn. The commentary is made by a man who knows what he likes, it is anti-academic and personal. The collection is predominantly early modern masters in a one or two-of-each way (Manet, Monet, Pissaro, Gauguin, Van Gogh, Matisse, Cézanne, Picasso, Modigliani, and, included because he portrays Wynn, Warhol). Each painting and each label is exhibited with a single framing spot isolating it from its immediate surroundings. At first glance the paintings hang in space. The walls seem to have de-materialized. Once one's eyes have become accustomed to the darkness, the walls reappear – covered in luxurious deep burgundy fabric. Steve's light and friendly, even intimate, chat heightens the intensity already created by the installation. In the press release accompanying the opening of the collection, Steve Wynn said 'Nobody owns these paintings. You just have custody. The pictures are bigger than we are, and we're simply the guardians.'

By the time this appears in print the Wynn Collection will be transformed in one way or another. Steve Wynn started to buy art again in May 2003. He paid $23 million for a Renoir, then the next day he bought a Cézanne for $17 million. Presumably these, like the rest of his collection are in transit, waiting for a new home in the casino that Wynn is building, called 'La Rêve', after the Picasso for which he is the

27. Rem Koolhaas, the walls of the Guggenheim Hermitage Museum behind the columns of the Venetian Casino.

guardian (no. 11 in the exhibition). But it is to be hoped that Wynn will, in the fullness of time, choose to be expensively frozen or embalmed in death. He can be exhibited in the midst of his collection, or, if the paintings have moved on, amongst the best reproductions that money can buy. He will act as a reminder of the melancholy of collecting and of gaining the thing that you most desire. He can remind us too that the city in which he made his fortune is just a dream-work, an ignoble ruin, consumed by its own volcano, already a Delirious Museum.

28. Found photograph album on fence, Glasgow (1979).

NOTES

Introduction

1 In Palais de Tokyo, 2001, p 51.
2 Ross, 1989. At a discussion in the Photographer's Gallery in London David Mellor said he had no objection to my re-use of his phrase.
3 Koolhaas, 1978, p 6.
4 Reprinted in Zone1/2, no date.
5 Kurimanzutto, in Palais de Tokyo, 2001, p 68.
6 Venturi, 1977, p 16.
7 The British Museum returns throughout this text in various disguises.

1 The Louvre: an absence

1 Quoted in Shattuck, 1967, p 264. This comment was made to Jacob on the occasion of Apollinaire missing his train.
2 From Baudelaire's collection *Tableaux Parisiens*. See Baudelaire, 1997.
3 Zola, 1970, p 91.
4 Apollinaire, 'Zone', in *Selected Poems*, 1965, p 20.
5 Quoted in Steegmuller, 1963, p 164.
6 Fernande Olivier, quoted in ibid., p 173.
7 Barring Apollinaire's own version – he insisted that Picasso was responsible.
8 Apollinaire, 'Zone', in *Selected Poems*, 1965, p 23.
9 In Apollonio, 1973, p 22–23. F. T. Marinetti, *The Founding and Manifesto of Futurism*, 1909.
10 An event recorded by the English painter William Nicholson in his work *Le Retour de la Joconde*. Needless to say in this painting, 'Mona Lisa' is virtually invisible behind a busy throng of people.
11 Quoted in McMullen, 1972, p 215.
12 *LHOOQ*. These letters pronounced in French approximate to 'She has a hot arse'. Later Duchamp was to re-work this image, removing the facial hair (that is, returning it to its 'original' state) but not the pun. This version was called *LHOOQ Shaved*.
13 Quoted in McMullen, 1972, p 225.
14 Quoted in Jukes, 1990, p 37.

2 The endless museum: a 'house of dreams'

1 This term was coined by the language theoretician Alford Korzybski.
2 Green and White, 1968, p 138.
3 There is a spectacular version of this type in Morningside, Edinburgh called both the Volunteer Arms and the Canny Man.
4 Altick, 1978, p 18.
5 Ibid., p 20.
6 John Updike describes the extended and renovated Museum of Modern Art as 'an invisible cathedral' in the New Yorker, 15 November 2004.
7 These comparisons are thoroughly drawn out in the relationship between the British Museum and Selfridges department store in Cummings and Lewandowska, 2000, and in their work 'Browse' presented as part of the exhibition 'Collected' in London, 1997. A more general overview is provided in Bayley, 1989.
8 W. Benjamin, 1999, p 415.
9 Ugrešić, 1999, p 1.
10 The essay, 'Wandering in the City' by Christel Hollevoet in Whitney Museum of American Art, 1992, was influential in setting up the structure for this chapter. Hollevoet extends this sequence of urban strategems into a discussion of the work of various artists who have used the idea of walking the city in their work.
11 Calvino, 2003, p 172.
12 Baudelaire, 1995, p 7. Curiously, Baudelaire's paraphrasing suggests that the man who sits watching the passers-by becomes the 'Man of the Crowd'. In Poe's story it is the old man whom he follows that is given this name. Furthermore Poe recognizes this 'man of the crowd' as being 'the type and the genius of deep crime'. Poe's story is set in London. See Poe, 1963.
13 Baudelaire, 1995, p 9.
14 Ibid., p 12.
15 'Some Motifs in Baudelaire', in W. Benjamin, 1997, p 129.
16 Ibid., p 128.
17 This suggests the possibility of the flâneuse. For various other discussions regarding this, see Tester, 1994.
18 See, for instance, Edmund White's 2001 book of reminiscences of Paris.
19 In London Review of Books, vol. 24, no. 1, 3 January 2002. The article is entitled 'At the Imperial War Museum'.
20 Missac, 1995.
21 Ibid., p 194.
22 In W. Benjamin, 1973.
23 'Eduard Fuchs, Collector and Historian', in W. Benjamin, 1992.
24 W. Benjamin, 1999, p 460.
25 W. Benjamin, 1992, p 169.
26 Ibid., p 170.
27 W. Benjamin, 1999, p 83.

28 W. Benjamin, 1992, p 230.
29 W. Benjamin, 1999, p 82.
30 Aragon, 1971, p 33.
31 Ibid., p 34.
32 Ibid.. p 63.
33 One of his photographs was used on the cover of the publication *La Révolution Surréaliste*. Atget insisted that it should be published without a credit line. Quoted in Nesbit, 1992, p 1.
34 Aragon, 1971, p 47.
35 Ibid., p. 47.
36 Zola, 1962, p 32.
37 Walter Benjamin to Theodore Adorno, 31 May 1935. Quoted in Buck-Morss, 1991, p 33.
38 Breton, 1960, p 52.
39 Breton, 1987, p 32.
40 In Waldberg, 1965, p 82.
41 Breton, 1960, p 112.
42 Ibid., p 152.
43 Quoted in Krichbaum and Zondergeld, 1985, p 177.
44 See Morton, 2000, pp 98–110.
45 Fiachra Gibbons, 'I don't have any cash. Do you take mackerel?', *Guardian*, 14 April 2003.
46 Quoted in Motherwell, 1989, p 115.
47 René Magritte, in 'Lifeline', *View*, December 1946. Quoted in Ford, 1991, p 244.

3 Beneath the museum, the street

1 Calvino, 2003, p 174.
2 See Chapter 4.
3 Yves Klein writing to his aunt, May 1958. Quoted in Stich, 1994, p 139.
4 Quoted in Altshuler, 1994, p 205.
5 Alexander Trocchi, 'Invisible insurrection of a million minds', in Blazwick, 1989, p 55.
6 From *Internationale Situationniste*, no. 1, June 1958. In Blazwick, 1989, p 22.
7 Published in English as *Society of the Spectacle*, 1987.
8 Reprinted in Blazwick, 1989, p 22.
9 Rumney was late delivering this piece for publication in the magazine. This was the excuse for his expulsion from the movement.
10 *The Leaning Tower of Venice*, reproduced in Blazwick, 1989, pp 45–49.
11 Rumney, 2002, p 47.
12 Khatib, Abdelhafid, 'Attempt at a psychogeographical description of Les Halles', *Internationale Situationniste*, no. 2, 1958. Reprinted in Andreotti and Costa, 1996, p 76.

13 'Détournement as negation and prelude', *Internationale Situationniste*, no. 3, December 1959. In Blazwick, 1989, p 29.
14 'Plan for Rational Improvements to the City of Paris', *Potlatch*, no. 23, 1955. Reprinted in Andreotti and Costa, 1996, pp 56–57.
15 See Wollen, 2001, p 130.
16 In Blazwick, 1989, p 24.

4 The Totalmuseum: exhibitions/experiments

1 In Lissitzky-Küppers, 1968, p 348.
2 From the essay 'Proun Space', in *G* magazine, 1923. In Dluhosch, 1970, p 139.
3 Ibid., p 149.
4 In a letter from Moscow dated 8 February 1926. In Lissitzky-Küppers, 1968, p 74.
5 Documented in Staniszewski, 1998, pp 16–22.
6 In Tupitsyn, 1999, p 23.
7 From text in archives of Lower Saxony Provincial Museum, Hanover. In Dluhosch, 1970, p 149.
8 Quoted in Gamard, 2000, p 26.
9 For a full description of the development of the Merzbau see Elderfield, 1985.
10 See Elderfield, 1985, and Gamard, 2000.
11 Quoted in Elderfield, 1985, p 150.
12 Dietrich, 1993, p 198.
13 Marcel Duchamp quoted in Bonk, 1989, p 257.
14 Duchamp said as much himself. See A. Schwarz, 2000, p 145.
15 Duchamp, 1999, pp 5–6. I have omitted certain typographic quirks included by the 'typotranslators'.
16 Ibid., p 7.
17 Duchamp, 1973, p 149.
18 For a description of the opening see Altshuler, 1994, pp 122 *et seq.*
19 For a full description of the individual mannequins see Kachur, 2001.
20 O'Doherty, 1976, p 69.
21 Interview with John Sweeney. Reprinted in Duchamp, 1973, p 136.
22 Stewart, 1993, p 65.
23 A. Schwarz, 2000.
24 In 2003 the British artist Cornelia Parker made her own re-interpretation of Duchamp's exhibition in her work *The Distance (a kiss with string attached)*. The string in this instance was wrapped around Rodin's famous sculpture at Tate Britain, *The Kiss*.
25 Quoted in IVAM Centre Julio Gonzalez, 1997, p 52.
26 See Chapter 9.
27 Kiesler, 1930, p 121.
28 Ibid., p 121.

29 Ibid., p 108.
30 Quoted in IVAM Centre Julio Gonzalez, 1997, p 70.
31 Ibid, p 77.
32 Guggenheim, 1960, p 101.
33 Ibid., p 99.
34 Quoted in IVAM Centre Julio Gonzalez, 1997, p 77.
35 Reprinted in Safran, 1989, pp 72–75.
36 Ibid., p 72.
37 Ibid., p 74.

5 This is not a museum

1 Smithson, 1996, p 42.
2 This latter connection has also been made in Hauptman, 2000.
3 The Joseph Cornell Study Center at the National Museum of American Art, Smithsonian Institution, Washington DC holds the archive.
4 Admission to the collection is free.
5 In conversation with Jon Bewley in Searle, 1993, p 23.
6 Ibid., p 23.
7 Marcel Broodthaers quoted by Douglas Crimp in the essay 'This is Not a Museum of Art', in Walker Art Center, 1989, p 71.
8 Author's note: Broodthaers' museum was also non-existent. It manifested itself from time to time and in various locations.
9 Quoted in McShine, 1999, p 225.
10 Broodthaers in an interview with Johannes Cladders, in INK-Dokumentation, 4, 1979. Quoted in Broodthaers, 1988, p 147.
11 For reasons of the building's history the galleries here are numbered anti-clockwise from the rear entrance.
12 Bloom, 1990.
13 Corrin, 1994.
14 See also a similar display device used to different ends by Carlo Scarpa at the Castelvecchio in Chapter 8.
15 Part of the multi-site exhibition, Collected, organized by Neil Cummings and Marysia Lewandowska.
16 Kosuth, 1992.
17 See the essay by Charlotta Kotik in Kosuth, 1992, p xiv.
18 Access to Room 1a is currently restricted to a route through the basement storage space. Apply to the Information Desk regarding location of staircase and lift and opening times.
19 The continued existence of these records does not fit with the current position of the museum as imaginary.
20 For a description and discussion of Boltanski's work see Chapter 7.
21 Haacke, 1999.
22 Ibid., p 17.

23 Ibid., p 19.
24 Detailed in Bronson and Gale, 1983, pp 151 *et seq.*
25 Haacke, 1999, p 13.
26 Also recorded by Joseph Arnold in his painting of 1668 from the Städtisches Museum, Ulm.
27 These include: Susan Hiller, Julian Walker, Joseph Beuys, René Magritte, Louise Lawler and Cornelius Gijsbrechts.
28 Kabakov, 1998.
29 Described fully in Wallach, 1996.
30 Van Bruggen, 1979, p 75.
31 Museum of Art, Rhode Island School of Design, 1970.
32 Warhol, 1989, p 577.
33 This list is from the Andy Warhol Museum website, 1998.
34 Ask at the Information Desk for times.
35 Oldenberg and Williams, 1967, p 8.
36 Check in the Shop for current availability.
37 Spoerri, 1991, p 55.
38 Arguably, Fluxus was Maciunas. Other artists submitted work that then became Fluxus works through their selection for various Fluxus publications and events.
39 *Fluxus Newsletter*, no. 6, April 1963.
40 Robert Filliou quoted in Bronson and Gale, 1983, p 89.
41 Also called the Festival of Misfits.
42 See Spoerri, 1991, p 115.
43 These are some examples of his 'snare' pictures – table-tops preserved or 'frozen' at particular moments in time. The entrance to the Café is in the north-east quadrant of the Rotunda.
44 The group was formed in 1982 by brothers Martyn and Stephen Young.
45 See also the contemporaneous work of Big Audio Dynamite.
46 From Kent Lundberg's website: http://web.mit.edu/klund/www/cboxtxt, 2004.
47 The making of this piece of music is detailed in Poschardt, 1998, p 261 *et seq.*
48 See www.jonimabe.com, 2003.
49 In Paolozzi, 1985, p 7.
50 The final year is represented by two vitrines.
51 For a full list of contents see Calle, 1999.
52 Calle and Baudrillard, 1988.
53 Calle, 1996.
54 Full documentation of this and other archaeological projects is in Coles and Dion, 1999.
55 Dion, 1997.
56 In Corrin, Kwon and Bryson, 1997. In interview with Miwon Kwon, p 17.
57 I would like to thank James Putnam for reminding me of the Filliou action and for drawing my attention to the work by Jeffrey Vallance. Both are

documented in Putnam, 2001, p 173. The Filliou work is also documented in McShine, 1999.

58 See Chapter 11.

6 From Soane to Soane

1 de Certeau, 1984, p 93.
2 'The Paris of the Second Empire in Baudelaire', in W. Benjamin, 1985, p 37.
3 This would have made this walk considerably shorter.
4 See Chapter 7.
5 These parallels are drawn out further in Chapter 7.
6 Trench and Hillman, 1984, p 39.
7 In 2003 Wellcome was the subject of a British Museum exhibition: 'Medicine Man'. A satellite of this project was Hawkins and Olsen, 2003, in which various writers create narratives, fictions and semi-fictions inspired by the collection.
8 Quoted in Tate Gallery, 1980, p 26.
9 See Chapter 7.
10 A scheme exists to unearth the museum from its current location and place it in a less obscure location.
11 There is a history and archive of the museum at www.pollocksweb.co.uk, 2004.
12 This event is described in greater detail with pictures in: Walker, 1995, pp 78–79.
13 Brennan, 2003.
14 Another (untitled) work by Terry Smith and the author, a re-reading of certain objects discovered during the creation of Capital may now reside in the archive or office of the Museum of Installation in Deptford, South London.
15 Hitchcock himself discusses this in Truffaut, 1978, p 24.
16 Sinclair, 1995, p 15.
17 Peter Ackroyd took his inspiration from Sinclair's poem, originally published in 1975, for his supernatural detective novel Hawksmoor, 1986.
18 See Chapter 7.
19 Altick, 1978, p 430.
20 Kent, 1937.
21 Bruno, 1977, p 115.
22 Ibid., p 125.
23 Ibid., p 126.
24 Yates, 1992, p 300.
25 'The Library of Babel', in Borges, 1970, p 78.
26 For a full description of this event see Dorey, 1991.
27 See Chapter 7.
28 In Sir John Soane's Museum, 1999, p 68.

29 Ibid., p 74.

7 The mausoleum: where death ends

1   Joyce, 1997, p 116.
2   Known in the United States as *Stairway to Heaven*.
3   Oliver, J. W., *The Life of William Beckford* (Oxford, 1932). Quoted in David Watkin, 'Monuments and Mausolea in the Age of Enlightenent', in Waterfield, 1996, p 14.
4   Ariès, 1983, p 61.
5   When I first visited the Paris Catacombs in 1974 there was no light in these passages; visitors were issued with candles to illuminate their way.
6   A different type of visit to the underground spaces of Paris, including parts of the Catacombs, is described in the journal of illicit urban exploration at www.infiltration.org. (2002). This details a journey into hidden parts of the Catacombs with the ever-present danger of detection by the authorities.
7   de Certeau, 1984, p 93.
8   See Chapter 8.
9   From the guidebook to the Catacombs. No publishing information available.
10 These resonances have been picked up by both Peter Ackroyd in *Hawksmoor*, 1986, and the renegade London writer, Stewart Home, in his novel *Slow Death*, 1996.
11 This engagement is not always so straightforward; the ancestors are not always 'ours'. The question of restitution of human remains is one that many museums have not yet resolved.
12 See Chapter 6.
13 I have to admit culpability: the displays of both bodies discussed here were designed by myself during my time working in the British Museum Design Office.
14 For a thorough description of Lenin's fate in death and those whose duty it was to preserve him, see Zbarsky and Hutchinson, 1998.
15 For a suitably alchemical interpretation of the Tradescant tomb see Iain Sinclair's *Lights Out for the Territory*, 1997. The relevant chapter is entitled 'Lord Archer's Prospects'. This psychogeographic diagram intersects with my own suggestion of an axis connecting Tate Britain (site of the Bentham-inspired Millbank Penitentiary) via the Tradescant tomb to the Imperial War Museum.
16 During one of his trips John Tradescant the Elder died. In the Ashmolean Museum, Oxford, there is a painting of him on his deathbed and wearing a shroud.
17 The Museum of Jurassic Technology in Los Angeles (see Chapter 11) has recorded a parallel story to that of the Tradescants in the pamphlet by Illera Edoh, *On the Foundation of the Museum*, 1969, reprinted in The Museum of Jurassic Technology, 2002.

18 Pocahontas is buried downriver at Gravesend, Essex on the Thames Estuary.

19 It is said to have belonged to the Algonquins of Virginia and is probably not a 'mantle' at all.

20 The walls of the church/museum are covered in plaques to the dead but many of these disappear behind display panels and are lost in the café and offices. One of these 'disappeared' plaques belongs to Elias Ashmole. High on the wall to the north of what was the altar is a plaque to the singer Anna Storace, designed by John Soane in 1817. Needless to say it is probable that it is no longer in its original form.

21 Ariès, 1983, p 503.

22 Curl, 1980, p 160.

23 Quoted in Waterfield, 1996, p 82. Soane arranged for one of his pupils to draw Père-Lachaise for his Royal Academy lectures.

24 As if to reinforce this, Abney Park's most extravagant tomb is that of the menagerist Frank Bostock. The tomb features a life-sized sculpture of a sleeping lion.

25 I only found this marker once. The cemetery is yet another labyrinth.

26 I would like to think that the car is a Zephyr.

27 Sontag, 1978, p 70.

28 Barthes, 1993, p 32.

29 Undated, reprinted in Boltanski, 1990. Boltanski has edited this text by scribbling out large sections of the interview. Rather than looking like censorship, this seems to refer back to the artist's interest in the idea of the 'missing'.

30 Reprinted in Perec, 1996.

31 Ibid., p 137.

32 Sir John Soane's Museum, 2001, p 31.

33 Summerson, 1978.

34 Ibid.

35 For a full description of the house, see Watkin, 1968, pp 95–123.

36 In *Thomas Hope and the Neo-Classical Idea,* David Watkin draws out parallels between this room and André Malraux's *Museé Imaginaire.*

37 In Summerson, 1978.

38 See Waterfield, 1996. Waterfield's own essay 'Dulwich Picture Gallery; An Artists Shrine' also draws attention to contemporaries of Soane who were buried in their own museums: the sculptor Bertel Thorvaldsen in Copenhagen and the history painter John Trumbull in New Haven.

39 See Waterfield, 1987.

40 In W. Benjamin, 1992, p 16.

41 Taylor and Lammerts, 2002, p 13.

8 Carlo Scarpa: the labyrinth in time

1 'The Garden of Forking Paths', in Borges, 1970, p 48.

2 *Potlatch*, 9/10/11, 17–31 August 1954. Quoted in Andreotti and Costa, 1996.
3 Quoted by Boris Podrecca, 'A Viennese Point of View', in Dal Co and Mazzariol, 1986, p 242.
4 Wright's design for the Guggenheim, New York provides a clue to his attitude to 'context'. Wright's building is often seen as a riposte to the dominant grid of the Manhattan street plan. New York did not correspond to Wright's prairie-based vision of America.
5 Vidler, 1992, p 11.
6 From the essay 'Naples', in W. Benjamin, 1992, p 169.
7 Ibid., p 170.
8 See Vigni, 1984.
9 Quoted in Murphy, 1990, p 18.
10 Ibid., p 19.
11 See Chapter 4.
12 Bataille, 1995 (from the entry for 'museum' in the 'Critical Dictionary').
13 For a detailed and thorough description of the development of Scarpa's work on Castelvecchio, see Murphy, 1990.
14 Dal Co and Mazzariol, 1986.
15 See, for instance, Richard Murphy's commentary to Murray Grigor's film *Carlo Scarpa* (VIZ for Channel 4 and the Arts Council of England, 1997).
16 Tafuri, 1989, p 113.
17 Quoted in Murphy, 1990, p 115.
18 Quoted in Dal Co and Mazzariol, 1986, p 287.
19 Ibid., p 287.
20 Though Tafuri in *History of Italian Architecture*, 1989, allies him with Guiseppe Samona as another designer operating with his own private 'codes'.
21 Quoted in Dal Co and Mazzariol, 1986, p 286.

9 The spiral in ruins

1 Borges, 1970, p 42.
2 See Chapter 5.
3 Le Corbusier, 1987, p 18.
4 Ibid., p 17.
5 Ibid., p 16.
6 This term is used by Bachelard, 1969, p 105.
7 Promotional brochure, quoted in Tim Benton's essay 'The Era of the Great Projects', in Arts Council, 1987.
8 Flaubert, 1976.
9 Crimp, 1993.
10 Eugenio Donato, quoted in Crimp, 1993.
11 In Borges, Silvina and Casares, 1988.
12 To bring this idea full circle, the High Museum has been used as the set for a high-security prison in the first Hannibal Lecter film *Manhunter* (dir. Michael Mann, 1986).

13 Aleksander Rodchenko, from 'Slogans', quoted in Harrison and Wood, 2003, p 340.
14 Mies van der Rohe, 'Museum for a Small City', in *Architectural Forum*, vol. 78, no. 5, May 1943. Quoted in Lambert, 2001, p 428.
15 See Lambert, 2001.
16 See Staniszewski, 1998.
17 There is a description of Geddes' ideas for city museums in Volker M. Welter's essay 'The Return of the Muses: Edinburgh as a *Museion*', in Giebelhausen, 2003. In the same collection Anthony Vidler connects Geddes' work with Le Corbusier's museum projects.
18 The Outlook Tower is the only vestige of Geddes' museum. The camera obscura is still in use.
19 Quoted in Lambert, 2001, p 373.
20 Vidler, 1992, p 93.
21 Ibid., p 94.
22 In *James Stirling Michael Wilford and Associates; Buildings and Projects, 1975– 1992*, p 14.
23 Crimp, 1993, p 314.
24 Vidler, 1992, p 95.
25 Vidler goes on to list the 'quiet structures [that] have preserved a space for architecture in a modern museum': Soane's Dulwich Picture Gallery, Kahn's Kimbell Museum, Fort Worth and Rafael Moneo's museum in Merida, Spain. Ibid., p 99.
26 Stirling, 1998, p 156.
27 Vidler, 1992, p 95. Coincidentally the Staatsgalerie was also used in an advertisement on British television to publicize a British car. The advertisement made much play of the fact that this was a building in Germany, designed by a British architect. The British car industry could now be said to be a ruin.
28 Crimp, 1993, p 282.
29 Stirling, 1998, p 140.
30 Vidler, 1992. The chapter discussing the Staatsgalerie is entitled 'Losing Face'.
31 Stirling, 1998, pp 211–12.
32 Ibid., p 222.
33 Ibid., p 259. In conversation with Charles Jencks.
34 Ibid., p 248
35 See Newhouse, 1998, p 120.
36 Reprinted in van Bruggen, 2001, p 23.
37 Foster, 2001.
38 Smithson, 1996, p 43.
39 Ibid., p 44.
40 See Gamboni, 1997.

41 He says this interest could be based on the carp that his grandmother bought live and with which he played in the bathtub before they were killed and cooked. See van Bruggen, 2001, p 49.

42 Quoted in ibid., p 115.

43 Debord, 1987, section 24.

44 Vidler, 2000, p 253.

10 After the Wall: Studio Libeskind

1 Perec, 1997, p 13.

2 'The Books of Groningen', in Libeskind, 2001, p 30.

3 W. Benjamin, 1992, p 298.

4 Borges, 1973, p 3.

5 Ibid., p 5.

6 I wrote this on 28 February 2003, 70 years after the process of 'cleansing' Berlin of its left-wing agitators was begun by the Nazis using the pretence of the fire to round up trouble-makers.

7 Ugrešić, 1999, p 169.

8 Libeskind, 2001b, p 187.

9 Daniel Libeskind, in Jewish Museum, 1998, p 9.

10 Libeskind, 2001b, p 55.

11 Daniel Libeskind, in BBC Radio interview, 1999.

12 Interview with Jason Oddy, in Oddy, 2002, p 87.

13 Libeskind, 1991, p 87.

14 Oddy, 2001, p 86.

15 Libeskind, 2001, p 92.

16 Ibid., p 96.

17 As does Libeskind's competition-winning entry for the World Trade Center site.

18 The Spiral project was abandoned by the V&A in 2004. Libeskind has shifted his own museum building endeavours to the project for the extension to Denver Art Museum.

19 Interview with Raymund Ryan, in Ryan, 1996.

20 Harbison, 1977, p 144.

21 Libeskind, 2001b, p 151.

22 Borges, 1999, p 361, 'Elegy', translated by Alastair Reid.

23 Ryan, 1996.

24 Libeskind, 2001b, p 155.

25 Libeskind, 2001a, no page numbers.

26 Ibid.

11 Los Angeles: the hidden museum

1 A Frommer's guide from about 1976.

2 Rugoff, 1995.

3 Ibid., p x.
4 At the time of writing it is being refurbished to house the display of ancient art from the Getty Center.
5 See J. Paul Getty Museum, 1992.
6 Ibid., p 7.
7 Quoted in Jencks, 1978.
8 As a local foretaste of the Getty, Meier completed the Museum of Television & Radio in Los Angeles in 1996. Unlike the Getty, this institution has almost no exhibits in the orthodox sense. It is, in effect, a museum in which to watch television.
9 See Chapter 12.
10 The Getty Center brochure 'Architecture and Gardens; A Tour of the Getty Center' also refers to the Bauhaus and to the pioneer modernists of Los Angeles: Richard Neutra, Frank Lloyd Wright and Rudolph Schindler.
11 Mangurian and Ray, 1999.
12 Ibid., p 105.
13 According to Wilson this type of interior is known locally as a 'Spanish Kitchen' after a restaurant that stood inexplicably abandoned for many years on Melrose Avenue.
14 Genesis, 6: 15 and 16.
15 Mangurian and Ray, 1999, p 106.
16 See Yates, 1992.
17 'The Delani / Sonnabend Halls', in Museum of Jurassic Technology, 2002, p 64.
18 Ibid., p 64.
19 For a fuller description of Kircher's life see Godwin, 1979.
20 Quoted by Paula Findlen in 'Science, History, and Erudition: Athanasius Kircher's Museum at the Collegio Romano', in Stolzenberg, 2001, p 17.
21 David Wilson, the director of the MJT, has written about Kircher in Cranbrook Art Museum, 1999.
22 Stolzenberg, 2001, p 22.
23 Norman Klein has called his book on shifting images of downtown LA *The History of Forgetting; Los Angeles and the Erasure of Memory*, 1997.

12 Las Vegas: the past sure is tense

1 The subtitle of this chapter comes from the Captain Beefheart composition on the 1982 album, *Ice Cream for Crow*.
2 Ivan Chtcheglov, 'Formulary for a New Urbanism', *Potlatch*, October 1953. Quoted in Blazwick, 1989, pp 24–25.
3 Quoted by Michael Ventura, in Tronnes, 1995, p 175.
4 Discussed in Chapter 3.
5 Such as Jean Baudrillard.
6 For a history of the architectural development of Las Vegas, see Hess, 1993.

7 Chaplin, Sarah and Eric Holding, 'Addressing the Post-Urban', in Leach, 2002, p 190.
8 Norman Klein, quoted in ibid., p 190.
9 Rugoff, 1995, p 28.
10 Andreotti and Costa, 1996, p 153.
11 In Taylor, 1997, 'Ground Zero', pp 219-67.
12 'Map of Luxor' leaflet. Circus Circus Enterprises, 1995.
13 Huysmans, 1959, p 35.
14 Ibid., p 143.
15 Venturi, Brown and Izenour, 1977.
16 Ibid., p 53.
17 Also discussed in Chapter 5.
18 This book has had a far longer gestation period than the life of some casinos. Even the relatively recent Luxor had undergone significant internal modifications between visits in 1995 and 2002.
19 Vallance also made sympathetic interventions in the Debbie Reynolds Museum and another popular venue in Vegas, the Magic and Movie Hall of Fame at O'Shea's Hilton Casino. In nearby Henderson he performed the same trick at Ron Lee's World of Clowns Museum.
20 Marc Cooper, 'Searching for Sin City and Finding Disney in the Desert', in Tronnes, 1995, p 329.
21 Originally published 1967, reprinted in Smithson, 1996, p 68.
22 Banham, 1982.
23 Ibid, p 43.
24 Taylor and Márquez, 1997.
25 Banham, 1982, p 42.
26 Rugoff, 1995, p 7.
27 Taylor, 1997, p 266.
28 Vallance, 1999, p 43. This article also provides a potted history of artists' interventions in the casinos of Las Vegas.
29 Koolhaas and Mau, 1995.
30 Ibid., p 936.
31 Chung, Inaba, Koolhaas and Leong, 2001.
32 Ibid.
33 Robert Venturi, in ibid., p 617.
34 Koolhaas, 2001.
35 The redeveloped Museum of Modern Art in New York allows for a similar reading but here the links are made vertically between floors.
36 His mission was to amend the Gaming Board rules so that corporations, as well as individuals, could hold casino licences.

BIBLIOGRAPHY

AA Files, 45/46 (London: Architectural Association, 2001).

Ackroyd, Peter, *Hawksmoor* (London: Abacus, 1986).

Altick, Richard D., *The Shows of London: A Panoramic History of Exhibitions, 1600–1862* (Cambridge, Mass.: Belknap/Harvard University Press, 1978).

Altshuler, Bruce, *The Avant-Garde in Exhibition; New Art in the 20th Century* (New York: Harry N. Abrams, 1994).

Andreotti, Libero, and Xavier Costa (eds), *Theory of the Dérive and Other Situationist Writings on the City* (Barcelona: ACTAR, 1996).

Apollinaire, Guillaume, *Selected Poems*, translated by Oliver Bernard (Harmondsworth: Penguin, 1965).

Apollonio, Umbro (ed), *Futurist Manifestos* (London: Thames and Hudson, 1973).

Aragon, *Paris Peasant*, translated by Simon Watson Taylor (London: Jonathan Cape, 1971).

Architectural Design: Surrealism, vol. 48, no. 2–3, 1978.

Ariès, Philippe, *The Hour of our Death,* translated by Helen Weaver (London: Penguin, 1983).

Arts Council, *Le Corbusier: Architect of the Century* (London: Arts Council, 1987).

Bachelard, Gaston, *The Poetics of Space*, translated by Maria Jolas (Boston: Beacon Press, 1969).

Banham, Reyner, *Scenes in America Deserta* (London: Thames and Hudson, 1982).

Banham, Reyner, *Los Angeles: The Architecture of Four Ecologies* (Harmondsworth: Penguin, 1990).

Banksy, *Cut it Out* (Banksy, 2004).

Barthes, Roland, *Camera Lucida*, translated by Richard Howard (London: Vintage, 1993).

Bataille, Georges, *Encyclopaedia Acephalica*, translated by Iain White (London: Atlas Press, 1995).

Baudelaire, Charles, *The Painter of Modern Life and Other Essays*, translated by Jonathan Mayne (London: Phaidon, 1995).

Baudelaire, Charles, *Baudelaire in English*, edited by Carol Clark and Robert Sykes (London: Penguin, 1997).

Bayley, Stephen, *Commerce and Culture* (London: The Design Museum, 1989).

Belloli, Andrea P., and Keth Godard, *Make Your Own Museum* (Santa Monica: The J. Paul Getty Museum, 1994).

Benjamin, Andrew, *Present Hope; Philosophy, Architecture* (London: Routledge, 1997).

Benjamin, Walter, *Illuminations*, translated by Harry Zohn (London: Fontana/Collins, 1973).

Benjamin, Walter, *Charles Baudelaire: A Lyric Poet in the Era of High Capitalism*, translated by Harry Zohn (London: Verso, 1985).

Benjamin, Walter, *One Way Street and Other Writings*, translated by Edmund Jephcott and Kingsley Shorter (London: Verso, 1992).

Benjamin, Walter, *Charles Baudelaire*, translated by Harry Zohn (London: Verso, 1997).

Benjamin, Walter, *The Arcades Project*, translated by Howard Eiland and Kevin Mclaughlin (Cambridge, Mass.: Belknap Press, 1999).

Blazwick, Iwona (ed), *An Endless Adventure . . . an Endless Passion . . . An Endless Banquet: A Situationist Scrapbook. The Situationist International, Selected Documents from 1957–1962* (London: Verso/ICA Publications, 1989).

Bloom, Barbara, *The Reign of Narcissism; Guide Book* (Stuttgart: Württembergischer Kunstverein, 1990).

Bloomer, Jennifer, *Architecture and the Text: The (S)crypts of Joyce and Piranesi* (New Haven, Conn., and London: Yale University Press, 1993).

Boltanski, Christian, *Reconstitutions; Christian Boltanski* (London, Eindhoven, Grenoble: Whitechapel, Van Abbemuseum, Musée de Grenoble, 1990).

Bonk, Ecke, *Marcel Duchamp: The Portable Museum*, translated by David Britt (London: Thames and Hudson, 1989).

Borges, Jorge Luis, *Labyrinths*, translated by Donald A. Yates and James E. Irby (London: Penguin, 1970).

Borges, Jorge Luis, *Other Inquisitions, 1937–1952,* translated by Ruth L. C. Simms (London: Souvenir Press, 1973).

Borges, Jorge Luis, *Selected Poems,* edited by Alexander Coleman (London: Allen Lane, 1999).

Borges, Jorge Luis, Silvina Ocampo and A. Bioy Casares, (eds), *The Book of Fantasy* (London: Xanadu Publications, 1988).

Boyer, M. Christine, *The City of Collective Memory; Its Historical Imagery and Architectural Entertainments* (Cambridge, Mass.: MIT Press, 1994).

Brandt, Bill, *Shadows of Light* (London: Gordon Fraser, 1977).

Brennan, Tim, *Museum of Angels, Guide to the Winged Creatures in the Collection* (London: Gli Ori, 2003).

Breton, André, *Nadja*, translated by Richard Howard (New York: Grove Weidenfeld, 1960).

Breton, André, *Manifestoes of Surrealism*, translated by Richard Seaver and Helen R. Lane (Michigan: Ann Arbor Paperbacks, University of Michigan Press, 1972).

Breton, André, *Mad Love*, translated by Mary Ann Caws (Lincoln, Nebr., London: University of Nebraska Press, 1987).

Bronson, A. A., and Peggy Gale, *Museums by Artists* (Toronto: Art Metropole, 1983).

Broodthaers, Marcel, *Writing, Interviews, Photographs*, edited by Benjamin H. D. Buchloh (Cambridge, Mass.: MIT Press, 1988).

van Bruggen, Coosje, *Claes Oldenburg: Mouse Museum/Ray Gun Wing* (Cologne: Museum Ludwig, 1979).

van Bruggen, Coosje, *Frank O. Gehry; Guggenheim Museum Bilbao* (New York: Guggenheim Museum Publications, 2001).

Bruno, G., *The Ash Wednesday Supper,* edited and translated by Edward A. Gosselin and Lawrence S. Lerner (Hamden, Conn.: Archon Books, 1977).

Buck-Morss, Susan, *The Dialectics of Seeing: Walter Benjamin and the Arcades Project* (Cambridge, Mass.: MIT Press, 1991).

Buskirk, Martha, and Mignon Nixon (eds), *The Duchamp Effect; Essays, Interviews, Round Table* (Cambridge, Mass.: OCTOBER/MIT Press, 1996).

Calle, Sophie, and Jean Baudrillard, *Suite Vénitienne/Please Follow Me*, translated by Dany Barash and Danny Hatfield (Seattle: Bay Press, 1988).

Calle, Sophie, *La Visite Guidée*, (with music by Laurie Anderson) (Rotterdam: Museum Boymans-van Beuningen, 1996).

Calle, Sophie, *Double Game* (London: Violette Editions, 1999).

Calvino, Italo, *Invisible Cities*, translated by William Weaver (London: Picador, 1979).

Calvino, Italo, *Hermit in Paris; Autobiographical Writings*, translated by Martina McLaughlin (London: Jonathan Cape, 2003).

Caws, Mary Ann, *Joseph Cornell: Theatre of the Mind* (London: Thames and Hudson, 1993).

Chung, Judy Chuihua, Jeffrey Inaba, Rem Koolhaas and Sze Tsung Leong (eds), *Project on the City 2; Harvard Design School Guide to Shopping.* (Cologne: Taschen, 2001).

Clark, T. J., *The Painting of Modern Life: Paris in the Art of Manet and his Followers* (London: Thames and Hudson, 1985).

Cohen, Margaret, *Profane Illumination: Walter Benjamin and the Paris of Surrealist Revolution* (Berkeley and Los Angeles: University of California Press, 1993).

Coles, Alex (ed), *The Optics of Walter Benjamin (de-, dis-, ex-. Volume 3)* (London: Black Dog, 1999).

Coles, Alex, and Mark Dion (eds), *Mark Dion, Archaeology* (London: Black Dog, 1999).

Cooke, Lynne, and Peter Wollen (eds), *Visual Display; Culture Beyond Appearances* (Seattle: Bay Press, 1995).

Corrin, Lisa G. (ed), *Mining the Museum: An Installation by Fred Wilson* (New York: The New Press, 1994).

Corrin, Lisa G. (ed), *Give and Take* (London: Serpentine Gallery, 2001).

Corrin, Lisa Graziose, Miwon Kwon and Norman Bryson, *Mark Dion* (London: Phaidon, 1997).

Cranbrook Art Museum, *Weird Science; A Conflation of Art and Science* (Broomfield Hills, Mich.: Cranbrook Art Museum, 1999).

Crimp, Douglas, *On the Museum's Ruins* (Cambridge, Mass.: MIT Press, 1993).

Cummings, Neil and Marysia Lewandowska, *The Value of Things* (London and Basel: August/Birkhauser, 2000).

Curl, James Stevens, *A Celebration of Death* (London: Constable, 1980).

Curl, James Stevens, *The Art and Architecture of Freemasonry* (London: Batsford, 1991).

Dal Co, Francesco. *Carlo Scarpa* (a+u Publishing, 1985. Quoted on www.StudioCleo.com, 2003).

Dal Co, Francesco, and Guiseppe Mazzariol, *Carlo Scarpa; The Complete Works*, translated by Richard Sadleir (London: Electa/Architectural Press, 1986).

Darley, Gillian, *John Soane; An Accidental Romantic* (New Haven, Conn.: Yale University Press, 1999).

Davis, Douglas. *The Museum Transformed: Design and Culture in the Post-Pompidou Age* (New York: Abbeville Press, 1990).

Debord, Guy, *Society of the Spectacle* (London: Rebel Press, Aim Publications, 1987).

de Certeau, Michel, *The Practice of Everyday Life*, translated by Stephen Rendall (Berkeley, Los Angeles and London: University of California Press, 1984).

Dietrich, Dorothea, *The Collages of Kurt Schwitters; Tradition and Innovation* (Cambridge: Cambridge University Press, 1993).

Dion, Mark, *Natural History and Other Fictions* (Birmingham: Ikon Gallery, 1997).

Dluhosch, Eric (translation), *Russia: An Architecture for World Revolution* (London: Lund Humphries, 1970).

Dorey, Helen, 'Sir John Soane's Acquisition of the Sarcophagus of Seti I', *Georgian Group Journal*, no. 1, 1991.

Downes, Kerry, *Hawksmoor* (London: Thames and Hudson, 1987).

Drake, Diana, Sarah Simons, M. Francis Rossi and David Wilson, *Tell the Bees . . . Belief, Knowledge & Hypersymbolic Cognition* (Los Angeles: Society for the Diffusion of Useful Information, 1996).

Duchamp, Marcel, *The Writings of Marcel Duchamp*, edited by Michel Sanouillet and Elmer Peterson (New York: Da Capo, 1973).

Duchamp, Marcel, *In the Infinitive*, typotranslation by Richard Hamilton and Ecke Bonk, translated by Jackie Matisse, Richard Hamilton and Ecke Bonk (the typosophic society, Northend Chapter, 1999).

Dulwich Picture Gallery, *Soane and After* (London: Dulwich Picture Gallery, 1987).

Edoh, Illera, *On the Foundation of the Museum: The Thums, Gardeners & Botanists* (West Covina, Calif.: Society for the Diffusion of Useful Information Press, 1969).

Elderfield, John, *Kurt Schwitters* (London: Thames and Hudson, 1985).

Elsner, John, and Roger Cardinal (eds), *The Cultures of Collecting* (London: Reaktion, 1994).

Flaubert, Gustave, *Bouvard and Pecuchet*, translated by A. J. Krailsheimer (London: Penguin, 1976).

Fluxus Newsletter, no. 6, April 1963.

Ford, Charles Henri (ed), *View: Parade of the Avant-Garde* (New York: Thunder's Mouth Press, 1991).

Foster, Hal, *Compulsive Beauty* (Cambridge, Mass.: MIT Press, 1993).

Foster, Hal, 'Why All the Hoopla?', *London Review of Books*, 23 August 2001.

Gamard, Elizabeth Burns, *Kurt Schwitters' Merzbau; The Cathedral of Erotic Misery* (New York: Princeton Architectural Press, 2000).

Gamboni, Dario, *The Destruction of Art; Iconoclasm and Vandalism since the French Revolution* (London: Reaktion Books, 1997).

Geist, Johann Friedrich, *Arcades; The History of a Building Type*, translated by Jane O. Newman and John H. Smith (Cambridge, Mass.: MIT Press, 1983).

Gibbons, Fiachra, 'I don't have any cash. Do you take mackerel?', *Guardian*, 14 April 2003.

Giebelhausen, Michaela (ed), *The Architecture of Museums* (Manchester, Manchester University Press, 2003).

Godwin, Joscelyn, *Athanasius Kircher; A Renaissance Man and the Quest for Lost Knowledge* (London: Thames and Hudson, 1979).

Green, Martin, and Tony White, *Guide to London Pubs* (London: Sphere Books, 1968).

Groys, Boris, David A. Ross and Iwona Blazwick, *Ilya Kabakov* (London: Phaidon, 1998).

Guggenheim, Peggy, *Confessions of an Art Addict* (London: André Deutsch, 1960).

Haacke, Hans, *Ansicht Sachen/Viewing Matters* (Düsseldorf, Richter, 1999).

Harbison, Robert, *Eccentric Spaces* (London: André Deutsch, 1977).

Harrison, Charles, and Paul Wood, *Art in Theory 1900–2000* (London: Blackwell, 2003).

Hawkins, Hildi, and Danielle Olsen, *The Phantom Museum and Henry Wellcome's Collection of Medical Curiosities* (London: Profile Books, 2003).

Hauptman, Jodi, *Joseph Cornell; Stargazing in the Cinema* (New Haven, Conn., London: Yale University Press, 2000).

Hess, Alan, *Viva Las Vegas: After-Hours Architecture* (San Francisco: Chronicle Press, 1993).

Hess, Thomas B., and John Ashbery, *The Grand Eccentrics* (New York and London: Collier-Macmillan, 1966).

Home, Stewart, *Slow Death* (London: Serpent's Tail, 1996).

Huysmans, J. K., *Against Nature*, translated by Robert Baldick (London: Penguin, 1959).

Impey, Oliver, and Arthur Macgregor, *The Origins of Museums; The Cabinet of Curiosities in Sixteenth- and Seventeenth-Century Europe* (London: House of Stratus, 2001).

IVAM Centre Julio Gonzalez, *Frederick Kiesler 1890–1965; Inside the Endless House* (Valencia: IVAM Centre Julio Gonzalez, 1997).

J. Paul Getty Museum, *Guide to the Villa and its Gardens* (Malibu: J. Paul Getty Museum, 1992).

James Stirling Michael Wilford and Associates; Buildings and Projects, 1975–1992 (London: Thames and Hudson, 1994).

Jappe, Anselm, *Guy Debord*, translated by Donald Nicholson-Smith (Berkeley: University of California Press, 1999).

Jencks, Charles, 'Don't Panic', *Architectural Review*, vol. 163, no. 972, February 1978.

Jencks, Charles, *Heteropolis: Los Angeles. The Riots and the Strange Beauty of Hetero-Architecture* (London: Academy Editions, 1993).

Jewish Museum Berlin, *Jewish Museum; Concept and Vision* (Berlin: Judisches Museum, 1998).

Joyce, James, *Ulysses*, edited by Danis Rose (London: Picador, 1997).

Joyce, Paul, *A Guide to Abney Park Cemetery* (London: Save Abney Park Cemetery Publications, 1984).

Jukes, Peter, *A Shout in the Street; An Excursion into the Modern City* (London: Faber & Faber 1990).

Kabakov, Ilya, *The Palace of Projects; 1995–1998* (London: Artangel, 1998).

Kachur, Lewis, *Displaying the Marvelous; Marcel Duchamp, Salvador Dali, and Surrealist Exhibition Installations* (Cambridge, Mass.: MIT Press, 2001).

Karp, Ivan and Steven D. Lavine (eds), *Exhibiting Cultures: The Poetics and Politics of Museum Display* (Washington: Smithsonian Institution Press, 1991).

Kellein, Thomas, *Fluxus* (London, Thames and Hudson, 1995).

Kent, William (ed), *An Encyclopaedia of London* (London: J. M. Dent & Sons, 1937).

Kiesler, Frederick, *Contemporary Art Applied to the Storefront and its Display* (London: Sir Isaac Pitman and Sons Ltd, 1930).

Klein, Norman, *The History of Forgetting; Los Angeles and the Erasure of Memory* (London: Verso, 1997).

Koolhaas, Rem, *Delirious New York: A Retroactive Manifesto for Manhattan* (London: Thames and Hudson, 1978).

Koolhaas, Rem, *OMA/AMO Projects for Prada, Part I* (Milan: Fondazione Prada Edizione, 2001).

Koolhaas, Rem, and Bruce Mau, *S, M, L, XL.* (Rotterdam: 010, 1995).

Kosuth, Joseph, *The Play of the Unmentionable* (London: Thames and Hudson, 1992).

Krichbaum, Jorg, and Rein A. Zondergeld, *Dictionary of Fantastic Art,* translated by Donna Pedini Simpson (Woodury, NY: Barron's, 1985).

Lambert, Phylis (ed), *Mies in America.* (Montreal, New York: CCA, Whitney, 2001).

Le Corbusier and Pierre Jeanneret, *The Complete Architectural Works: Volume I, 1910–29,* edited by W. Boesiger and O. Stonorow (London: Thames and Hudson, 1964).

Le Corbusier, *The Complete Architectural Works: Volume IV, 1938–46,* edited by W. Boesiger (London: Thames and Hudson, 1966).

Le Corbusier, *The Complete Architectural Works: Volume V, 1946–52,* edited by W. Boesiger (London: Thames and Hudson, 1966).

Le Corbusier, *The Decorative Art of Today,* translated by J. Dunnet (London: Architectural Press, 1987).

Leach, Neil (ed), *The Hieroglyphics of Space; Reading and Experiencing the Modern Metropolis* (London: Routledge, 2002).

Libeskind, Daniel, *Countersign* (London: Academy Editions, 1991).

Libeskind, Daniel, *Libeskind at the Soane* (London: Sir John Soane's Museum, 2001a).

Libeskind, Daniel, *The Space of Encounter* (London: Thames and Hudson, 2001b).

Libeskind, Daniel, and Cecil Balmond, *Unfolding* (Rotterdam: Netherlands Architecture Institute, 1997).

Lissitzky-Küppers, Sophie, *El Lissitzky; Life, Letters, Texts,* translated by H. Aldwinckle and M. Whittall (London: Thames and Hudson, 1968).

Lucan, Jacques, *OMA Rem Koolhaas* (New York: Princeton Architectural Press, 1991).

Mabe, Joni, *Joni Mabe's Museum Book* (no bibliographic details available).

McClellan, Andrew, *Inventing the Louvre* (Cambridge: Cambridge University Press, 1994).

McMullen, Roy, *Mona Lisa; the Picture and the Myth* (London: Macmillan, 1972).

McShine, Kynaston (ed), *Joseph Cornell* (New York: The Museum of Modern Art/ Prestel, 1990).

McShine, Kynaston, *The Museum as Muse; Artists Reflect* (New York: The Museum of Modern Art, 1999).

Mangurian, Robert and Mary-Ann Ray, *Wrapper: Faces Looking for the Future from the Past, 40 Possible City Surfaces for the Museum of Jurassic Technology* (San Francisco: William Stout Publishers, Houston: Rice School of Architecture, 1999).

Marcus, Greil, *Lipstick Traces: A Secret History of the Twentieth Century* (London: Penguin, 1993).

Melly, George, *Paris and the Surrealists* (London: Thames and Hudson, 1991).

Miller, Edward, *That Noble Cabinet: A History of the British Museum* (London; André Deutsch, 1973).

Miller, Paul D., *Rhythm Science* (Cambridge, Mass.: MIT Press, 2004).

Missac, Pierre, *Walter Benjamin's Passages,* translated by Shierry Weber Nicholsen (Cambridge, Mass.: MIT Press, 1995).

Montaner, Josep, *New Museums* (London: Architecture, Design & Technology Press, 1990).

Montaner, Josep Maria, *Museums of the 21st Century*, translated by Mary Black (Barcelona: Gustavo Gili, 2003).

Mordaunt Crook, J., *The British Museum; A Case Study in Architectural Politics* (London: Penguin, 1973).

Morton, Patricia A., *Hybrid Modernities; Architecture and Representation at the 1931 Colonial Exposition, Paris* (Cambridge, Mass.: MIT Press, 2000).

Motherwell, Robert, *The Dada Painters and Poets* (Harvard: Belknap Press, 1989).

Muensterberger, Werner, *Collecting: An Unruly Passion* (Princeton: Princeton University Press, 1994).

Murphy, Richard, *Carlo Scarpa & the Castelvecchio* (London: Butterworth Architecture, 1990).

Museum of Art, Rhode Island School of Design, *Raid the Icebox 1 with Andy Warhol* (Providence: Rhode Island School of Design, 1970).

Museum of Jurassic Technology, *The Museum of Jurassic Technology, Primi Decem Anni, Jubilee Catalogue* (West Covina, Calif.: Society for the Diffusion of Useful Information Press, 2002).

Nadeau, Maurice, *The History of Surrealism*, translated by R. Howard (Harmondsworth: Penguin, 1973).

Nesbit, Molly, *Atget's Seven Albums* (New Haven, Conn.: Yale University Press, 1992).

Newhouse, Victoria, *Towards a New Museum* (New York: Monacelli Press, 1998).

Noever, Peter (ed), *The Discursive Museum* (Ostfildern-Ruit: MAK/Hatje Cantz, 2001).

O'Doherty, Brian, *Inside the White Cube; The Ideology of the Gallery Space* (Santa Monica, Calif.: Lapis Press, 1976).

Oddy, Jason, 'A Spatial Art', *Modern Painters*, vol. 15, no. 1, Spring 2002.

Oldenburg, Claes, and Emmet Williams, *Store Days; Documents from the Store (1961) and Ray Gun Theatre (1962)* (New York: Something Else Press, 1967).

Palais de Tokyo, *What Do You Expect from an Art Institution in the 21st Century?* (Paris: Palais de Tokyo, 2001).

Paolozzi, Eduardo, *Lost Magic Kingdoms* (London: British Museum Press, 1985).

Perec, Georges, *Three*, translated by Ian Monk (London: Harvill Press, 1996).

Perec, Georges, *Species of Spaces and Other Pieces*, translated by John Sturrock (London: Penguin, 1997).

Phillpot, Clive and Jon Hendricks, *Fluxus: Selections from the Gilbert and Lila Silverman Collection* (New York: The Museum of Modern Art, 1988).

Plant, Sadie, *The Most Radical Gesture: The Situationist International in a Postmodern Age* (London and New York: Routledge, 1992).

Poe, Edgar Allan, *Tales of Mystery and Imagination* (London: Dent, 1963).

Polano, Sergio, *Carlo Scarpa: Palazzo Abatellis* (Milan: Electa, 1989).

Polizzotti, Mark, *Revolution of the Mind: The Life of André Breton* (London: Bloomsbury, 1995).

Poschardt, Ulf, *DJ Culture*, translated by Shaun Whiteside (London, Quartet, 1998).

Purcell, Rosamond Wolff, and Stephen Jay Gould, *Finders, Keepers: Eight Collectors* (London: Hutchinson Radius, 1992).

Putnam, James, *Art and Artifact; The Museum as Medium* (London: Thames and Hudson, 2001).

Richie, Alexandra, *Faust's Metropolis; A History of Berlin* (London: HarperCollins, 1999).

Ross, Richard, *Museology* (Santa Barbara: Aperture, 1989).

Rugoff, Ralph, *Circus Americanus*, (London and New York: Verso, 1995).

Rumney, Ralph, *The Consul*, translated by Malcolm Imrie (London: Verso, 2002).

Ryall, Tom, *Blackmail* (London: BFI, 1993).

Ryan, Raymund, 'English Spoken Here', *Blueprint*, no. 130, July/August 1996.

Sadler, Simon, *The Situationist City* (Cambridge, Mass.: MIT Press, 1998).

Safran, Yehuda (ed), *Frederick Kiesler 1890–1965* (London: Architectural Association, 1989).

Schaffner, Ingrid, and Matthias Winzen (eds), *Deep Storage; Collecting, Storing and Archiving in Art* (Munich: Prestel-Verlag, 1998).

Schubert, Karsten, *The Curator's Egg* (London: One-Off Press, 2000).

Schwarz, Arturo, *The Complete Works of Marcel Duchamp* (New York: Delano Greenidge Editions, 2000).

Schwartz, Vanessa R., *Spectacular Realities; Early Mass Culture in Fin-de-Siècle Paris* (Berkeley: University of California Press, 1998).

Searle, Adrian (ed), *Talking Art* (London: ICA, 1993).

Serota, Nicholas, *Experience or Interpretation; The Dilemma of Museums of Modern Art* (London: Thames and Hudson, 1996).

Sharpe, William, and Leonard Wallock (eds), *Visions of the Modern City* (Baltimore: Johns Hopkins University Press, 1987).

Shattuck, Roger, *The Banquet Years* (New York: Vintage, 1967).

Sheman, Daniel J., and Irit Rogoff (eds), *Museum Culture: Histories, Discourses, Spectacles* (London: Routledge,1994).

Sheringham, Michael (ed), *Parisian Fields* (London: Reaktion, 1996).

Sinclair, Iain, *Lud Heat and Suicide Bridge* (London: Vintage, 1995).

Sinclair, Iain, *Lights Out for the Territory* (London: Granta, 1997).

Sir John Soane's Museum, *Soane: Connoisseur & Collector* (London: Sir John Soane's Museum, 1995).

Sir John Soane's Museum, *Visions of Ruin; Architectural Fantasies & Designs for Garden Follies* (London: Sir John Soane's Museum, 1999).

Sir John Soane's Museum , *A New Description of Sir John Soane's Museum* (London: Sir John Soane's Museum, 2001).

Smithson, Robert, *The Collected Writings*, edited by Jack Flam (Berkeley: University of California Press, 1996).

Solomon, Deborah, *Utopia Parkway; The Life and Work of Joseph Cornell* (London: Jonathan Cape, 1997).

Sontag, Susan, *On Photography* (Harmondsworth: Penguin, 1978).

South Bank Centre, *Worlds in a Box* (London: South Bank Centre, 1994).

Spalding, Julian, *The Poetic Museum; Reviving Historic Collections* (Munich: Prestel, 2002).

Spector, Jack J., *Surrealist Art and Writing 1919/39: The Gold of Time* (Cambridge: Cambridge University Press, 1997).

Spies, Werner, *Max Ernst. Loplop; The Artist's Other Self* (London: Thames and Hudson, 1983).

Spoerri, Daniel, *Daniel Spoerri from A to Z* (Milan: Fondazione Mudima, 1991).

Spoerri, Daniel, *An Anecdoted Topography of Chance*, translated by Emmett Williams and Malcolm Green (London: Atlas Press, 1995).

Staniszewski, Mary Anne, *The Power of Display; A History of Exhibition Installations at the Museum of Modern Art* (Cambridge, Mass.: MIT Press, 1998).

Steegmuller, Frances, *Apollinaire; Poet Among the Painters* (London: Rupert Hart-Davis, 1963).

Stewart, Susan, *On Longing: Narratives of the Miniature, the Gigantic, the Souvenir, the Collection* (Durham, NC: Duke University Press, 1993).

Stich, Sidra, *Yves Klein* (London: Hayward Gallery/Cantz, 1994).

Stirling, James, *Writings on Architecture*, edited by Robert Maxwell (Milan: Skira, 1998).

Stolzenberg, Daniel (ed), *The Great Art of Knowing: The Baroque Encyclopedia of Athanasius Kircher* (Stanford, Calif.: Stanford University Libraries, 2001).

Storr, Robert, *Dislocations* (New York: The Museum of Modern Art, 1991).

Summerson, John, *A New Description of Sir John Soane's Museum* (London: Sir John Soane's Museum, 1954).

Summerson, John, 'Soane and the Furniture of Death', *Architectural Review*, March 1978.

Summerson, John, et al, *John Soane* (London: Academy Editions, 1983).

Tafuri, Manfredo, *History of Italian Architecture, 1944–1985*, translated by Jessica Levine (Cambridge, Mass.: MIT Press, 1989).

Tate Gallery, *Marcel Broodthaers* (London: Tate Gallery, 1980).

Taylor, Mark C., *Nots* (Chicago: University of Chicago Press, 1993).

Taylor, Mark C., *Hiding* (Chicago: University of Chicago Press, 1997).

Taylor, Mark C., and Dietrich Christian Lammerts, *Grave Matters* (London: Reaktion Books, 2002).

Taylor, Mark C., and José Márquez, *The Réal, Las Vegas, Nevada* (CD-ROM) (Williamstown, Mass.: Williams College Museum of Art/MASS Moca, 1997).

Tester, Keith (ed), *The Flâneur* (London and New York: Routledge, 1994).

Tillman, Lynne, *The Madame Realism Complex* (New York: SEMIOTEXT(E), 1992).

Timms, Edward, and David Kelley (eds), *Unreal City: Urban Experience in Modern European Literature and Art* (Manchester: Manchester University Press, 1985).

Tomkins, Calvin, *Duchamp* (London: Chatto and Windus, 1997).

Trench, Richard and Ellis Hillman, *London Under London; A Subterranean Guide* (London: John Murray, 1984).

Tronnes, Mike (ed), *Literary Las Vegas* (New York: Henry Holt, 1995).

Truffaut, François, *Hitchcock* (London: Paladin, 1978).

Tschumi, Bernard, 'Architecture and its Double', *Architectural Design*, vol. 48, no. 2–3, 1978.

Tupitsyn, Margarita, *El Lissitzky; Beyond the Abstract Cabinet* (New Haven, Conn.: Yale University Press, 1999).

Ugrešić, Dubravka, *The Museum of Unconditional Surrender*, translated by Celia Hawkesworth (London: Phoenix, 1999).

Vallance, Jeffrey, 'The Greatest Art Show on Earth', *LA Weekly*, 23–29 April 1999.

Vaniegem, Raoul, *The Revolution of Everyday Life*, translated by Donald Nicholson-Smith (London: Left Bank Press & Rebel Press, 1983).

Venturi, Robert, *Complexity and Contradiction in Architecture* (London: Architectural Press, 1977).

Venturi, Robert, Denise Scott Brown and Steven Izenour, *Learning from Las Vegas* (Cambridge, Mass.: MIT Press, 1977).

Vidler, Anthony, *The Architectural Uncanny* (Cambridge, Mass.: MIT Press, 1992).

Vidler, Anthony, *Warped Space* (Cambridge, Mass.: MIT Press, 2000).

Vigni, Giorgio, *Carlo Scarpa: il progetto per Santa Caterina a Treviso* (Treviso: Vianello Libri, 1984).

Waldberg, Patrick, *Surrealism* (London: Thames and Hudson, 1965).

Walker Art Center, *Marcel Broodthaers* (Minneapolis/New York: Rizzoli, 1989).

Walker, John A., *John Latham – The Incidental Person; His Art and Ideas* (London: Middlesex University Press, 1995).

Wallach, Amei, *Ilya Kabakov; The Man Who Never Threw Anything Away* (New York: Abrams, 1996).

Warhol, Andy, *The Andy Warhol Diaries*, edited by Pat Hacket (New York: Warner Books, 1989).

Waterfield, Giles, *Soane and After; The Architecture of Dulwich Picture Gallery* (London: Dulwich Picture Gallery, 1987).

Waterfield, Giles (ed), *Palaces of Art: Art Galleries in Britain 1790–1990* (London: Dulwich Picture Gallery, 1991).

Waterfield, Giles (ed), *Soane and Death: The Tombs and Monuments of Sir John Soane* (London: Dulwich Picture Gallery, 1996).

Watkin, David, *Thomas Hope and the Neo-Classical Idea* (London: John Murray, 1968).

Webster, Gwendolen, *Kurt Merz Schwitters; A Biographical Study* (Cardiff: University of Wales Press, 1997).

Weschler, Lawrence, *Mr. Wilson's Cabinet of Wonder* (New York: Pantheon Books, 1995).

White, Edmund, *The Flâneur; A Stroll Through the Paradoxes of Paris* (London: Bloomsbury, 2001).

Whitney Museum of American Art, *The Power of the City/The City of Power* (New York: Whitney Museum of American Art, 1992).

Williams, Emmett and Ann Nöel (eds), *Mr. Fluxus; A Collective Portrait of George Maciunas 1931–1978* (London: Thames and Hudson, 1997).

Williams, Rosalind H., *Dream Worlds: Mass Consumption in Late Nineteenth-Century Paris* (Berkeley: University of California Press, 1982).

Wollen, Peter, 'A Psychogeography of Chance', *New Left Review*, 8, March–April 2001.

Worth, Valentine, *Bernard Maston, Donald R Griffith and the Deprong Mori of the Tripiscum Plateau* (West Covina, Calif.: Society for the Diffusion of Useful Information Press, 1964).

Yates, Frances A., *The Art of Memory* (London: Pimlico, 1992).

Zbarsky, Ilya and Samuel Hutchinson, *Lenin's Embalmers*, translated by Barbara Bray (London: Harvill Press, 1998).

Zola, Émile, *Thérèse Raquin*, translated by Leonard Tancock (Harmondsworth: Penguin, 1962).

Zola, Émile, *L'Assomoir*, translated by Leonard Tancock (Harmondsworth: Penguin, 1970).

Zone I & II (New York: Urzone Inc., no date).

PICTURE CREDITS

INDEX